Changing Electoral Politics in Delhi

Changing Electoral Politics in Delhi

FROM CASTE TO CLASS

Sanjay Kumar

$SAGE www.sagepublications.com
Los Angeles • London • New Delhi • Singapore • Washington DC

First published in 2013 by

 SAGE Publications India Pvt Ltd
B1/I-1 Mohan Cooperative Industrial Area
Mathura Road, New Delhi 110 044, India
www.sagepub.in

SAGE Publications Inc
2455 Teller Road
Thousand Oaks, California 91320, USA

SAGE Publications Ltd
1 Oliver's Yard, 55 City Road
London EC1Y 1SP, United Kingdom

SAGE Publications Asia-Pacific Pte Ltd
33 Pekin Street
#02-01 Far East Square
Singapore 048763

Published by Vivek Mehra for SAGE Publications India Pvt Ltd, Phototypeset in 10/12 Times New Roman by RECTO Graphics, Delhi, and printed at Saurabh Printers Pvt Ltd.

Library of Congress Cataloging-in-Publication Data Available

ISBN: 978-81-321-1374-4 (PB)

The SAGE Team: Sutapa Ghosh, Shreya Chakraborti, Nand Kumar Jha, and Rajinder Kaur

Contents

List of Tables	vii
List of Figures	ix
List of Abbreviations	xi
Preface	xiii
Acknowledgements	xix
Introduction	1
1. Delhi: A City of Migrants	12
2. Social Cleavages	30
3. The Voting Patterns: Caste or Class?	56
4. The Electoral Verdict	73
5. Popular Perception about Leaders and Parties	86
6. Unheard Voices	97
7. The New Definition of Delhi	117
Appendix 1: Detailed Results of Delhi Assembly Election, 2008	139
Appendix 2: Detailed Results of Delhi Assembly Elections, 1993–2003	157
References	210
Index	214
About the Author	217

List of Tables

1.1   Decadal Growth Rate of Urban Population in Mega Cities   13
of India

1.2   Pattern of Migration in Delhi during Last Few Decades   17

1.3   State-wise Pattern of Migration in Delhi: 1971–2008   18

1.4   Settlement Pattern of Migrants from Select States   19

1.5   What Attracts Migrants to the City of Delhi?   21

1.6   Occupational Pattern of Migrants from Select Regions   22

1.7   Educational Attainment among Migrants from Select   23
Regions

1.8   Economic Prosperity of Migrants from Select Regions   24

3.1   The Class Divide among Brahmin Voters   69

3.2   The Class Divide among Punjabi Khatri Voters   69

3.3   The Class Divide among Jat Voters   70

3.4   The Class Divide among Sikh Voters   70

3.5   The Class Divide among Dalit Voters   71

4.1   Party Performance in Delhi: Lok Sabha Elections,   74
1952–2009

4.2   Party Performance in Delhi: Assembly Elections,   75
1993–2008

4.3   Region-wise Vote Shares of Political Parties in Delhi: 80
Assembly Election, 2008

4.4   Vote Shares of Political Parties in Different Types of   81
Constituencies

5.1   Increasing Popularity of Sheila Dikshit, 1998–2009   88

5.2   Popularity of Madan Lal Khurana   91

5.3   Malhotra's Popularity (Caste-wise), Election 2008   92

5.4   BJP Leaders' Popularity (Class-wise), 1998–2008   92
5.5   Sheila Dikshit's Popularity (Class-wise), 1998–2009   93
5.6   Sheila Dikshit's Popularity (Caste-wise), 2003–09   94

7.1   Public Opinion on Privatization of DTC (Class-wise)   123
7.2   Public Opinion on the BRT Corridor (Class-wise)   128
7.3   Public Opinion on Privatization of Electricity in Delhi 134
        (Class-wise)
7.4   Public Opinion on Government Hospitals (Class-wise)   134
7.5   Inequitable Provision of Basic Services in Delhi   136

List of Figures

2.1   The Brahmin Vote in Delhi: Assembly Elections,   38
1993–2008

2.2   The Punjabi Khatri Vote in Delhi: Assembly Elections,   40
1993–2008

2.3   The Rajput Vote in Delhi: Assembly Elections,   42
1993–2008

2.4   The Vaishya Vote in Delhi: Assembly Elections,   43
1993–2008

2.5   The Gujjar–Yadav Vote in Delhi: Assembly Elections,   45
1993–2008

2.6   The Jat Vote in Delhi: Assembly Elections, 1993–2008   47

2.7   The OBC Vote in Delhi: Assembly Elections,   49
1993–2008

2.8   The Dalit Vote in Delhi: Assembly Elections,   51
1993–2008

2.9   The Muslim Vote in Delhi: Assembly Elections,   53
1993–2008

2.10   The Sikh Vote in Delhi: Assembly Elections,   54
1993–2008

3.1   The Chief Approaches to Class   59

3.2   Voting Pattern of Delhi's Upper-class Voters: Assembly   64
Elections, 1998–2008

3.3   Voting Pattern of Delhi's Middle-class Voters: 66
Assembly Elections, 1998–2008

3.4   Voting Pattern of Delhi's Lower-class Voters: Assembly   68
Elections, 1998–2008

7.1 Attitude of Delhi's Voters towards Privatization 122

7.2 Public Support for the Right to Buy and Drive a Car in Delhi 125

7.3 Public Opinion on Jhuggis in Delhi (Class-wise) 130

7.4 Public Opinion on Regularization of Unauthorized Colonies (Class-wise) 131

7.5 Public Opinion on How Police Should Deal with Beggars (Class-wise) 133

7.6 Public Opinion on the Right to Vote (Class-wise) 137

List of Abbreviations

BJP	Bharatiya Janata Party
BJS	Bharatiya Jana Sangh
BLD	Bharatiya Lok Dal
BRT	Bus Rapid Transit
BSP	Bahujan Samaj Party
CRRI	Central Road Research Institute
CSDS	Centre for the Study of Developing Societies
CTI	Centre for Transforming India
DDA	Delhi Development Authority
DTC	Delhi Transport Corporation
HUDCO	Housing and Urban Development Corporation
ICESCR	International Covenant on Economic, Social and Cultural Rights
JJ	jhuggi jhopri
LIG	Low-income Group
MCD	Municipal Corporation of Delhi
MIG	Middle-income Group
MLA	Member of Legislative Assembly
NCR	National Capital Region
NDMC	New Delhi Municipal Council
NHHP	National Housing and Habitat Policy
NGO	non-governmental organization
OBC	Other Backward Class
RJD	Rashtriya Janata Dal
RSS	Rashtriya Swayamsevak Sangh
SC	Scheduled Caste
ST	Scheduled Tribe
UDHR	Universal Declaration of Human Rights
ULCRA	Urban Land (Ceiling and Regulation) Act

UNHRC	United Nations Human Rights Commission
UNOHCHR	United Nations Office of the High Commissioner for Human Rights
UP	Uttar Pradesh

Preface

Caste plays an important role in Indian electoral politics. This is not a new phenomenon which has come to play during the last few decades, but a close relationship of caste and politics has existed ever since the first election was held after Independence. The early years of national politics and in many states of India was characterized by dominance of the upper castes. The post-Mandal period witnessed the rise of the Other Backward Classes (OBCs) in the politics of many North Indian states, especially Uttar Pradesh (UP) and Bihar. The last few decades have witnessed the political mobilization of the Dalits. The OBC and the Dalits have gradually acquired political dominance, which is largely the result of their numerical size and their political mobilization. Regional parties tend to have their support bases more amongst the lower castes. Since the lower castes (the OBCs and the Dalits) are numerically very large, the regional parties have naturally come to occupy a vital place in present-day politics. The regional parties have posed an electoral challenge to the mainstream national parties in many states, like the Dravida Munnetra Kazhagam and the All India Anna Dravida Munnetra Kazhagam in Tamil Nadu, the Asom Gana Parishad in Assam, the Trinamool Congress in West Bengal, the Shiv Sena in Maharashtra, the Samajwadi Party and the Bahujan Samaj Party (BSP) in UP, the Janata Dal (United) and the Rashtriya Janata Dal (RJD) in Bihar, the Akali Dal in Punjab and in a few other regional parties in other states. The electoral politics in many states of India has moved from a bipolar contest to a multipolar contest. The puzzle is that even though Delhi has a large Dalit population, a sizeable Muslim population and large number of people from the OBC, the politics in Delhi still remains largely bipolar between the Congress and the Bharatiya Janata Party (BJP). In the recent Assembly election (2008), the BSP has made some inroads in the city's politics largely because a large number of migrants from the lower-income-and-poor group, amongst whom sizeable numbers belong to the Dalit community, voted for the BSP. But still the Congress and the BSP are competing for the support of the Dalits. Why is the BSP, which is so popular amongst the Dalit voters of UP, unable to mobilize the Dalits in Delhi? Is caste-based political mobilization missing in Delhi? If caste is not the primary factor for voters' mobilization in Delhi, what are the other social cleavages for political mobilization?

Using empirical evidence from large-scale surveys of a cross section of people conducted during the last few Assembly elections, the book tries to look at the relationship between caste and electoral politics in Delhi. The evidence used in explaining this relationship of caste and voting pattern, and the shift in voting patterns from caste to class, adds strength to the book since there is hardly any empirical study which focuses on the contemporary electoral politics of the city of Delhi. The data used in the book helps the reader to understand the voting patterns of voters of Delhi and the analysis suggests, more than caste, it is class which matters in Delhi's electoral politics.

This book also tries to explore how large-scale migration to the city of Delhi has changed the social profile of voters, with a large number of voters belonging to migrant community, largely from the lower-income-and-poor class. While the data from the census tells us the story of migration in different cities, the survey data analyzed in this book helps us in going beyond that and to look at the social and economic profiles of the migrants. The book also focuses on the impact of migration on the changing electoral politics in Delhi over the last few years. Unlike many of the other Indian states, Delhi's population mainly comprises migrants. Delhi has always attracted a very high number of migrants from other states. This book tries to analyze as to what extent migration has an impact on electoral politics of the state and is responsible for the shift in electoral behaviour of the voters of Delhi, from caste to class. One explanation of this shift could be that people's association on caste lines starts weakening due to migration and class takes over the social identity, that is, caste. This shift was noticed during the 2003 Delhi Assembly election as well when the class division among Delhi voters was sharp enough to even influence the voting choices of voters from different classes within the same caste or community. One saw the divide in voting preferences between the rich and the poor even among the Brahmins and the Punjabis.

The recent migrants to Delhi, especially from Bihar and UP, largely belong to the lower/poor class who migrated to Delhi mainly in search of better livelihood opportunities, though some even came for better educational opportunities. Of all the migrants from Bihar, nearly 63 per cent are poor while another 30 per cent belong to the middle class. Similarly of those who migrated from UP, 46 per cent are poor while 45 per cent belong to the middle class. A large proportion of the people who migrated to the city as refugees at the time of Partition of India now belong to the upper and middle classes. Clearly the class character of Delhi has changed with rapid migration over the last several decades. Delhi no more remains a city of the rich people; it has a sizeable middle-class population and a large number of poor people living in slums and unauthorized colonies. These slums and unauthorized colonies are spread all over the city, and the previous classifications of Delhi—into New Delhi and Old Delhi, or South Delhi being a synonym of upper-class people and Yamuna Paar being seen as lower-class localities—no longer hold true. Even the most recent division of Delhi into nine administrative zones is not so meaningful. Delhi, in my opinion, is three cities being merged into one city: the city of the upper class, the city of the middle class and the city of the lower class. People belonging to the Punjabi Khatri community are the most affluent people in Delhi, but they no longer are the majority community. There is a very large migrant population, a large Dalit population (17 per cent) and also a sizeable Muslim population (12 per cent). The Muslim population is largely concentrated in localities like Okhla, Chandni Chowk, Seelampur, Karawal Nagar, Badarpur, Zafrabad, Nand Nagri and Geeta Colony. The changed social profile of the people also has an impact on the profile of the voters. There are 16 Assembly constituencies which have a sizeable proportion of Punjabi Khatri voters. But at the same time, the migrants constitute a sizeable proportion of voters in many Assembly constituencies like Burari, Adarsh Nagar, Wazirpur, Uttam Nagar, Dwarka, Palam, Ambedkar Nagar (SC), Sangam Vihar, Tughlakabad, Badarpur Trilokpuri (SC), Kondli (SC), Seemapuri (SC), Gokalpur (SC), Mustafabad and Karawal Nagar. Due to sheer numerical strength, they are in a position to influence the electoral battle in many constituencies. There are some Assembly constituencies like Chandni Chowk, Ballimaran and Okhla with sizeable Muslim voters.

These three cities are spread across Delhi and do not have clearly demarcated geographical boundaries, but have sharply demarcated social and political boundaries. The political boundaries between these three are reflected in their political attitudes and preferences exhibited by their voting patterns across the last three Assembly elections held in 1998, 2003 and 2008. The upper-class voters voted for the BJP in big numbers while the middle-class and lower- class (poor) voters voted for the Congress in sizeable proportions. Though voters belonging to different castes like Punjabi Khatri, Jat, Dalit, Brahmin, or the OBCs have their political preferences and sizeable numbers of them vote for one or the other political party, they seemed divided more on class lines rather than on caste lines. The lower-class Punjabi Khatri and the upper-class Punjabi Khatri vote differently. The lower-class Jat and the lower-class Punbaji Khatri vote similarly while the upper-class Punbjai Khatri and the upper-class Dalit vote in a more or less similar manner, even though the Dalits are largely in favour of the Congress.

The changed social profile of Delhi's voters (sizeable proportions of lower-class or poor voters and migrants) and the nature of political preference guided largely on class lines had benefited the Congress as the party is relatively more popular amongst the poor and lower-class voters. The poor voters voted in much bigger numbers for the Congress compared to the upper-class voters and that helped the party in winning three successive Assembly elections—in 1998, 2003 and 2008. Even though the vote share of the Congress declined from 48 per cent during the 1998 and 2003 Assembly elections to 40 per cent during the latest victory in 2008, we did not witness a corresponding increase in the vote share of its main rival party, the BJP. The Congress also benefited from the able leadership of Sheila Dikshit, who is not only much more popular compared to any BJP leader but also amongst other Congress leaders. If on the one hand, after the exit of Madan Lal Khurana, the BJP had the handicap of leadership, it kept trying various options in various elections: Sahib Singh Verma, Sushma Swaraj, Vijay Kumar Malhotra, Vijay Jolly and most recently, Vijay Goel. On the other hand, the Congress was placed pretty well with Sheila Dikshit in command, whose popularity cuts across caste and class lines.

But the 2008 Assembly elections witnessed a change in voting patterns, visible more on class lines rather than on caste lines. The Congress lost its traditional vote back amongst the lower/poor class who moved towards the BSP resulting in about 8 per cent decline in the vote share of the Congress between 2003 and 2008. On the other hand, the BSP's vote share increased to 14 per cent. With sizeable presence of Dalit voters, mainly poor migrants, there is a possibility for the emergence of the new third force in the city's politics and BSP is emerging as the party to fill this gap.

The various classes of people living in the city of Delhi do not only have different political preferences; the social boundaries between the three classes of people are even much sharper. The opinions of the people belonging to the three different classes differ sharply on issues like privatization of electricity in Delhi, the regularization of unauthorized colonies, the regularization of jhuggis (shacks) in Delhi, the Bus Rapid Transport (BRT) system, the privatization of government hospitals and similar such issues which concern the common man on the street.

The story of the city of Delhi would remain incomplete without a mention of the large number of houseless people in the city, who sleep on payments, parks, roadside and similar such open spaces. They hardly have any role to play in the city's political life. These houseless people are the marginal citizens who hardly enjoy any political rights. Most of them do not have any identity proof, as they do not have any residence proof and, hence, are denied of various political rights which a normal citizen enjoys. The government hardly bothers about them except providing a few shelter homes. The political parties hardly pay attention to their concerns and problems as they do not form the vote bank for them. There is a need for not only providing material benefit to them but also making an effort to bring them into the mainstream of democratic process. The law does not debar houseless people from being enrolled as voters, so there is a need to think about how to integrate them in the social and democratic process.

Acknowledgements

This is one book which I wanted to write for quite some time, but that some time actually turned out to be a long time. Writing this book took much more time than I had expected. The large data set which we at the Centre for the Study of Developing Societies (CSDS) collected during the 1998 Delhi Assembly election as part of the *Hindustan Times*–CSDS Delhi Survey encouraged me to do an in-depth analysis of the voting behaviour of Delhi's voters. The reason behind this delay was first it took me some time to think about how to use this huge data set for academic output and then when I started the analysis, the next Assembly election was very close, and I preferred waiting for the data to be updated after the 2003 Assembly election. The CSDS team conducted the HT–CSDS Delhi survey even during the 2003 Assembly election and collected information from about 15,000 voters. The temptation of looking at more data and more analysis could not be contained, and I decided to use the data for another round of Assembly election, which was held in Delhi in 2008. A time series data of three elections (1998, 2003 and 2008) is what has been used for the analysis of Delhi's electoral politics in this book. Rarely would a researcher have access to time series data for doing an analysis and from that point of view, keeping in mind the nature of data used, this book is important for making sense of politics in Delhi.

The journey has been long but I am happy to see this book being published by SAGE. My continued research on Delhi's elections spanning a period of three Assembly elections may not have been possible without the support of a large number of people, some of whom were with me in the initial stages of my research, some travelled considerable distance with me, while some stood beside me even till the time of writing the last bits of the book. My sincere thanks to all those who helped me at different stages of writing this book. I must begin by extending my thanks to all the respondents who agreed to spare time for sharing their views on politics, elections and related issues. Thanks are also due to the team of investigators who worked hard in the field for data collection. Without the hard work of field investigators, the collection of reliable data may not have been possible, and I would have struggled hard to make sense of electoral politics in Delhi.

But I must confess that this long journey may not have been possible without the support and encouragement I received from my colleagues at the CSDS, especially V. B. Singh, D. L. Sheth and Yogendra Yadav. The directors of the CSDS at various points of time—V. B. Singh, R. K. Srivastava, Suresh Sharma and Rajeev Bhargava—provided me the opportunity to work independently, which helped me complete this book. I would also like to express my gratitude to Suhas Palshikar who always encouraged me to write this book.

Several researchers working at Lokniti helped me at different times and different stages of writing this book, some of whom are Banasmita Bora, Kinjal Sampat, Jyoti Mishra, Vibha Attri, Shreyas Sardesai, Preeti Singh Gautam, Anwesha Dutta and Sharib Zey. Thanks are also due to the data unit team of the CSDS which includes Himanshu Bhattacharya, Kanchan Malhotra and K. A. Q. A. Hilal. It may be unjust if I do not mention the names of Dhananjay Kumar Singh and Anuradha Singh, who extended various kinds of administrative and logistics support to me whenever needed.

Last, I would like to thank my wife Rashmi who always supported and encouraged me not in only writing this book but in anything which gets published under my name. I am sure that without her moral support it would have not been easy for me to complete this book. My two daughters, Vishakha Nandini and Manavi Nandini, need special mention. Their curious questions at late hours (late night) while writing this book—especially from the younger daughter Manavi about why this book, why I need to sit for long hours for writing the book, about my work, my writing, my teaching and overall about my office—have always been a source of inspiration for me. I must thank all other family members who provided moral support to me in writing this book. There may be a few others who provided different kinds of support to me while writing this book; I may not have mentioned their names, but my sincere thanks to all of them as well.

Introduction

The city of Delhi occupies an important place not only in recent decades but even in the past going back to the ancient period. The history of Delhi could be traced since Harappan Civilization (*Economic Survey of Delhi* 2005–06); even in the Mahabharata there are some descriptions about Delhi (Indraprastha), the capital of the Pandavas, and the struggle for capturing power could also be traced since that period. The Delhi which has been ruled by various rulers from time to time has witnessed many social, cultural, architectural and political developments. Various small cities within Delhi were constructed by the rulers during their reign and some of them still exist in Delhi, namely, Quila Rai Pithora, Mehrauli, Siri, Tughlakabad, Firozabad, Shergarh and Shahjehanabad.[1] The city of Delhi was captured by the British government after the 1857 mutiny, the imperial government shifted its capital from Calcutta (now Kolkata) to Delhi in 1911 and the new capital was named 'New Delhi' in 1927. The city was planned by two British architects, Sir Edwin Lutyens and Sir Herbert Baker who used different kinds of architecture from the previous rulers of the medieval age.

Historically, the city of Delhi can be divided into two cities: one 'Old Delhi' and the other 'New Delhi'. The city Old Delhi has a culture and architecture (having a web of congested lanes and old havelis) which are very different from New Delhi, which has spacious and wide roads, tree-lined avenues and grand government buildings. It has the memories of freedom struggles and also the Partition of India in 1947. It was at the time of Partition that Delhi received large numbers of refugees, which added a significant number to its already existing population. Many places were converted into refugee camps which were later made permanent housing for refugees, like Lajpat Nagar, Rajinder Nagar, Nizamuddin East, Punjabi Bagh, Rehgar Pura, Jungpura and Kingsway Camp (Kaur 2007).

During the past six decades, the city has expanded both geographically and numerically. Old Delhi has witnessed several changes with regard to architecture, culture and people; the Asian Games (1982) and more recently the Commonwealth Games (2010) have changed even those localities known as New Delhi. But some people still see Delhi as two cities, Old Delhi and New Delhi, while some even see this as Yamuna Paar and the rest of Delhi. But the city of Delhi has moved much beyond that not only geographically (National Capital Territory and more recently National Capital Region), but has also witnessed changes in its architecture, culture and social and economic profiles of the people living in Delhi. The changed class profile of the people living in Delhi has an impact on the nature of electoral politics of this city. The focus of this book is to map the changes which the city of Delhi has witnessed in terms of people, and show in great detail how the electoral politics of Delhi has changed after Delhi became a state in 1993.

The city of Delhi does not merely have a historical memory or past, but even after Independence, the city has remained the hub of various cultural, social and political events. Delhi is a home for people practising various religions: Hindus (82.0 per cent), Muslims (11.7 per cent), Sikhs (4.0 per cent), Jains (1.1 per cent), Christians (0.9 per cent) and Buddhists (0.2 per cent) (Government of Delhi 2012). In terms of language diversity, 81.1 per cent of the people speak Hindi, followed by 7.2 per cent Punjabi and 6.3 per cent Urdu. Other than these major languages, people speak other state-specific languages too, like Bengali, Oriya, Malayalam, Tamil and Telugu (ibid.). The explanatory fact for this could be the migration. As per the 2001 census, Delhi has 6,014,458 migrated population and this is from the various states of India. Despite this social and cultural variation, Delhi is also known for its class variations. If on the one hand some of the richest families live in Delhi, on the other hand there are a large number of houseless—mainly migrants from Bihar, UP and other states—who have no shelter and no house to spend their nights; they sleep on the roadsides, pavements and similar public spaces. Some people live extremely luxurious lives and there are some who do not have the basic amenities or the necessary human conditions to live. As per the *Delhi Statistical Handbook*, there are 43,813 households in Delhi who do not have a single room to live (ibid.). This book tries to address the issues related to the houseless in Delhi.

The city of Delhi is not only the social and cultural centre of India but it is also the hub of all political activities, from protests, demonstrations, rallies and dharnas on issues which may or may not be an issue concerning the people of Delhi. The anti-Emergency movement (1975–77), popularly known as the J. P. Movement, was spread across almost the entire northern India, but Delhi remained the epicentre of the anti-Emergency movement. Similarly, the anti-Mandal movement (1990) was widespread, but again Delhi city witnessed most of the action. In recent years (2012) the city of Delhi witnessed large-scale participation of people, with a large number of youth, in the anti-corruption movement led by Anna Hazare and the protest against the gruesome rape incident (Nirbhaya) which happened in the city recently. Studies have been conducted and books have been written on Delhi's culture and history, and on social and political movements which the city witnessed in the past, but it is difficult to find any book on Delhi's electoral politics, more so on the electoral politics in the city in recent years after Delhi became a state and the first Assembly election was held in 1993. This book on Delhi's changing electoral politics analyzes in great detail how the electoral politics of this city has changed in recent years.

It is not that elections began in Delhi in recent years; we have had elections in Delhi ever since the first Lok Sabha election held in India in 1952. People of Delhi have been voting to elect seven Lok Sabha members representing different Lok Sabha constituencies. The city has also witnessed municipal elections for a very long time. But the interest and focus on Delhi's electoral politics actually emerged among the people after Delhi became a state with 70 seats in the State Legislative Assembly. Soon after Delhi became a state, the first Assembly election was held in 1993 and the BJP formed the first government in Delhi. There have been three more Assembly elections in Delhi after that—in 1998, 2003 and 2008. The Congress was defeated during the first Assembly election, but after that the Congress has managed to win all the three Assembly elections, and Sheila Dikshit has been the chief minister for the past 15 years. Why was the BJP badly defeated? How did the Congress manage to register three successive victories by defeating the BJP? Is it because of the leadership of the Congress or is it because of the party being very popular amongst some sections of voters? The book tries to answer some of these questions.

The earliest election witnessed a bipolar contest between the BJP and the Congress, but the last few elections have witnessed the emergence of the BSP. The BSP performed very well during the 2008 Assembly election, won two seats (Gokalpur and Badarpur) and its candidates were runners-up in another five Assembly constituencies. How has the BSP managed to make inroads into Delhi politics? The voters of Delhi vote more on class lines rather than caste lines and Delhi at present is a home to broadly three classes of people—the upper class, the middle class and the lower/poor class—each class being of more or less equal numbers/ size but with very different social and political orientations. The recent migration to Delhi has added a large number of migrants, mainly from the lower-and-poor class to the city's original habitants. Not only has the population of the city changed, the profile of voters in different con- stituencies has also changed, resulting in a change in the nature of elec- toral contest and electoral politics in the city of Delhi. The book tries to analyze the factors, the process and the result of change in the city's electoral politics.

This book looks into great detail how the electoral politics of Delhi has changed and the factors resulting in such change. The analyses of voting behaviour of Delhi's voters—the shifts in their political choices and preferences—is done using two types of data sources, both second- ary data and primary data. The secondary data used for analysis are the constituency-wise detailed results of all the four Assembly elections held in Delhi since 1993 (constituency-wise detailed results are appended to the book as appendix) while the primary data used for the analysis of voting behaviour are from the surveys conducted by the CSDS during the 1998, 2003 and 2008 Assembly elections. During the 2008 Assembly election, the data was collected from interviews of 1,674 respondents/ voters spread across 29 Assembly constituencies, which was a represent- ative sample of the voters of Delhi. The sample surveys during the 2003 and 1998 Assembly elections were much bigger (12,311 voters in 1998 and 14,460 voters in 2003) from all the 70 Assembly constituencies of Delhi. As far as possible, the surveys were conducted scientifically, that is, the sample of 20 locations within each Assembly constituency was drawn using systematic random sampling technique and the sample of voters (respondents) at each selected location was drawn from the most updated electoral roll using systematic random sampling technique. The sample of voters from whom the data was collected was representative of the voters of Delhi during all the surveys. Soon after the survey was completed, some newspaper reports were generated and published in a national newspaper, but the detailed academic analyses of the primary data collected from the benchmark survey of Delhi, both in 1998 and 2003, are being used and published in this book for the first time.

The very first chapter of the book (Chapter 1) analyzes how Delhi's demographic profile has changed during the past couple of decades as a result of large-scale migration to the city. While the data from the censuses of India 2001 and 2011 tell us the story of migration in different cities, the findings of the survey data analyzed in this chapter help us in going beyond the mere number of migrants and help in unfolding the story of the social and economic profiles of the migrants who settled down in Delhi during the past couple of decades. Unlike many of the other Indian states, Delhi's population mainly comprises migrants. Delhi has always attracted a very high number of migrants from other states. A recent report of the Indian Institute of Human Settlement shows that Delhi receives the largest flow of migrants anywhere in urban India (*Times of India* 2011). There are various reasons for people migrating to Delhi, like better employment opportunities, better facilities of health care, education and several such civic amenities. Large-scale migration to this city has resulted in an enormous increase in the city's population from 1.75 million in 1951 to more than 2 million people as per the latest census (2011) estimates. The two largest streams of migration to urban India are from UP to Delhi and from Bihar to Delhi (ibid.).

In the past, various studies have been done on migration, its causes and how it has an impact on electoral outcome. There are studies which focus on how rapid growth and development of Delhi is resulting in opportunities of livelihood support for the poor, unskilled/ semi-skilled rural population in the secondary and tertiary sectors of the economy within Delhi (National Capital Region Planning Board n.d.: Chapter 3). Some attribute the highest per capita income and income growth, a huge concentration of wealth, resources, infrastructure and a relatively high quality of urban services as the reasons for this high flow of migration to Delhi (*Times of India* 2011). That a large number of poor or so-called lower-caste migrants head to Delhi in search of livelihood is obvious; many 'upper-caste' folk also migrate to Delhi. According to one explanation,

> The same caste system that inhibits lower castes from rising up the economic ladder prevents the upper castes from performing menial jobs to earn a living. The anonymity of cities like Delhi allows a Brahmin to work as a rickshaw-puller, whereas the caste hierarchy would make it hard for him to do so in his hometown, even if his family is starving. (ibid.)

Much of the work that has been done on migration focuses on what are the various reasons why people move from one place to another. Migration is said to have a lot of effect in electoral politics. It is often said to be one of the several factors underlying political change (Gimpel and Schuknecht 2001). Migration has always been happening through-out the world for various reasons. It has always been a major source of human survival and adaptation. Apart from moving from one place to another, migration can result in willing and unwilling exchange of ideas, attitude, skills and genes (Roy and Debnath 2011). Niranjan Roy and Avijit Debnath in their work talk about how internal migration in India is of particular interest because of the strong heterogeneous character of the country (ibid.).

The second chapter of the book begins with a discussion on caste and politics and caste-based voting. The Assembly constituencies of Delhi have changed to a great extent, both geographically and socially. If the redrawing of boundaries of Assembly constituencies by way of delimitation exercise resulted in change in geographical boundaries of Assembly constituencies, the rapid migration has changed the social profile of Assembly constituencies. This chapter of the book maps in great detail the social profile of different Assembly constituencies and who matters most in different Assembly constituencies in terms of their number. There is a very large migrant population, a large Dalit population (17 per cent) and also a sizeable Muslim population (12 per cent). The changed social profile of the people also has an impact on the profile of the voters. The Muslims are largely concentrated in localities like Okhla, Chandni Chowk, Seelampur, Karawal Nagar, Badarpur, Zafrabad, Nand Nagri and Geeta Colony. There are 16 Assembly constituencies which have a sizeable proportion of Punjabi Khatri voters. But at the same time the migrants constitute a sizeable proportion of voters in many Assembly constituencies like Burari, Adarsh Nagar, Wazirpur, Uttam Nagar, Dwarka, Palam, Ambedkar Nagar (SC), Sangam Vihar, Tughlakabad, Badarpur, Trilokpuri (SC), Kondli (SC), Seemapuri (SC), Gokalpur (SC), Mustafabad and Karawal Nagar. Due to sheer numerical strength, they are in a position to influence the electoral battle in many constitu-encies. There are some Assembly constituencies like Chandni Chowk, Ballimaran and Okhla with sizeable Muslim voters. Using evidence from surveys, this chapter essentially focuses on how voters from differ-ent caste backgrounds have voted in Delhi during the last four Assembly elections. Caste plays an important role in Indian electoral politics. This is not a new phenomenon which has come to play during the past few decades, but a close relationship of caste and politics has existed ever since the first election was held after Independence. Many studies have been done on caste and its impact on electoral politics. Caste affects electoral politics in India at all levels and elections in turn have redefined the meaning of caste (Deshpande 2000: 267). Rajni Kothari also focuses on its importance and says, "It is not politics that gets caste-ridden; it is caste that gets politicized" (Kothari 1970: 225). Importance of caste-based mobilization can also be seen in Rudolph and Rudolph's work in which they talk about three kinds of mobilization that take place in Indian politics on the basis of caste, which they connote as vertical, horizontal and differential mobilizations (Rudolph and Rudolph 1967).[2] The second chapter of the book analyzes in great detail the relationship of caste and politics in the city of Delhi.

The focus of the third chapter of the book is on one big question of what matters more in Delhi politics—caste or class? The book tries to focus on the shift from caste-based political mobilization to class-based mobilization. Using empirical evidence the book explains how class is a more important social cleavage in Delhi compared to caste. The evidence used in explaining this relationship of caste and voting pattern, and the shift in voting patterns from caste to class, add strength to the book since there is hardly any empirical study which focuses on the electoral politics of a city. The data used in the book helps the reader to understand that in Delhi it is class more than caste which matters in electoral politics.

The electoral politics in many states of India has moved from a bipolar contest to a multipolar contest. The puzzle is, even though Delhi has a large Dalit population, a sizeable Muslim population and large number of people from the OBCs, the politics in Delhi is largely a bipolar contest between the Congress and the BJP, and the third political force—first in the form of Janata Dal (United) and now in the name of BSP—has largely remained marginalized. In recent Assembly elections the BSP has made some inroads in the city's politics largely because a large number of migrants from lower and poor income groups, amongst whom large numbers belong to the Dalit community, voted for the BSP. The Congress and the BSP are competing for the support of the Dalits in Delhi. The changes in the social bases of parties have also led to a sharpening of polarization between the Congress and the BJP, leaving less room for the BSP and making it a third force (Pai 2003).Why is the BSP, which is so popular amongst the Dalit voters of UP, unable to mobilize the Dalits in Delhi? Is caste-based political mobilization missing in Delhi? If caste is not the primary factor for voters' mobilization in Delhi, what are the other social cleavages for political mobilization?

It is not that caste is not an important factor for voters' mobilization; it is important but more in rural areas compared to the urban areas (Ahmed 1970: 980). For mobilizing support on caste lines in a rural area, patron–client relationships and kinship networks are some of the channels used (ibid.: 981) which are not as visible in urban areas. He further added a reason that in urban areas there are other attributes than caste which influence the electoral behaviour of voters, like regional and linguistic identities, class and occupational interests, and considerations of governmental policies and performance. A study of Delhi slums indicates that there are a large number of Dalits who have migrated to Delhi from different states, they are divided along regional and subcaste lines and, hence, political mobilization along caste identity becomes difficult. They do not have strong party preferences. They select candidates who have done something for their areas (Antony and Maheshwaran 2001).

The fourth chapter of the book maps the electoral trajectories of the two main political parties (the Congress and the BJP) and the recent rise of the BSP. Going beyond merely which party won how many seats and what percentage of votes in different elections, the chapter analyzes the election results by different types/classification of constituencies using caste and migrant population as variables. The vote share of the Congress declined from 48 per cent during the 1998 and 2003 Assembly elections to 40 per cent during the latest victory in 2008, though we did not witness a corresponding increase in the vote share of its main rival party, the BJP. But things seem to have changed a little bit with regard to the electoral performance of the BSP in Delhi. The 2008 Assembly election in Delhi witnessed changing political preferences amongst different classes of voters, but more so amongst the lower-and-poor-class voters. Large proportions of lower-class (and poor) voters moved from the Congress to the BSP, resulting in decline in about 8 per cent vote share of the Congress between 2003 and 2008. The large proportion of lower-class (and poor) voters, of which an overwhelming numbers are migrants, voted for Mayawati's BSP. In about 16 Assembly constituencies with a large proportion of migrant voters, the BSP polled 18.9 per cent votes compared to its average 14 per cent votes in that election. It also managed to win two Assembly seats—Gokalpur reserved seat by a decent margin of over 3,000 votes and the Badarpur general seat by a huge margin of over 13,000 votes (the BSP candidate Ram Singh Netaji defeated a stalwart of Delhi politics, Ram Singh Bidhuri of the Congress)—during the 2008 Assembly election. Apart from that, the BSP was also the runner-up in another five Assembly constituencies—Narela, Badali,

Deoli, Tughlakabad and Babarpur. In all these constituencies the BSP polled a sizeable proportion of the votes. The BSP did make its presence felt even during the previous Assembly election held in Delhi in the year 2003. With sizeable Dalit voters and a large proportion of migrants mainly poor, there is a scope for the rise of the new third force in the city's politics and BSP is emerging as the party to fill this gap. There are clear signals of Delhi's politics moving from bipolarity to a situation of a three-cornered contest.

The fifth chapter discusses the personality factor in city politics and using empirical evidence over a period of time analyzes why Congress has an upper hand over its main rival the BJP in the city's politics. It is true that the changed social profile of Delhi's voters (sizeable proportions of lower-class-and-poor voters and migrants) and the nature of political preference guided largely on class lines had benefited the Congress as the party is relatively more popular amongst the poor and the lower-class voters. But besides that the Congress also benefited from the able leadership of Sheila Dikshit. While on the one hand, after the exit of Madan Lal Khurana, the BJP had the handicap of leadership and kept trying various options in various elections (Sahib Singh Verma, Sushma Swaraj, Vijay Kumar Malhotra and Vijay Jolly), on the other hand, the Congress was placed pretty well with Sheila Dikshit in command, whose popularity cuts across caste and class lines.

The sixth chapter focuses on people who live in Delhi but do not have voting rights, those who live on the footpaths and hardly enjoy any political right due to lack of identity. There are only newspaper stories with photographs of the houseless, whose estimates vary but they are in sizeable numbers. The state pays little attention to them, that too seasonal (only during winter), but after that the city hardly pays any attention to their problems. This chapter of the book tries to analyze the social and economic conditions of the houseless in Delhi. While it is true that Delhi largely has three classes of people—the upper class, the middle class and the lower class—who play important social and political roles and have their views and opinions on social and political issues, it would be an incomplete story of Delhi. The city is also home to a very large population (there are various estimates about their numbers) who do not have a home. These are houseless people, who sleep on pavements, parks, roadsides and similar open spaces and who hardly have any role to play in the city's political life. Besides the differences of caste communities and class, this is another kind of difference which extends to those who vote and those who are unable to vote, not as a matter of choice but due to impinging constraints and impediments. The former category may be described as the 'de facto' citizens while the latter could be called the 'dormant' or the marginal citizens of democracy. The category of 'dormant citizens' stands excluded from the democratic and participatory process of the state. This is not due to a matter of choice but largely due to the existential preoccupations of bare survival. The state in such situations has remained a mere spectator and has hardly tried to intervene. The people, in this context, are actually the marginal citizens who hardly enjoy any political rights—most of them do not have any identity proof, as they do not have any residence proof and, hence, are denied various political rights which a normal citizen enjoys. Due to the very fact that most of them are not counted as voters and are unable to vote, the government hardly bothers about them, except providing a few shelter homes. The political parties hardly pay attention to their issues as they do not form the vote bank for them. There is a need for not only providing material benefits to them but also to make efforts to bring them into the mainstream of the democratic process. The law does not debar houseless people from being enrolled as voters. There has been a beginning—some non-governmental organizations have made some effort in enrolling the houseless as voters and some of them have also voted during the last national election. Rather than thinking of policies about how to move them out of the city, there is a need to think about how to integrate them into the social and democratic processes. This chapter of the book also tries to bring into focus those who are on the margins of the society and left out of the political process—the houseless in Delhi.

The last chapter offers a new explanation of the city of Delhi and builds up the argument that Delhi is not just one city, but three cities merged into one, namely, the city of the upper class (rich), the city of the middle class and the city of the lower-class (poor) people. Delhi has witnessed enormous change during the past few decades. The class character of Delhi has changed with rapid migration over the past several decades. Delhi no more remains a city of the rich people, it has a sizeable middle-class population, and a large number of poor people living in slums and unauthorized colonies. These slums and unauthorized colonies are spread all over the city and the previous classifications of the city into 'New Delhi' and 'Old Delhi', or 'South Delhi' being a synonym of upper-class people and 'Yamuna Paar' being seen as lower-class localities no longer hold true. Even the most recent division of Delhi into nine administrative zones is hardly meaningful. At present, neither the different geographical boundaries of the city with certain notions of a class hold ground, nor does the administrative division of the city seem meaningful; there is a need to relook at the city more carefully. I see Delhi as three cities being merged into one city—the city of the upper class, the city of the middle class and the city of the lower class. These three cities are spread across Delhi and do not have clearly demarcated geographical boundaries, but have sharply demarcated social and political boundaries. The political boundaries between these three are reflected in their political attitudes and preferences exhibited by their voting patterns across the past three Assembly elections held in Delhi in 1998, 2003 and 2008. The upper-class voters voted for the BJP in big numbers while the middle-class and lower-class-and-poor voters voted for the Congress in sizeable proportions. Though voters belonging to different castes like Punjabi Khatri, Jat, Dalit, Brahmin, or OBC have their political preferences and sizeable numbers of them vote for one or the other political party, they seem divided more on class lines rather than on caste lines.

Notes

1. These are still listed in government records and available at the Government of Delhi website. Retrieved from http://delhigovt.nic.in/dept/prj/visitor/places.asp?opt=2.
2. Vertical mobilization is the regimenting of the sustenance by traditional person in local societies that are instituted and unified by rank, mutual reliance and of traditional authority. Horizontal mobilization engages the regimenting of political sustenance by class or community leaders and their specialized establishments. Differential mobilization employs the regimenting of direct or indirect political encouragement by political parties and other integrative structures from practicable but intrinsically categorized communities through corresponding pledges to ideology, sentiment and interest.

1

Delhi: A City of Migrants

Delhi has seen an enormous increase in its population mainly due to massive migration of people from various parts of the country. As per an estimate, nearly 40 per cent of the city's population is constituted of the migrants, accounting for nearly 3–3.5 million migrant voters in Delhi. Delhi's first *Human Development Report* indicated that in the recent years, Delhi, not Mumbai, was the most sought-after city of dream for the common Indian. The report indicated that Delhi's population has been growing at a rate which is more than one-and-a-half times the national average. As per the estimates, 665 people migrate to this city every day. Contrary to the popular perception of Biharis constituting the maximum number of migrants, it is the neighbouring state UP from where the largest numbers of people migrate to Delhi. This, however, does not refute the fact that a large number of people from Bihar migrate to Delhi and the NCR daily. In a study it was found that there are approximately 20,000 people who come to Delhi and the NCR every day for a job or to study. Going by this calculation, approximately 15,000 people from Bihar migrate to Delhi and the NCR and live there for a long time. Based on these statistics it can be summed up that in one month 450,000 people add to the existing populace of Delhi and the NCR.

During the past few decades, the population of this city has more than doubled. The latest census of 2011 counted Delhi's population as 13.7 million. A decade back, the population of Delhi was a little more than nine million. The rapid increase in Delhi's population has been mainly due to a very high growth rate of population. During the last three decades 1981–91, 1991–2001 and 2001–11, the city of Delhi has witnessed the growth of population at 51.4, 47.02 and 20.96 per cent respectively, much higher compared to the national growth rate of 36.5 and 31.3 and 31.8 per cent in corresponding decades (see Table 1.1). This has resulted in high density of Delhi's population, which at present is 9,294 persons per square km, compared to the national density of 324 persons per sq km in the year 2001. This was much lower a decade back at 6,352 persons per square km. By 2015, Delhi is expected to be the third-largest agglomeration in the world after Tokyo and Mumbai.

Table 1.1:
Decadal Growth Rate of Urban Population in Mega Cities of India

	1981–91	*1991–2001*	*2001–11*
All India	36.5	31.3	31.8
Delhi	46.9	52.6	26.69
Mumbai	33.7	30.2	12.1
Kolkata	19.9	21.1	6.8
Chennai	26.4	19.8	32.56
Bangalore	41.4	39.1	47.56
Hyderabad	39.3	29.2	34.96

Source: Data for 1981–91, Census of India 1991, 1991–2001, Census of India 2001 Data for 2001–2011, India's 2011 Census, a population turning point. Available at http://makanaka.wordpress.com/2011/04/01/indias-2011-census-a-population-turning-point/.
Note: All figures are in per cent.

The contribution of migration to the mounting population of Delhi cannot be skipped. The issue needs to be focused in a way that the undercurrents of the phenomenon in consideration get proper attention.

Theorizing Social Migration in Delhi

Migration, interestingly, has been studied variedly by different disciplines. Disciplines like sociology, anthropology, demography, economics and political science deal with the issues of migration differently but it is hard to demarcate the boundaries of these disciplines in the domain of the studies in migration, which cuts itself out separately from other overlapping disciplines, thereby making the subject a multidisciplinary field. It is up to the researcher to streamline the issues to be looked into, or overlooked, as per the need and purpose of the research.

Studying migration patterns of the city so as to coherently understand the dynamics of migration, demands two broad questions to be dealt systematically. First, a theoretical understanding of why Delhi witnessed more migration on its soil, compared to other metropolises of the country. This will encompass all the social, economic and political causes and determinants which made the city a lucrative option to migrate for a large number of the population. The study will include the chronological analyses of the emergence of migration to the city and the development of the factor which gave impetus to the phenomenon. Second, making a further enquiry on the social, economic and political repercussions of the migration in the city, so as to understand the social, cultural and organizational patterns which became the object of study for the classical sociological theorists like Marx, Durkheim and Weber.

It was after the Second World War that the phenomenon of migration began in India, as it did in most of the countries of the world. It was at this juncture that many nations achieved independence and embarked on their programmes aimed at social and economic development (Premi 1986). The studies in migration since the days of E. G. Ravenstein have explained the dynamics of migration on the basis of push and pull factors that vary temporally and spatially. However, to truly comprehend the pattern of migration it is important not to look just at the push and pull factors; rather, what is required is an analysis based on the relation between these factors. For instance, arguing the causes for migration in Delhi, Dupont (2000) considers employment to be the main reason for migration. For him "the specific pull of the labour market" of Delhi has attracted both the rural as well as urban migrants to its land.

To be fully equipped to answer the question in consideration, delving deeper into this crucial aspect is of paramount importance for any student of migration studies. Thus, when we look for the causes for Delhi being characterized by a higher rate of migration as compared to other metropolises of the country, we consider not just the presence of certain 'pull factors' in the city (place of destination), but also the 'push factors' present in the major states or region from where people migrate (the places of origin). Neither does the physical condition of Delhi have any stark difference with that of UP or Bihar, nor have these states suffered any natural calamity which Delhi has not. But the opportunities—be they economic, social or educational—are in plenty for the migrants here as compared to their native states. This situation of contrast is not so stark in other metropolitan cities of the country.

One more reason that could be attributed to this increasing rate of migration is the geographical distance that Delhi has with other metropolitan cities. It occupies a solitary seat in North India thereby serving a bigger geographical area as well as a larger population of the country than any other metropolis of India.

Dupont writes,

[S]uch a demographic growth occurred together with the spatial expansion of the urban zone in all directions, including to the east of the Yamuna River. The official urban area doubled between 1941 and 1961. The geographical location of Delhi in the Gangetic plain, and, moreover, the absence of any significant physical barrier to the progress of urbanization (the Aravalli hills—the Delhi Ridge—in the west and south do not constitute an effective obstacle) favoured multidirectional urban expansion and this trend continued in the decades that followed. (Dupont 2000: 230–31)

Cadene (2000) traces the development of Delhi since Independence, and the major component for this advancement being Delhi as the capital city, thereby gaining the most important place in the political and the administrative systems. He acknowledges Mumbai's domain in the urban landscape, and its role and dominance in economic sectors, but Delhi follows the city. "Delhi, alongside Mumbai, occupies the top position as the headquarters of fertilizers and construction companies; it comes second after Mumbai in the field of transport equipment and electronics; second after Calcutta for mechanical consumer goods" (Cadene 2000: 243). In economic domains other than the industrial sector, for instance, in the banking sector, Delhi precedes any other city in the country. "In the field of education, research and communication, Delhi plays a major role largely because of its political position. If research and development in private sector takes place mainly in Mumbai, Delhi clearly dominates in research and development initiated by the central government" (ibid.: 243–44).

Locating Migration: A Historical View

Tracing the history of migrant population in Delhi, people always emphasize the recent migrants, who have moved to Delhi for enhanced education facilities or for employment opportunities. This history is relatively new and it discounts the old history of the city which emerged in the medieval age and nourished itself as the capital city of the country. People are of the view that migration to this city began soon after the Partition of India when large numbers of refugees came and settled down in Delhi.

> Just after 1947 Delhi, whose population was about 9,00,000 at the time, received 4,70,000 refugees from western Punjab and Sindh, while 3,20,000 Muslims left the capital and migrated to Pakistan. Not surprisingly, 1941–51 is the period of highest demographic growth in the history of the capital which expanded from almost 7,00,000 inhabitants in 1941 to 1.4 million in 1951, corresponding to an annual growth rate of 7.5 per cent which has not been equaled since. (Dupont 2000: 229)

But the truth is that Delhi started witnessing migration to its territory even before Partition. Delhi was the capital city of the British Raj as well as the Mughal rule. The city being the hotbed of political and administrative conduct cannot be denied.

Development in Delhi is linked to four different periods. These periods are precolonial (before 1911), pre-Independence (1911–47), post-Independence (1947–61) and Master Plan period (1961–81). During each of these periods, migration to Delhi has been circumstantial. The precolonial period was based on traditions, cultures and religious lifestyles promoted by invaders. Pre-Independence was related to migration of the British and the development of trade. Post-Independence was based on migration from partitioned West Pakistan. The Master Plan period refers to the temporary migration from rural areas in search of employment. At present, it has become an alternative, central place for international trade as well as a seat of power. The increase in Delhi's population from 4.1 million in 1911 to 16.7 million in 2011 shows a sharp increase in the city's population. The major increase during the Master Plan period has been in the past two decades, from 5.2 million to 13.7 million.

The large-scale migration which occurred in the period 1946–47 did not stop the migration after that. Rather migration became an unending phenomenon in the city, where initially people from all over the country, and later from all over the globe, travelled and stayed for a significant time. Figures indicate that the significant migration to Delhi which began in the mid-1940s continued in subsequent decades as well, with more or less similar proportion of people migrating to this city. During the period 1971–90 the pace of migration to Delhi actually picked up and it was during these two decades that the maximum number of people (19 and 21 per cent of the total migrants) migrated to Delhi. In other words, of the total migrants in Delhi, nearly 40 per cent migrated to this city between these 20 years (Table 1.2). Thus, the overcrowding of the city in recent years may make some believe that the migration to this city has increased over the past few decades but the data on migration gives us altogether a different picture of the demographic state of affairs.

Table 1.2:
Pattern of Migration in Delhi during Last Few Decades

Year of migration	Per cent migration
Before Partition	11
During Partition	11
1951–60	10
1961–70 ·	13
1971–80	19
1981–90	21
1991–2001	15
2007–08	24

Source: HT–CSDS Delhi Survey 2003[1] and Survey Office Report for the years 2007–08.
Note: All figures are in per cent.

Migrant Politics or Politicizing Migrants: The Voting Behaviour

"The problem of ethnicity has assumed an important place in migration studies especially in the urban context" (quoted in Rao 1986) but studies on the electoral behaviour of these migrants have not been emphasized upon. Though the period 1971–90 witnessed large-scale migration, and by this time a large migrant population was already significant to the city, they were not perceived as a vote bank by any political party. Looking at the predominance of the Congress in the city's politics one could, with common sense, imagine a strong support for the Congress amongst the migrant voters during that period. Except for the 1977 Lok Sabha election, when there was an anti-Emergency wave, the Congress had performed relatively well in most of the Lok Sabha elections. We do not see political parties attracting the migrant voters by alluring them with migrant-favouring policies. One of the reasons why the political parties did not exploit them as serious vote bank in the past, despite their living in clusters and concentrated in a few localities, was that they did not form sizeable numbers, crucial in electoral contest. But affairs seem to have changed dramatically as well as drastically during the past couple of decades.

Over the years, the pace of migration from different states has been slightly different. During the last two decades, there has been a rapid migration in Delhi of people from Bihar, eventually leading to an increase in Bihari voters in Delhi. Of those who migrated to Delhi during the decade 1991–2001, nearly one-fourth were from Bihar (Table 1.3). The proportion of people who migrated from Bihar to Delhi during the previous decade (1981–91) was much higher. During that period, of all the migrants, nearly one-third were from Bihar.

Table 1.3:
State-wise Pattern of Migration in Delhi: 1971–2008

States	1971–80	1981–91	1991–2001	2007–08
Bihar	19	33	24	18
UP	22	24	14	10
Other Hindi states	17	17	15	2
North Indian states	19	17	14	8

Source: Census of India and National Sample and Survey Office report for the years 2007–08.
Note: All figures are in per cent.

It is not that there are differences among migrants from Bihar and UP only in terms of their period of migration; they also differ in terms of their social and economic backgrounds. While there may be several indicators for the economic status of these migrants, one thing more or less sound indicator of economic status is the place of residence—the kind of house, and whether owned or rented. The settlement pattern is a clear indicator of the economic status of the person. One can more or less successfully guess the economic status of the Delhi voter, or his family, by his place of residence. Living in South Delhi indicates that the family or the person is economically affluent, while on the other hand Trans Yamuna is considered a synonym for a lower-middle-class lifestyle. The settlement in Trans Yamuna developed in early 1980 when the people could not afford a house in any other part of the city. This was the lowland area across the Yamuna, which was available for residential purpose at a relatively very low price. People with lower income started settling down in Trans Yamuna localities in big numbers in the early and mid-1980s. With a large number of housing societies coming up in Trans Yamuna localities, especially in the Patparganj localities as well as Mayur Vihar area, there has been a great change in the image and profile of those who live in Trans Yamuna localities. From a lower-class locality, now it has turned into an upper-middle-class locality.

It is precisely because of this that the poor who migrated to the city started looking for new localities for their living and started settling down in large numbers on the periphery of Delhi. Since they settled down in large numbers, it ultimately led to big working-class colonies coming up on the outskirts of the city. In recent times, these working-class colonies on the edges of the city are considered a synonym for the lower-and-poor-class settlements. Those living in localities mainly on the outskirts of the city are people from lower-income-class families, mainly migrants from Bihar and UP. Besides these, there are villages on the edges of the city where large numbers of people still live.

As mentioned, the migrants from Bihar somewhat differ from the migrants from UP or other states in terms of their settlement patterns. Large numbers of migrants from Bihar having settled down in the working-class periphery or in Trans Yamuna localities speaks of their economic status in general. This is somewhat true of those who have migrated from UP, but the only difference is that 46 per cent of the migrants from UP have settled down in Trans Yamuna, while only 19 per cent are living in working-class localities at the periphery of the city (Table 1.4). While this indicates that the migrants from UP are slightly better off in their economic condition, large numbers of them settling down in Trans Yamuna may also be because of the physical proximity and contiguity of the Trans Yamuna locality, with its bordering state UP.

Table 1.4:
Settlement Pattern of Migrants from Select States

Region of origin	Trans Yamuna	Working-class periphery	Periphery	Rest
Bihar	21	25	17	37
UP	46	19	9	26
Pakistan	19	11	7	63
Delhi population	26	20	15	39

Source: HT–CSDS Delhi Survey, 2003.
Notes: All figures are in per cent. 'Working-class periphery' = Badli, Shahbad, Sultanpur Majra, Mangolpuri, Vishnu Garden, Saket, Ambedkar Nagar, Tughlakabad, Badarpur, Wazirpur and Adarsh Nagar. 'Rest' includes all other colonies of South Delhi, West Delhi and North Delhi.

The settlement pattern of the migrants has remained essentially the same as what we observe now. The new migrants settled in localities where they knew someone who had migrated to the city some time back. M. S. A. Rao writes that

> migrants belonging to a particular region, language, religion, caste and tribe tend to live together in separate neighbourhoods in cities and they form ethnic groups on the basis of shared elements of culture and ideology, merging lower levels of differences based on subcaste or subreligion. The earlier migrants help the fresh ones in getting jobs and houses, and initiate them into urban ways of life. (Rao 1986: 21)

Delhi attracts people from all over the country. Most of those who migrate to the city in search of employment are adults. They have the potential of adding to the city's electoral strength even though there are some who are left out of the democratic process due to lack of political awareness or due to their casual approach towards their voting rights. The rapid migration has added more voters to the city's electoral register; at the same time, it has also added more and more houseless on the streets of this city.[2]

Reasoning Migration: A Preliminary Analysis

Although there are various reasons for migration, employment is the basic driving force of migration. Data from the *Census of India* suggests that at the all-India level, 44 per cent migrated due to marriage, 21 per cent migrated due to shifting of the household, 7 per cent mentioned moving soon after their birth while another 3 per cent mentioned migrating from one place to another due to education. Apart from all these reasons, 15 per cent mentioned employment as the main reason for their migration from one place to another. When it comes to the reason behind migrating to Delhi, the driving force attracting people to Delhi from different states somewhat varies, though employment opportunities remain an overarching concern. Among those who have migrated to Delhi, 38 per cent mentioned employment as the main reason for migration, while another 37 per cent mentioned moving to this city with the household permanently. Only 14 per cent of the people seemed to have moved to this city due to marriage. Educational attainment has been the concern of less than 3 per cent of the migrants in Delhi. Among those who migrated to Delhi from Bihar 51 per cent migrated to this city looking for work, employment and opportunities for livelihood, while another 30 per cent seemed to have migrated to this city with the entire family from Bihar with their household belongings (see Table 1.5).

Table 1.5:
What Attracts Migrants to the City of Delhi?

Reasons	*1981–91*	*1991–2001*	*2007–08*
Employment	31.29	37.6	34.5
Education	2.28	2.7	1.7
Family moved	41.45	36.8	39.7
Marriage	15.62	13.8	14.7
Others	5.16	8.6	7.8

Source: Census of India 1991, 2001 and Economic Survey of Delhi, 2007–2008.
Note: All figures are in per cent.

But a large number of them do not seem to have had great success, since of those who migrated from Bihar, 34 per cent got engaged in semi-skilled and unskilled manual work, while another 9 per cent got engaged in petty business like selling vegetables, paan on roadside or tea shop to earn their livelihood. Only a few managed to get a decent job—6 per cent managed to get employed as higher professionals and 14 per cent got employed at lower grades (Table 1.6). The situation of those who migrated from UP is slightly better since only 27 per cent are engaged in skilled and unskilled work. Nearly 8 per cent of them managed to enter high-class occupations while another 18 per cent managed to qualify for lower professional work or equivalent. Among those who migrated from southern, eastern or northeastern states, large numbers have managed to enter higher professional jobs. Among those who migrated to this city from Pakistan at the time of Partition, large numbers are engaged in either big or small business. In the case of women who are mostly illiterate, they either work as domestic workers, babysitters or daily wage labourers, or also in some cases stayed back at home which accounted as 'unpaid work'. If occupation helps in assessing people's economic and social status, clearly, among the migrants, the Biharis seem to be at the lowest while those who migrated from Pakistan seem to be well off.

Table 1.6:
Occupational Pattern of Migrants from Select Regions

State or region	Higher professional	Lower professional	Big or medium business	Small business	Petty business	Skilled and unskilled work
Delhi (native)	9	16	13	17	7	16
UP	8	18	5	14	9	27
Bihar	6	14	3	10	9	34
South	30	24	6	4	3	10
East & Northeast	21	20	4	9	4	22
Pakistan	13	17	23	21	5	9

Source: HT–CSDS Delhi Survey, 2003.
Notes: All figures are in per cent. South = Andhra Pradesh, Karnataka, Kerala, Pondicherry and Tamil Nadu. East and Northeast = Arunachal Pradesh, Assam, Bangladesh, Manipur, Meghalaya, Mizoram, Nagaland, Odisha, Sikkim, Tripura and West Bengal. Rest are engaged in various other kinds of occupation.

The phenomenal surge of Delhi's physical growth and the underdevelopment of its surrounding areas is primarily a problem of relationship rather than a problem of scarcity. For example, the total journey time from Delhi to the farthest towns in the region is so short that no big centre of transportation and trading activities has developed in the outer ring of the NCR. The entire region outside the Delhi Metropolitan Area has thus registered a relatively slow growth rate leading to lopsided development of the region characterized by the 'Metropolis–Satellite' syndrome, where part of the economic surplus of the periphery is extracted by the core and whatever development takes place in the periphery mostly reflects the expanding needs of the core. Under this phenomenon, the region, rather than adding or accelerating its growth, supported the growth and prosperity of Delhi, thereby setting an uneven system tied up in a chain of 'centre–periphery' relationship. This relationship helped to raise the income levels in Delhi. Delhi with a per capita income of Rs 19,779 at current prices (1995–96), as compared to the all-India per capita income of Rs 9,321, has the distinction of having the highest per capita income in the country. Thus, ample job opportunities coupled with higher wages and earnings have provided enough opportunities for the people who migrate to Delhi.

The occupational engagement to a great extent is linked to the level of educational attainment. While some occupations, especially entering into higher and lower professions, are directly linked to individual educational attainment, others like small or petty business may not be directly linked to the level of educational attainment. The difference in terms of engagement in different occupations also reflects the level of educational attainment among migrants from different states. There seems to be a vast difference in terms of the level of educational attainment among migrants from different states. Those who have migrated from the southern states as well from the eastern and northeastern states seem to be much more educated compared to those who have migrated from Bihar or UP. Nearly one-fifth of the migrants from Bihar and UP are non-literate, which in a way explains why a large number among them are engaged in skilled and semi-skilled work for their livelihood in Delhi. On the contrary, a large number of graduates or of much higher education explains how the migrants from the southern states have managed to get higher and lower professional jobs (Table 1.7).

Table 1.7:
Educational Attainment among Migrants from Select Regions

State or region	Non-literate	Primary school	High school	Graduate
Delhi (native)	13	11	28	47
UP	21	15	29	34
Bihar	20	18	32	30
North (others)	9	9	29	52
South	8	5	16	71
Pakistan	4	8	27	60

Source: HT–CSDS Delhi Survey, 2003.
Notes: All figures are in per cent. Other North Indian states include Rajasthan, Haryana, Punjab, Himachal Pradesh, Jammu and Kashmir, Chhattisgarh, Jharkhand, etc. South states include Andhra Pradesh, Karnataka, Kerala, Pondicherry and Tamil Nadu.

Income of the individual is directly linked to employment. The nature of gainful employment determines to a great extent the level of income of the individual. Higher the occupation or bigger the business, greater is the possibility of having a higher income. The estimates of the survey indicate that the majority of the people who have migrated from Bihar still remain poor and very few of them have managed to earn a decent livelihood (Table 1.8). This is not surprising since large numbers of them are engaged in skilled or unskilled manual work that helps little in earning a decent income or livelihood. The economic condition

Table 1.8:
Economic Prosperity of Migrants from Select Regions

State or region	Rich	Middle	Poor
Delhi (native)	20	53	27
Bihar	7	30	63
UP	9	45	46
North (others)	27	53	20
South	26	54	20
Pakistan	36	52	12

Source: HT–CSDS Delhi Survey, 2003.
Note: All figures are in per cent. Other North Indian states include Chandigarh, Chhattisgarh, Haryana, Himachal Pradesh, Jammu and Kashmir, Punjab, Rajasthan, Jharkhand, etc. South states include Andhra Pradesh, Karnataka, Kerala, Pondicherry and Tamil Nadu.

of those who have migrated from UP is slightly better, which may be explained in terms of their longer stay in Delhi, since a large number of them migrated to Delhi much before the pace of migration picked up from Bihar. More so, many among them are also employed in higher or lower professional jobs, or professions.

But this is not to say that the migrants from UP are very well off economically. Compared to those who have migrated to Delhi from the southern states or from the eastern and northeastern states, the economic condition of the migrants from UP is still very bad. Those who settled down in this city on Partition came almost empty handed but after years of struggle have managed to earn decent lives for their families.

The migrants from Pakistan constitute the richest people in Delhi. This is also because large numbers of them are engaged in big or small business, which normally bring greater economic returns compared to what one could earn being gainfully employed. While it seems that those who migrated to Delhi from Pakistan over the years have worked hard and attained a decent life, the migrants from the southern states are also economically well off, since sizeable proportions amongst them have managed to occupy relatively decent positions in the government or private sector. On the other hand, among the migrants from Bihar and Jharkhand, a large number are poor and only 7 per cent are rich. Similarly, most migrants from UP and Uttaranchal too are poor. But those who migrated to this city at the time of Independence have become very rich—87 per cent among them are rich or belong to the middle class.

The Landscape of Migration: Profiling Delhi

The rapid migration of people, mainly from Bihar and UP, has resulted in a change in the social composition of Delhi voters. Amongst Delhi's voters there are sizeable proportions of Jats and Punjabis—the original inhabitants or those who migrated to this city at the time of Partition or from western UP in the early phases of migration. But during the later phase of migration that saw a large number of migrants coming to Delhi from Bihar, the proportion of Jats and Punjabis in Delhi population declined. The Punjabi and Jat voters are still in sizeable proportions but they no more remain the most dominant sections amongst Delhi's voters. After the large-scale migration in this city, now it is the migrants who have become numerically dominant. Though these migrant voters are not a homogeneous lot and are extremely diverse in respect of their place of original residence, their caste and their language, one thing which helps them bind together is a sense of being dislocated from their original homeland where they were unable to meet their daily needs.

The large-scale migration to Delhi has resulted not only in a change in the social profile of Delhi's voters, but also in a change in the city's voters in terms of class character. Large-scale migration has added a large number of poor people in Delhi since the majority of the migrants from Bihar and UP, especially those who migrated to this city during the last couple of decades, belong to the poor economic class. A sizeable number of voters in Delhi (nearly 40 per cent) would belong to the poor economic class. At the same time, there are also people who would be considered extremely wealthy, like those who migrated to this city at the time of Partition and have prospered with the expansion of their business. Apart from these two poles there is a sizeable proportion of voters who would be considered belonging to the middle class.

The migrants' form a sizeable proportion of voters in many Assembly constituencies and are seen as a powerful political force in the city's politics. Their relative importance in the city's politics is more than their proportionate share in Delhi's electorate mainly because of their concentration in a few Assembly constituencies, at times large enough to tilt the electoral outcome with their support. As per a rough classification, after the fresh delimitation of Assembly constituencies, there are 16 Assembly constituencies which are dominated by migrants from Bihar and UP. Due to large-scale migration of (mainly poor) people from Bihar and eastern UP, they form a sizeable proportion of voters in Burari, Adarsh

Nagar, Wazirpur, Uttam Nagar, Dwarka, Palam, Ambedkar Nagar, Sangam Vihar, Tughlakabad, Badarpur, Trilokpuri, Kondli, Seemapuri, Gokalpur, Mustafabad and Karawal Nagar Assembly constituencies. Even though the proportion of voters belonging to the Punjabi community has declined due to the influx of migrants, they are still a sizeable proportion in 17 Assembly constituencies, namely, Timarpur, Badali, Shalimar Bagh, Shakur Basti, Wazirpur, Patel Nagar, Madipur, Rajouri Garden, Tilak Nagar, Hari Nagar, Janakpuri, Jangpura, Malviya Nagar, Kalkaji, Vishwas Nagar, Krishna Nagar and Shahdara. Besides these there are 11 Assembly constituencies, namely, Narela, Bawana, Mundka, Kirari, Vikaspuri, Matiala, Najafgarh, Bijwasan, Mehrauli, Chhattarpur and Deoli, which are dominated by voters from peasant communities (Jats and Gujjars). Apart from these, there are another 27 Assembly constituencies, which can be seen as mixed type of constituencies. The delimitation has not only changed the social profile of Assembly constituencies, but also of Lok Sabha constituencies. Prior to delimitation, West Delhi largely had a mix of Punjabi and Khatri voters. But after the delimitation, there has been an addition of rural voters, voters from new housing societies in Dwarka and a large number of migrant voters living in nearly 100 unauthorized colonies. This new addition of voters has changed the nature of this constituency from Punjabi-dominated to one which has a sizeable proportion of migrant voters. Out of 1.6 million voters, nearly 22 per cent voters are Poorvanchali or migrants from Bihar and UP. Nine per cent are mixed, middle-income class, 20 per cent OBCs, 13 per cent Punjabi, 6 per cent Vaish, 12 per cent SCs, 9 per cent Brahmin, 9 per cent Sikh and 8 per cent Jat. After the delimitation, the West Delhi parliamentary constituency includes Janakpuri, Hari Nagar, Tilak Nagar and Rajouri Garden from South Delhi, and Madipur and Najafgarh from Outer Delhi. Now the constituency has a mix of urban and rural voters, with posh residential areas like Janakpuri, Rajouri Garden, Vikaspuri and Dwarka on one side, and the rural areas Madipur, Matiala and Najafgarh on the other. The area also has a large percentage of population from unauthorized colonies in Uttam Nagar, Dwarka and Matiala. Over the years a large number of migrants—especially from UP, Bihar and other states—who are economically not well off have usually been dwelling in the jhuggi jhopris of Delhi. People living in such jhuggis also form a large part of the electorate in this constituency (Kaur 2004).

The Jats and Punjabi Khatris still have their hold on city politics, but over a period of time, different political parties have come to see the migrants as a vote bank and tried to woo them for their support. Initially, leaders of political parties tried to woo the migrants by facilitating and participating in religious festivals and other public gatherings organized mainly by the migrants from Bihar and UP.[3] But things seem to have changed somewhat. Not only do political parties try to facilitate the festivals celebrated mainly by migrants from Bihar and UP, they now also try to blame each other for neglecting these festivals and failing in making any arrangements for the celebration of Chhat festival, which is mainly celebrated by the migrants from the Poorvanchal. During the 2008 Assembly election, the BJP tried to rake up the issue of neglect of migrant voters in Delhi. To mobilize the migrant voters, mainly from Bihar and UP, the BJP attacked Sheila Dikshit for not making any preparation for the Chhat puja and also reminded Delhi's voters about her negative remarks about the migrants from Bihar and UP—Dikshit had once blamed the migrants from Bihar and UP for the scarcity of basic amenities and had hinted at stopping people from Poorvanchal coming to Delhi. The political parties pay a lot more attention now in mobilizing the votes of the Poorvanchali, compared to the past. The 2008 election campaign witnessed both the Congress and the BJP trying to show their concern for the problems which people face while living in jhuggi jhopri (JJ) clusters, underdeveloped colonies and the suburbs. Top leaders made it a point to visit the slums every day, and promised food security and regular water and power supply. Such measures ahead of the elections are common in states where provision of basic amenities is an issue. Despite the ever-increasing migrant population, Delhi's progress and development are generally measured by mega projects such as Metro Rail, air-conditioned buses, flyovers, the Commonwealth Games, and the introduction of compressed natural gas in the public transport system, and not basic issues which undoubtedly arise before each election. This was however taken care of by the Congress party by identifying the issues early. Sheila Dikshit's government made an effort in the NCR to systematically address the housing and drinking water problems of these colonies, where more than 50 per cent of Delhi's population live.

In recent times, the political parties have adopted a more pro-migrant approach by even nominating a few migrants to contest elections on the party ticket, in the hope that this might help in mobilizing the migrants towards other candidates put up by the party in other constituencies. It was only with an eye on a large number of Poorvanchal votes that the Congress fielded Mahabal Mishra, the Poorvanchal voice in Delhi, from the West Delhi parliamentary constituency, over Mukesh Sharma, who had a strong base amongst the Jat and Brahimn votes in the rural locations of Delhi. After the new delimitation, large numbers of migrant votes were added to this Punjabi-dominated constituency. The decision of the Congress to nominate a Poorvanchali from this constituency paid dividends. Not only did Mahabal Mishra get elected from this constituency by a margin of 129,010 votes, but it also helped in mobilizing the votes of the Poorvanchal voters in favour of the Congress in other constituencies. Another trend reflected in Delhi in recent elections has been the focus on local issues; bread-and-butter issues have gained importance over national issues. L. K. Advani's 'strong leadership' qualities and terrorism found mention in the BJP's campaign, but soon the twitter was about basic issues. Except among a certain section of the educated middle class, issues such as terrorism and leadership of the country seem to have become non-issues in Delhi. Delhi's demographic structure in terms of class, caste and community composition explains this trend. The poor, unemployed and rural people are more concerned about their bread-and-butter issues compared to the big national issues. The scales are tilted in favour of the poor, uneducated, unemployed and rural poor, and the large number of people living in slums and less developed colonies, who outnumber those living in posh, middle-class areas.

Migration has not only changed the social and economic profiles of the voters in Delhi, but it has also had an impact on political preferences. The city seemed to be divided into three broad categories—the city of the upper class, the city of the middle class and the city of the lower class. The upper-class voters seemed to be inclined more towards the BJP while the lower-class voters seemed to favour the Congress. But recent elections have witnessed some shifts in the voting preferences of the lower-class voters. The BSP is emerging as a popular party amongst the lower-class voters and large numbers of them have voted for it, cutting into the lower-class vote of the Congress. At the same time, the Congress has managed to make up its loss amongst the lower-income-class voters by increasing its popularity amongst the middle-class voters, though they still remain somewhat divided between the Congress and the BJP.

Notes

1. The HT–CSDS Delhi Survey is one of the largest surveys of social and political opinions and attitudes of people living in Delhi. This is probably

the largest survey undertaken in any city of the world. The data for this survey was collected from 1,700 locations spread over all the 70 Assembly constituencies of Delhi. In each Assembly constituency, 20 per cent of the polling booths were randomly selected using the probability proportionate to size technique. In each of the selected locations, 2 per cent respondent voters were randomly selected from the electoral rolls. A total of about 38,000 voters were approached for interview, of which a total of 14,460 voters were successfully interviewed during September–October 2003. The chapter draws heavily from the findings of this survey.

2. The number of total electors in Delhi has increased during the past 15 years. The number of total registered voters in Delhi increased from 5,850,545 in the 1993 Assembly election to 10,722,800 in the 2008 Assembly election. The number of total electors in Delhi during the 2003 Assembly election was 8,420,141.

3. Various leaders of political parties try to provide as much facility as possible at the time of Chhat puja, a sacred festival celebrated largely amongst the migrants from Bihar and eastern UP.

2

Social Cleavages

A Glimpse into the Relation between Caste and Politics

India is a land of diversities. One of the biggest challenges to Indian politics has been, as such, to successfully integrate these numerous diversities within the canopy of the larger Indian nation state. Owing to this, a significant cornerstone of Indian democracy has been the use of politics as a tool to knit together this highly diverse nation.

Though India's diversity can be looked at in terms of a plethora of categories, it has nonetheless, primarily been understood in terms of language, tribe, religion and caste. Whereas linguistic and tribal communities are defined as being geographically concentrated, caste and religious groups are spread across the length and breadth of the country. The latter categories, because of their geographical diffusion, have not been successfully dealt with through federalism, unlike the former. These social differentiations have continued to affect the political behaviour of the people, though in varied intensity in different time and space.

The relation between caste and politics is not a new phenomenon. But it was always present since the day caste was defined as the hierarchical division of society based on the concepts of purity and pollution, and leaving the groups unavailable or limitedly available for each other to marry, keeping the Brahmins at the top of the ladder followed by the Kshatriyas, the Vaishyas, and the Shudras, and keeping the untouchables out of the ladder. But the power relations between the caste groups were largely local in nature. The entrance of caste into national politics came after the emergence of the idea of 'India as a nation' and gained significant place in postcolonial Indian politics.

Colonial India saw caste entering into politics both as a unifying factor and a bone of content in the struggle for freedom. Hindu nationalism emerged against the divide-and-rule policy of the British. V. D. Savarkar was the main proponent of the idea of Hindutva—an ideology "which seeks to fuse all the distinct particularities and differences of religious minorities (Muslims and Christians) and ethnocultural minorities (Dalits and Adivasis) into its Brahmanic construction of an Indian nation" (Clarke 2002: 200). Thus Hindutva saw India as a homogeneous community and threatened all minorities who saw themselves as distinct from this imagined whole. For Savarkar, Hindutva was able to provide "a broad basic foundation on bedrock on which a consolidated and mighty Hindu Nation could take a secure stand" (Savarkar 1969: vii).

The bigger question regarding Savarkar's writings was to place the caste divisions in this common nation, common race and common civilization. And the question was: do the Brahmins and the Dalits share these between them as well? He wrote that not only the Dalits but also the Adivasis (the tribes) share these.

Clarke writes that there is reason to believe that the notion of the four-fold hierarchy of caste system is maintained in the philosophy of Savarkar. He quotes him writing of twice-born castes as "noble bloods," the Dalits as "poor and barren" and referring to Manu as "saintly and patriotic law-giver." But one thing that this Hindutva ideology did was that it put all other divisions aside and presented India as one entity. Savarkar, however, was never successful in his ambitions as the leading figures in the national struggle never identified themselves with his philosophy.

Two of the leading figures of the national struggle for independence, who had huge differences on caste politics, were Ambedkar and Gandhi. Dirks writes,

> Gandhi saw caste system as an organic, unifying and inclusive system that could divest itself of all hierarchical ideologies while Ambedkar saw caste system as the part of the problem and not as the part of the solution and rejected Gandhi's call for the untouchables to be included within the compass of the caste system [as "Harijans"]. (Dirks 2001: 216)

The main issue of difference came in 1932, after the civil disobedience movement led by Gandhi, when it was planned to bring provincial rule in

India. The negotiations reached a stalemate because of the issue of separate electorates. Ambedkar wanted a separate electorate for the Dalits, to which Gandhi did not agree. Dirks writes that

> although Gandhi and Ambedkar shared a fundamentally anthropological view of caste, they had very different idea about politics. While Ambedkar was committed to the need to politicise caste, using it as the basis for organising political constituencies and waging political battles, Gandhi was perhaps more concerned than any other major nationalist leader about the possibility that caste would become basis for political and social conflict. Thus Gandhi felt the need to minimize caste differences and underplay caste identity. Ambedkar, on the other hand, was convinced that caste (or, rather, untouchable) identities had to be fostered in order to combat centuries of oppression by collective organisation of political struggle. (Dirks 2001: 218)

Although Ambedkar lost the political battle against Gandhi in the early 1930s, later his position was triumphant, which is obvious from the fact that the "reservations were established for SCs and Scheduled Tribes (STs), and despite some resentment and debate, there has been general unanimity about the importance of these constitutional provisions and guidelines" (ibid.: 218). This reservation policy did not limit itself only to the SCs and STs but extended itself to the backward classes as well.

Soon after Independence, in 1953, Kaka Kalekar was asked to head the Backward Classes Commission to investigate the possibility of establishing reservation for OBCs. But the confusion was how to determine or identify a backward class as there was no data available because of the fact that earlier reservations were on caste identity. Many of the leaders at that time did not want reservations to be caste-based, as according to Nehru, they wanted to put an end to all those infinite divisions that have grown up in Indian society like the caste system and religious divisions. But academics like N. K. Bose were of the opinion that what was called backward classes was nothing else but a collection of certain castes.

In 1956, the commission submitted its report with the conclusion given by the chairman that "it would have been better if we could determine the criteria of the backwardness on principles other than caste". The Ministry of Home Affairs gave its discontent citing that the emphasis on caste demonstrated the dangers of separatism. The minister added that the caste system was undeniably "the greatest hindrance in the way of our progress toward an egalitarian society, and the recognition of specified castes as backward may serve to maintain and perpetuate the existing distinctions on the basis of caste". Even though sociologists like M. N. Srinivas put forward the idea of neutral indices for backwardness—like literacy, landownership or income—that was impractical in a sense.

Kalekar commission's list contained as many as 2,399 communities, of which 913 alone accounted for an estimated population of 116 million. All women were regarded as backward but they were not regarded as a backward class because they could not be classified as a separate community. It was practically impossible to give privilege to that large part of the population. A majority of the members of the commission were of the opinion that caste determined the degree and extent of backwardness (Srinivas 1957: 547–48).

But the demand for privileges to the backward castes did not die and it came up again during the prime ministership of Morarji Desai in 1978, when he appointed a five-member commission headed by B. P. Mandal with the same task as that of the Kalekar commission in 1953, in order to ensure that the minorities, SCs and STs and OBCs do not suffer from discrimination and inequality.

Apart from the discourses revolving around the policy of affirmative action, this period saw the birth of many political parties based on caste, the most prominent among them being the BSP formed by Kanshi Ram. The establishment of the BSP (literally, Party of the Majority) in UP clearly shifted the foci of caste-based politics. The BSP was instrumental in gradually expanding the term 'Dalit' into 'Dalit–Bahujan', borrowing terminology from the non-Brahmin movements of the 1920s in order to forge a political unity between the Dalits, the OBCs and (religious) minorities. But the rhetoric of Dalit–Bahujan social critique was growing ever stronger, and it was focused far less on class than on caste. One BSP slogan claims "*Brahmin, Bania, Thakur Chor / Baki Sab DS–Four*" naming all the upper castes thieves and all the rest victimized—but now politically organized—Dalits. Even a cursory analysis of the BSP rhetoric indicates that the party saw only one line of battle, and it fell between the upper castes and the Dalit–Bahujans. Kanshi Ram argued that ruling ideologies were still Brahminical, and that it was this Brahmin hegemony, far more than caste structures themselves, that needed to be dismantled. Although wide caste alliances had become important in the early 1970s and all the more so in the 1980s, the BSP's initial successes were still limited, indicating, among other things, that the idea of caste-based politics had not yet firmly taken root (Reddy 2005: 552–53).

The second Backward Classes Commission—also known as the Mandal Commission—was constituted in 1978 by the Janata Party, keeping the promise made in their election manifesto of establishing an independent and autonomous civil rights commission as a challenge to Indira Gandhi's infamous Emergency. Despite upper-caste discontentment over reservation policies rising in the background, the Commission's report identified 3,743 'backward' communities, and recommended 27 per cent reservation for the OBCs, apart from the constitutionally mandated 22.5 per cent quota for SC/ST communities in government and public sector jobs, and government-supported educational institutions. These recommendations, if implemented, would bring the total reservations to 49.5 per cent, just under the Supreme Court cap (given in a 1963 ruling) of 50 per cent. But the Janata Party government was not able to do much on that as the government lost power. The Mandal report did not play much of a role in the growing debate over caste reservations until 1991 when the V. P. Singh government made an announcement of its implementation; Mandal again became the focus of furious national debate. This was not by any means the first time that reservation policies had been publicly protested against. But they had not been as furious and intense as it was this time. What was perhaps unique about these agitations and what stuck in the mental images of the time, was one aspect of their method—self-immolation—images of which were carried far and wide by the print media, requiring almost no language to convey meaning. On 19 September 1990, Rajeev Goswami, a student from Delhi University poured kerosene on his body and set himself on fire. This example was followed in many parts of North India. Within one month, more than159 young people had followed this act of attempting suicide by self-immolation and 63 had succeeded. Another 100 people were killed in police firings and clashes that accompanied the widespread protest (Dirks 2001: 213). Photographs of upper-caste youth dousing themselves with kerosene and then setting themselves alight in public protest of Mandal reservation quotas, and then pictures of burned and charred bodies on hospital stretchers were a daily front-page feature in all the Indian papers, and on several foreign ones as well. Accompanying these images was a storm of rhetoric on the 'Mandalization' of India, the brain drain the country would suffer and the absolute devaluation of any idea of 'merit'. So fierce was the rhetoric and so powerful the images that it is no wonder that the word 'Dalit', and with it an entirely new political understanding of caste, came into vogue following the Mandal agitations (Reddy 2005: 553).

The debate on Mandal brought to light many new arguments regarding the centrality of caste in Indian politics. It was very different from what the country had seen soon after Independence and it proved that the politics revolving around caste in the country was much more complex than thought of (that caste would lose its hold in Indian society after Independence) by national leaders and academics.

One of the biggest political issues of this period was the BJP's 'Ram Janmabhoomi' or 'Babri Masjid' campaign. Interestingly, the incidents tried to reunite Indian society which had seen a serious disintegration on the basis of caste on the Mandal issue. In September 1990, the then BJP President L. K. Advani began a rath yatra of visiting sites at which Hindu temples had been destroyed (and sometimes replaced by mosques) by Muslim invaders and rulers of various dynasties. The BJP pledged to replace the existing Babri mosque at Ayodhya with a Hindu temple. Advani never completed his journey because of controversies but the rath yatra did, in some senses, succeed in its mission of unifying a Hindu community fractured as the result of clashes on the streets for supporting or opposing Mandal. The implications of this contradiction were not lost on the Dalit intellectual community. As Kancha Ilaiah would write, in the "Mandal Yuga [era of Mandal]... [upper caste Hindus] abuse us as meritless creatures, but in their Ramrajya [ideal state] we are defined again as Hindus" (quoted in Reddy 2005: 554).

The post-Mandal debates on caste, politics and class point not only to the primacy of caste as a vital factor in politics, but also to the persistent influence it has had over the public–political sphere in the country. The issues then are the extent to which caste is recognized as an apparatus of sociopolitical change, and how caste-centred political movements of the 1980s and 1990s have assisted caste-centred public–political life by giving it a secular purpose and a modern value.

It cannot be denied that democracy, as a form of political system and governance, privileges 'number'. The lower castes have come to take advantage of their gradually acquired political dominance. Owing to the multiparty system and the emerging trend of fractured mandate at the national political scene, regional parties have come to play an instrumental role in the formation of the national government. Regional parties continue to exercise influence on regional politics but the era of coalition politics has enabled them to exercise influence even at the national level.

Regional parties tend to have their support bases amongst different caste groups. Since caste is one of the most important determinants of voting behaviour, the regional parties have naturally come to occupy a vital place in present-day politics. Thirty-five years ago, M. N. Srinivas wrote that caste is so tacitly and so completely accepted by all, including those who are most vocal in condemning it, that it is everywhere the unit of social action.

Besides, in the very modern, small and urban areas in India, the unit of mobility is not the individual; the unit of mobility is caste. For any party, the decision about its choice of candidate is decided by caste; considerations of disposition, aptitude and skill come later.

Romancing with Caste in the Political Beauty of the National Capital

All the developments in the relation between caste and politics have had a direct impact on the political behaviour of the people of Delhi. Over the years, caste has grown in appeal, the manifestation of which can be seen in the voter's ever-increasing passion towards it. The electorate is now drawn out into 'caste blocks'. The rise of caste-based politics has led to the emergence of a disintegrated verdict by the electorate. The emergence of the RJD in Bihar, the Samajwadi Party and the BSP in UP, and various other parties in different states is attributed to the growing appeal of the party among the voters belonging to the caste of the leader of the party. Empirical evidence from the CSDS surveys indicate that the RJD draws large support amongst the Yadavs in Bihar, its leader Lalu Prasad himself being a Yadav. The Samjawadi Party is equally popular amongst the Yadavs of UP, Mulayam Singh Yadav being a Yadav himself. The BSP draws large support amongst the Dalit voters from UP. Many attribute the increased fragmentation of politics with the rise of caste identities as well as the rise of various regional parties.

Delhi's politics over the years has largely witnessed a bipolar contest between the Congress and the BJP. During the past few decades, both in the Lok Sabha and Assembly elections, more than two-third of the votes have been cornered by the two main political parties. The bipolarity was reflected more in the Lok Sabha elections compared to the Assembly elections. The BJP used to get many votes by default because Delhi was earlier dominated by refugees from Pakistan. The blood bath and communal hatred that they faced in Pakistan during Partition made them staunch Rashtriya Swayamsevak Sangh (RSS) followers. Most of the leaders also came from this community. The BJP had a considerable hold over the trading community of Delhi. But the situation changed during the last two decades and now, no party can emerge victorious without garnering votes from every section of the society. Another reason for BJP's steady erosion has been the changing social composition of Delhi's electorate over a period. Earlier, the Jan Sangh (and later the BJP) found overwhelming support amongst the migrants of 1945–47, hailing from western Punjab who brought with them the trauma of Partition and sympathized with the BJP. The BJP has not been able to transcend the label of being a Bania–Brahmin–Punjabi party in Delhi. The party so far has had no important leaders from the ranks of either the Dalits or the Muslim community.

The results of various Assembly elections held in the state since 1993 indicate that there has been some presence of the third force in the city's politics, first in the form of the Janata Dal, and then during the last few years, in the BSP, which has successfully occupied the place of the third force in the city's politics. It has managed to replace the Janata Dal and its splinters, which had been seen as the emerging third force in the city's politics, besides the Congress and the BJP. The results of various Assembly elections clearly indicate that the BSP has slowly, but steadily, increased its political presence in Delhi. The results of the 2008 Assembly election indicate that the BSP's elephant had marched into this city and made its presence felt in the city's politics. But Delhi's politics is still not fragmented to the extent that we witness in states like Bihar, UP or Tamil Nadu. Does this lack of political plurality suggest that Delhi has not witnessed political mobilization on caste lines? Are there no caste cleavages in Delhi's politics?

The Brahmin Vote

The political elite which assumed power in 1947 comprised the upper castes, primarily Brahmins, Rajputs, Kayasthas, Bhumihars, Vaishyas and other forward castes. The Brahmin vote bank has seen its importance dwindle considerably in the electoral arena over the past few years. Even though Brahmins are no longer as visible on the political landscape as in the past, a closer look at political parties across the political spectrum throws up an interesting insight. Most of the country's political strategists and party advisor–officials are Brahmins. The number of party tickets issued by the Congress to Brahmins, in the Assembly elections, points to the fact that the political influence of the Brahmin community has hardly diminished. Political parties are still looking to Brahmins for their support in strategizing their victory in the polls.

While there are no official estimates, the findings from the CSDS surveys indicate that Brahmins constitute 10–12 per cent of Delhi's electorate, and prior to the delimitation had a sizeable presence in about seven Assembly constituencies.[1] After the fresh delimitation, their share among Delhi's electors remained unchanged, but due to changes in the boundaries of the Assembly constituencies, there has been some change in the constituencies where their numerical strength matters. The Brahmins are in sizeable numbers in about 10 Assembly constituencies and are an important vote bank for political parties.[2]

Voting patterns across the four Assembly elections held in Delhi since it got statehood suggest that the Brahmin voters in Delhi have had a strong preference for the BJP. Over the years, they have voted for the BJP in large numbers. Soon after the creation of the state in 1993, the first Assembly election witnessed 58 per cent of the Brahmins voting for the BJP, while only 31 per cent voted for the Congress (Figure 2.1). This was also an election in which the BJP won and formed the government in Delhi. What is interesting to note is that even in the elections the BJP did not do well; the party attracted more Brahmin votes,

Figure 2.1:
The Brahmin Vote in Delhi: Assembly Elections, 1993–2008

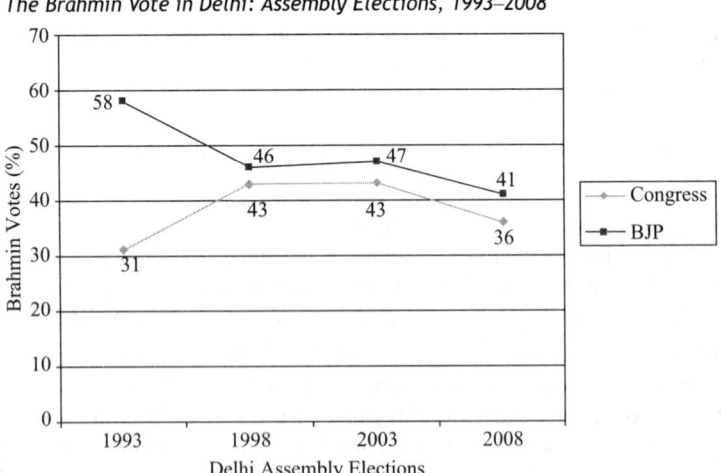

Sources: HT–CSDS Delhi Survey, 1998 and 2003; Post-poll Survey, 2008.

compared to the Congress. In the 1998 Assembly election, the BJP was defeated and its popularity amongst the Brahmin voters declined; still, most Brahmin voters in Delhi voted for the BJP. While 46 per cent of the Brahmin voters voted for the BJP, only 43 per cent of them voted for the Congress. The 2003 Assembly election hardly witnessed any shift in the political choices of the Brahmin voters, with only marginal increase in their preference for the BJP.

The 2008 Assembly election witnessed the emergence of the BSP in the city's politics. The BSP, which polled more than 14 per cent votes, cut into the support base of both the Congress and the BJP. This resulted in declining support both for the Congress and the BJP amongst the Brahmin voters, since some of them voted for the BSP. During the period 2003 to 2008, support for the BJP amongst the Brahmin voters declined by 6 per cent and support for the Congress declined by 7 per cent. Even though the BJP did not perform well and the Congress retained power, the BJP maintained its lead over the Congress amongst the Brahmin voters. Over the years it seems that the BJP has remained the first choice amongst a large number of Brahmin voters.

The Punjabi Khatri Vote

The Punjabi Khatri community in Delhi, represented by Madan Lal Khurana in the BJP, has always been the core constituency of the party in Delhi. The politics of Delhi has mostly centred on the Punjabi Khatri–Baniya–Jat dominance. Since most of the Jats and Punjabis have been economically well off, they have been able to dominate Delhi's politics. Like the Brahmins, the Punjabi Khatris also have a sizeable presence in Delhi, as they constitute about 7–9 per cent of Delhi's electorate. Numerically they are not as large as the Brahmins, but they are more concentrated compared to the Brahmins. Prior to delimitation, the Punjabi Khatris constituted about one-third of the electorate in three Assembly constituencies, while in another 16 Assembly constituencies they comprised 20–34 per cent of the electorate.[3] After the new delimitation, with the change in the boundaries of the Assembly constituencies, the Punjabi Khatri voters seem to be a little more dispersed, but still constitute more than one-fifth of the electorate in about 18 Assembly constituencies.[4]

The Punjabi vote forms the backbone of the BJP support base in Delhi. Over the years in various elections, the Punjabi voters voted for the BJP in an overwhelming majority. In the 1993 Assembly election which the BJP won, about two-third of the Punjabi voters voted for the BJP (Figure 2.2). The fortunes of the BJP have declined since the 1998 Assembly election—the party has lost three Assembly elections in a row—but its popularity amongst the Punjabi Khatri voters has not declined to a great extent. Between 1993 and 1998, the popularity of the BJP amongst the Punjabi Khatri voters did witness a 12 percentage point decline (from 64 per cent to 52 per cent), but in the 2008 Assembly election, 58 per cent of the Punjabi Khatri voters voted for the BJP, an increase in the party's popularity compared to previous elections. Over last four Assembly elections, even though the BJP performed badly, the majority of the Punjabi Khatri voters voted for the BJP. The share of the Punjabi vote for the Congress has always remained low. During the 1998 and 2003 Assembly elections, when the Congress vote share increased, its share amongst the Punjabi vote also increased, while in the 1993 Assembly election, its vote share amongst the Punjabi Khatris remained low at 31 per cent. Even though the Congress managed to win the 2008 Assembly election, its popularity amongst the Punjabi Khatri voters remained very low—it was less than the Congress average vote share in the state.

Figure 2.2:
The Punjabi Khatri Vote in Delhi: Assembly Elections, 1993–2008

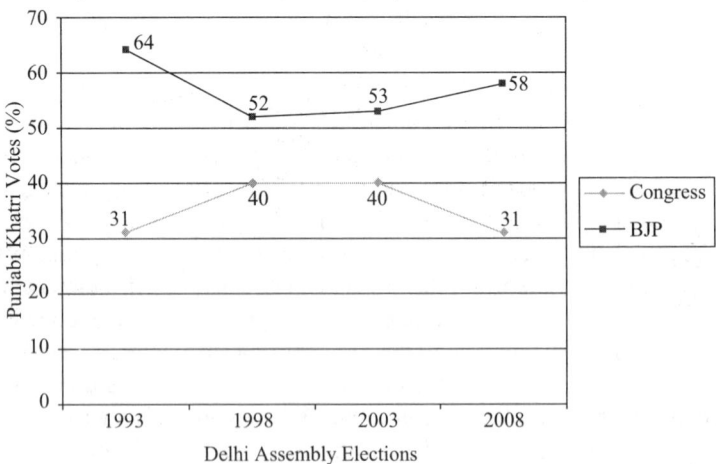

Sources: HT–CSDS Delhi Surveys, 1998 and 2003; Post-poll Survey, 2008.

The Rajput Vote

There is hardly any discussion of the Rajput vote in Delhi even though they constitute 5–6 per cent of Delhi's voters. Two factors have resulted in not putting the Rajputs on Delhi's political map. First, they are widely spread all over Delhi, which puts them in a disadvantageous position in electoral politics. Since they are not concentrated, they do not form a critical number which can help a party win the election by their support. Prior to the new delimitation, they were in sizeable numbers only in R. K. Puram and Nasirpur Assembly constituencies. After the new delimitation, they form a sizeable proportion of voters in Malviya Nagar and Dwarka Assembly constituencies, which are adjacent to the old R. K. Puram and Nasirpur Assembly constituencies. Second, the absence of leadership among Rajputs, both within the BJP and the Congress, put them in a disadvantageous position. Political parties hardly saw the Rajputs as a vote bank and no political party made an effort to woo the Rajput voters in Delhi. But does that mean that Rajput voters have remained divided and they did not form a vote bank for any political party?

The findings of the CSDS surveys indicate that compared to the Brahmins or the Punjabi Khatri voters, the Rajput voters in Delhi are less polarized in favour of one political party. There seems to be some competition between the Congress and the BJP for the Rajput vote, but largely they seem to favour the BJP. Over the last few elections, more Rajput voters have voted for the BJP, compared to the Congress (Figure 2.3). In the 1993 Assembly election, which the BJP won, the majority of Rajput voters voted for the BJP. The support for the BJP amongst the Rajput voters declined in successive elections, but it has remained marginally ahead of the Congress. The 2008 Assembly election witnessed a decline in the popularity of the Congress amongst Rajput voters, and a marginal increase in the popularity of the BJP among them. But overall, it seems that the Rajput voters do not form a vote bank for any political party in Delhi. An effort to mobilize the Rajput voters can easily swing the Rajput votes in their favour.

The Vaishya/Bania Vote

The Vaishyas, nearly 7–8 per cent of Delhi's population, are numerically as big as the Punjabi Khatris in Delhi. But the voting pattern with

Figure 2.3:
The Rajput Vote in Delhi: Assembly Elections, 1993–2008

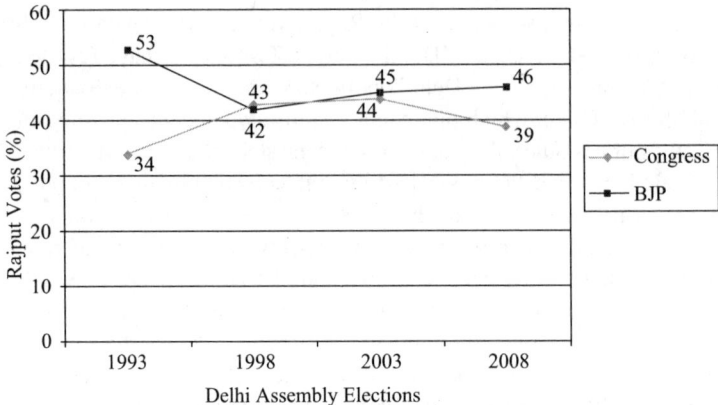

Sources: HT–CSDS Delhi Surveys, 1998 and 2003; Post-poll Survey, 2008.

regard to the Vaishya community has not received significant attention. One of the reasons for this is that while the Punjabi Khatri voters had pockets of influence, were concentrated in some Assembly constituencies and wielded enormous political influence in those constituencies, people belonging to the Vaishya community, despite being concentrated in various locations of Delhi, were not in sizeable numbers in many Assembly constituencies so as to matter in the electoral contest. Before the redrawing of the boundaries of Assembly constituencies, the voters from the Vaishya community were extremely spread out across various Assembly constituencies, comprising a little more than 10 per cent of the total electorates of these constituencies. But there was hardly any constituency where they could tilt the balance for or against a party with their solitary support. Things seem to have gone slightly in favour of voters belonging to the Vaishya community after the redrawing of the boundaries of Assembly constituencies, by way of the fourth delimitation exercise. Now they are in sizeable numbers in constituencies like Rohini, Shakur Basti, Shalimar Bagh, Tri Nagar, Wazirpur, Model Town and Sadar Bazar on the northern side of the city, and also in Vishwas Nagar, Krishna Nagar, Gandhi Nagar and Shahdara, the constituencies in the Trans Yamuna area. Apart from these constituencies, the voters from the Vaishya community are in significant numbers in Rithala and Adarsh Nagar Assembly constituencies. Even though in various elections, a sizeable number of legislators belonging to the Vaishya community get elected and large numbers of the community have also voted for the BJP, they are not perceived as a vote bank for any political party. Compared to their polarization in favour of the BJP during the first Assembly election held in 1993 (Figure 2.4), the support for the BJP amongst the voters from the Vaishya community has declined; still, a majority of them have voted for the BJP in all the Assembly elections which followed after that. Congress has won the last three Assembly elections, but since the 1998 Assembly elections, there had been some decline in the support for the Congress amongst voters from the Vaishya community.

Figure 2.4:
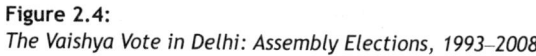
The Vaishya Vote in Delhi: Assembly Elections, 1993–2008

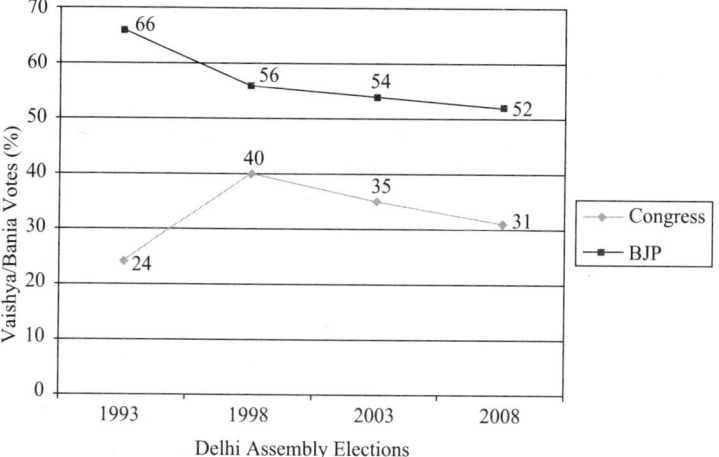

Sources: HT–CSDS Delhi Surveys, 1998 and 2003; Post-poll Survey, 2008.

The Gujjar Vote

To begin with, the Jats and the Gujjars had ample landed property in the city, making them part of the propertied class, giving them the bargaining power in the realm of political representation and securing a good place in Delhi's power structure. The most aggressive ticket seekers in the Delhi elections have been the Jats and the Gujjars who have emerged as the most determined of political climbers despite their modest population—about 5 per cent and 4.5 per cent respectively. During the 2008 Assembly election, the Jats and the Gujjars figured prominently in the list of candidates of both the Congress and the BJP. Thirteen candidates from the BJP and 14 from the Congress belonged to either of the two communities, making them about 20 per cent of the total contestants from the two parties. In the 2003 election, there were 19 Jat or Gujjar candidates from the two parties. The number of ticket seekers that year was in hundreds as the Jats and the Gujjars seem to have more political interests than many of the other communities. Political research in current times reveals that the rise of the two communities in the political arena has been happening for a while now; the booming property market has left many of them with surplus cash which acts as an aiding agent in making their political ambitions possible. The spatial concentration of the community in about 15-odd constituencies and their political awareness regarding their voting rights make them discernible. The recent Gujjar agitations for OBC status have also resulted in further consolidation of this voting behaviour.

The Gujjars are not as dominant a political force as they are in Rajasthan, but they play an important role in the city's politics. They are about 5 per cent of Delhi's electorate. Prior to the delimitation, they were concentrated in constituencies mostly on the southern fringes of the city, like Mahipalpur, Mehrauli, Badarpur, Delhi Cantonment, and in a few other Assembly constituencies like Badali and Najafgarh extending on the northwestern side of the city. Besides these constituencies, there are sizeable numbers of Gujjar voters in a few other constituencies in the Trans Yamuna locality, like Mandawali, Ghonda, Yamuna Vihar and Karawal Nagar. Since the geographical boundaries of the Assembly constituencies have changed after the fourth delimitation, there is some change in the pockets of influence of Gujjar voters. They are in sizeable numbers in the newly demarcated constituencies of Badali, Matiala, Najafgarh and Bijwasan on the northwestern side of the city, Chhatarpur, Tughlakabad, Badarpur and Okhla on the southern end of the city, and in Trans Yamuna in the Ghonda and Babarpur Assembly constituencies. But there are many others like Rithala, Rajouri Garden, Delhi Cantonment and Model Town, where Jat/Gujjar candidates are pitted against opponents from other communities, with the balance weighed in their favour. Party insiders say that it is a sign of how money power and the time at their disposal make the prosperous Jats and Gujjars important players in the political arena, even in areas where their presence may not be too significant in terms of numbers.

In the city's politics, even though the Gujjars occupy an important role, their allegiance is to the mainstream political parties, but not to the extent seen among voters of other caste communities. Over the years, nearly 70 per cent of the voters from the Gujjar community have voted for mainstream political parties, the Congress getting the larger share, and the BJP taking the smaller share. Nearly 30 per cent of the Gujjars have voted for either smaller parties or independents, depending upon the candidates in various constituencies. During the 1993 Assembly election, when the BJP became victorious, a little more than one-third of the Gujjars voted for the BJP, while a little more than one-quarter of them voted for the Congress (Figure 2.5). The situation was different in the 1998 Assembly election, when the Congress came to power defeating the BJP. In that election, 44 per cent of the Gujjar votes went in favour of the Congress while 29 per cent voted for the BJP. Since then, the Gujjar vote has remained tilted in favour of the Congress, but a large proportion of Gujjar votes has remained divided amongst other parties, BJP taking the largest share amongst them.

Figure 2.5:
The Gujjar–Yadav Vote in Delhi: Assembly Elections, 1993–2008

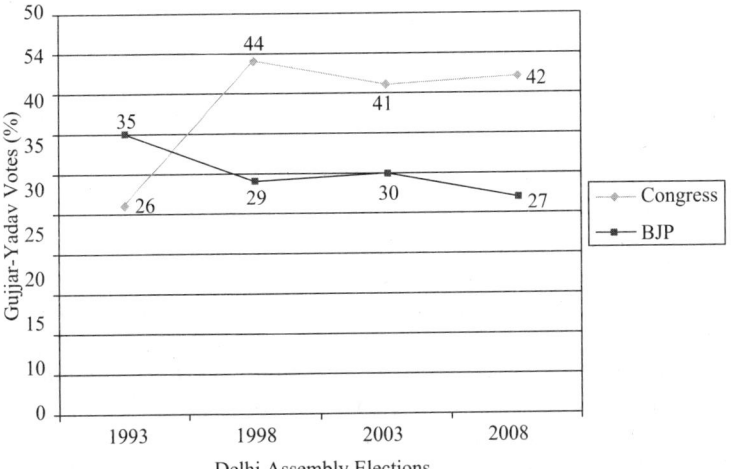

Sources: HT–CSDS Delhi Surveys, 1998 and 2003; Post-poll Survey, 2008.

The Jat Vote

Two faces that represented the Jat politics in Delhi over a long period were the senior Congress leader Sajjan Kumar and the late senior BJP leader Sahib Singh Verma. While Sajjan Kumar was elected to the national parliament several times as a Congress candidate, Sahib Singh Verma was the chief minister of Delhi for a brief period when the BJP was in power in Delhi between 1993 and 1998. Later he was also a central minister in the BJP-led National Democratic Alliance government. Even though the Jats are not numerically very large, Delhi's politics is always talked about in the name of the Jat vote mainly due to the tall stature of these two political leaders and also because of the community's extreme concentration in a few Assembly constituencies. Before the redrawing of the boundaries of Assembly constituencies, the constituencies in which the Jats held the key were Bawana, Najafgarh, Hastsal, Palam, Nangloi Jat, Mahipalpur and Narela, all on the southwestern side of the city. In these constituencies, the Jats were numerically large and they constituted more than one-fifth of the total voters. Due to their concentration, they could augment or deny the prospect of any candidate contesting from these constituencies. These constituencies hardly witnessed any non-Jat leadership for a long time. Besides these constituencies, the Jats were about 10 per cent of the total voters in Narela and Shahbad Assembly constituencies.

After the new delimitation and redrawing of the boundaries of Assembly constituencies, there has been some shift in the constituencies where they are in sizeable numbers. Post-delimitation, the Jats are in sizeable numbers in Bawana, Mundka, Kirari and Nangloi Jat Assembly constituencies, all on the outskirts of North Delhi, Vikaspuri, Uttam Nagar and Matiala in West Delhi, and Najafgarh, Bijwasan and Mehrauli on the south west end of Delhi. But the Jats do not seem to have a hold on the city's politics as it used to in the past. This is mainly because both the national parties, the Congress and the BJP, have lost their Jat face due to different reasons. The BJP has been unable to find a suitable replacement for Sahib Singh Verma, as the new Jat face for the city, after his untimely death, while the Congress Jat face has lost its shine and glamour due to Sajjan Kumar's alleged involvement in the 1984 anti-Sikh riots.[5] Both parties have tried to fill the void of the Jat leadership—the BJP by portraying Parvesh Verma, son of Sahib Singh Verma, as their new Jat face, and the Congress by bringing up Ramesh Kumar, brother of Sajjan Kumar, as the new Jat leader of the party. While Parvesh Verma failed to get the party ticket to contest the Lok Sabha election, Ramesh Kumar got elected to the Parliament from the South Delhi seat as the Congress candidate. But neither of them has been able to match the stature of their father and brother respectively.

Findings of the studies conducted by the CSDS indicate that the BJP has been the popular choice amongst the Jat voters ever since the first Assembly election after Delhi attained statehood. Barring the 2003 Assembly election, the majority of the Jat voters have voted for the BJP in various elections (Figure 2.6). But there is some decline in Jat support for the BJP now, compared to what it used to be in earlier Assembly elections. It is important to note that even in elections that the BJP had performed relatively badly, and were not able to come back to power, and the Congress retained the dominant political position, more Jats voted for the BJP, compared to the Congress. The Congress has gained some popularity amongst the Jat voters in Delhi over the last few elections, but still the BJP remains the first choice amongst a large number of Jat voters in this city. A young Jat face within the city unit of the party can help in a sizeable shift amongst the Jat voters in favour of the BJP.

Figure 2.6:
The Jat Vote in Delhi: Assembly Elections, 1993–2008

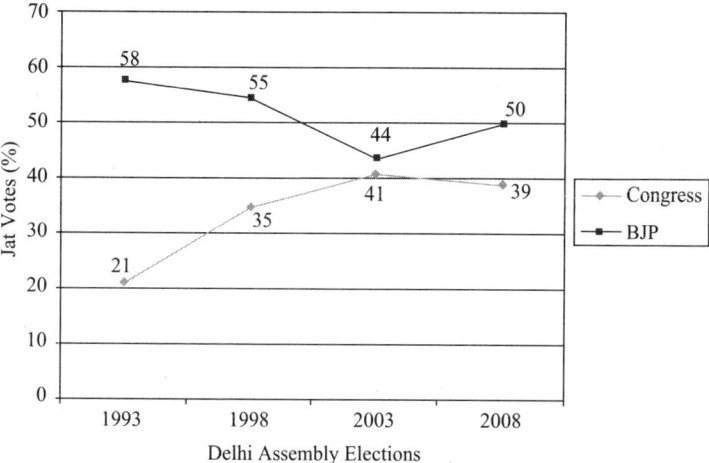

Sources: HT–CSDS Delhi Surveys, 1998 and 2003; Post-poll Survey, 2008.

The OBC Vote

Post-Mandal politics, especially in North India, is largely perceived in terms of the intense mobilization of the OBC voters. The OBC, which comprises a large number of castes, constitute a sizeable proportion of voters in many states, and Delhi is no exception to that. Since there is a large number of castes within the OBC category, usually the more influential castes within the OBC are seen as a separate political category and they are seen as a separate political block, like the Yadavs in the case of Bihar and UP, the Kurmis in the case of Bihar and the Loadh in the case of UP. The Gujjars belong to the dominant OBC caste, but their contributions to the political activities in the city are apprehended as distinct from the OBC for the reason that the Gujjars alone constitute about 12–14 per cent of the city's electorate.

This broad category 'OBC' (other than the Gujjars) comprises various castes and they are widely spread all over the city, not surprisingly having a presence in various Assembly constituencies. Prior to the fresh redrawing of boundaries of Assembly constituencies, the OBC constituted more than 15 per cent of the electorate in Bawana, Mangolpuri, Palam, Mahipalpur, Badarpur, Mandawali, Karawal Nagar, Narela, Bhalswa Jahangirpuri and Adarsh Nagar Assembly constituencies. There were a few other Assembly constituencies, like Sarojini Nagar, Gole Market, R. K. Puram, Rajouri Garden, Tri Nagar, Sultanpur Majra, Nangloi Jat, Hastsal, Nasirpur, Ambedkar Nagar, Tughlakabad, Trilok Puri, Gandhi Nagar, Shahdara, Seemapuri, Nand Nagri, Babarpur Seelampur, Ghonda, Yamuna Vihar, Wazirpur, Paharganj, Matia Mahal, Model Town and Sadar Bazar, where the proportions of OBC voters were between 10 to 15 per cent of the total voters in these constituencies. Since the proportion of the OBC voters is large enough and spread all over Delhi, the redrawing of boundaries has hardly altered their numerically dominant position and they are still in sizeable numbers in the freshly drawn Assembly constituencies of Burari, Badali, Bawana, Adarsh Nagar, Sultanpur Majara and Kirari in northwest Delhi, and Uttam Nagar, Dwarka, Matiala, Najafgarh, Bijwasan, Delhi Cantonment and Palam in the southwestern side of the city. On the southern end of the city, the OBC voters are in sizeable numbers in Chhatarpur, Devli and Ambedkar Nagar. Besides, there are also pockets of influence of OBC voters in a few Assembly constituencies in central Delhi, like Sadar Bazar, Chandni Chowk, Ballimaran, Karol Bagh, Patel Nagar, Moti Nagar and Madipur. The OBC voters are also in sizeable numbers in a few Assembly constituencies in East Delhi, like Patparganj, Shahdara, Seemapuri and Mustafabad.

Over the years, while voters of different castes more or less seemed to have shown their preference for one political party, the OBC votes seemed to be somewhat floating. After the first Assembly election when a large number of them voted for the BJP, there has been a shift among them in favour of the Congress; the majority of the OBC voters voted for the Congress during the 1998 and 2003 Assembly elections (Figure 2.7). The 2008 Assembly election witnessed a keen contest between the political parties for the OBC vote. The entry of the BSP in the city's politics attracted a sizeable proportion of OBC voters, resulting in the decline of the popularity of the Congress amongst the OBC voters. In recent years, to some extent the delimitation of constituencies and to a great extent the natural demographic shifts have changed the character of the seven Lok Sabha seats of Delhi, redefining the traditional electoral calculations. The exodus of the middle class to the National Capital Region towns of Noida, Gurgaon and Faridabad, and the proliferation of unauthorized colonies (there are 4 million residents in the 1,600-odd colonies) all across the city, coupled with the permutation-combination of colonies worked out by the Election Commission have meant that in all seven constituencies the largest percentage of voters are from the SC and the OBC. So essentially, Delhi as a whole has emerged first and foremost an SC–OBC stronghold, with all other caste and community identities taking a back seat. The SC and OBC population ranges from nearly 27 per cent in East Delhi to 50 per cent in South Delhi.

Figure 2.7:
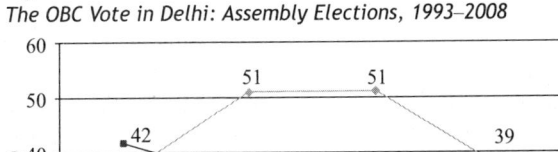
The OBC Vote in Delhi: Assembly Elections, 1993–2008

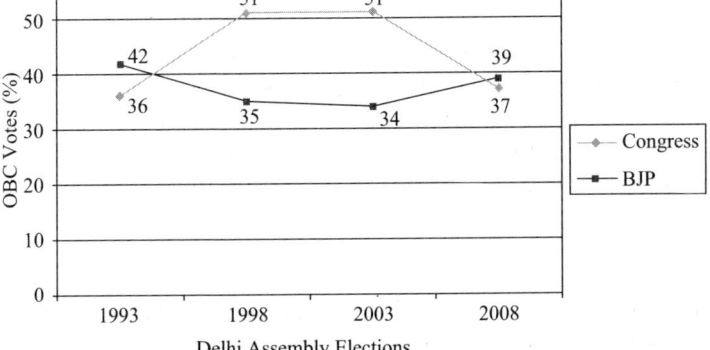

Sources: HT–CSDS Delhi Surveys, 1998 and 2003; Post-poll Survey, 2008.

The Dalit Vote

The broad categorization 'Dalits' encompasses many castes and in Delhi the Dalits constitute 17 per cent of the city's population (Census of India 2001). As per constitutional requirement, Assembly seats are to be reserved for people belonging to the Dalit community. Thirteen Assembly constituencies were reserved for Dalits; after the fresh redrawing of boundaries of Assembly constituencies the number of reserved constituencies has come down to 12. The Assembly constituencies reserved for the Dalits before delimitation were Madipur, Bawana, Sultanpur Mazara, Mangolpuri, Ambedkar Nagar, Trilok Puri, Patparganj, Seemapuri, Nand Nagri, Narela, Karol Bagh, Ram Nagar and Baljeet Nagar. After the redrawing of the boundaries of Assembly constituencies, the reserved Assembly constituencies are Bawana, Sultanpur Majara, Mangol Puri, Karol Bagh, Patel Nagar, Madipur, Deoli, Ambedkar Nagar, Trilok Puri, Kondli, Seemapuri and Gokalpur. Even though there have been some changes in the boundaries of most of these constituencies, most of these constituencies existed earlier with similar names, while a few new constituencies have been created with new names. In addition to the seats that are reserved for the Dalits, there are a few other assembly constituencies where the Dalits are in sizeable numbers. These Assembly constituencies are Badali, Nangloi Jat, Wazirpur, Model Town, Rajendra Nagar, Chhatarpur and Shahdara. These Assembly constituencies remain unreserved but in these the Dalits constitute about 15–20 per cent of the electorate.

Even though they are sizeable in number, the Dalits were not seen earlier as a vote bank by political parties. Political parties in various states make an effort to mobilize the Dalits for their vote, but their role in politics has not been understood as a major stakeholder in the elections. The Dalits seemed to be a natural political ally of the Congress before the BSP made its serious presence in the city's politics during the 2008 Assembly election (Figure 2.8). Even though the Congress could not perform well in the first Assembly election held in 1993, a large number of the Dalits had voted for the Congress. The popularity of the Congress increased amongst the Dalits soon after that and the Assembly elections which followed witnessed much sharper polarization of the Dalits in favour of the Congress. During the 1998 and 2003 Assembly elections, the majority of the Dalits voted for the Congress while only 17 per cent voted for the BJP. About one-quarter of the Dalits voted for smaller parties or independents, depending upon the candidates in various

Figure 2.8:
The Dalit Vote in Delhi: Assembly Elections, 1993–2008

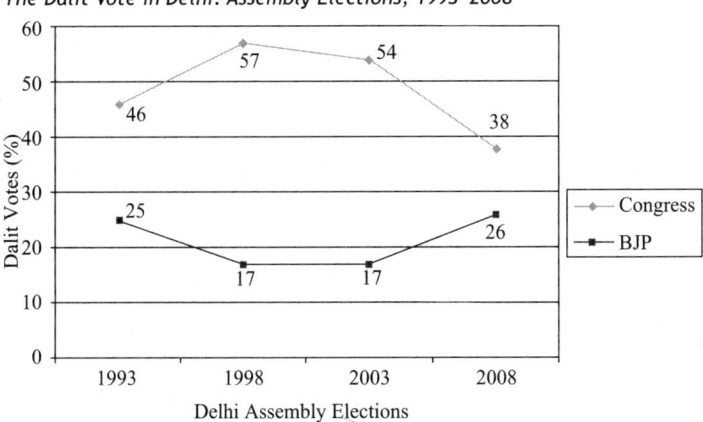

Sources: HT–CSDS Delhi Surveys, 1998 and 2003; Post-poll Survey, 2008.

Assembly constituencies. But the 2008 Assembly election witnessed a change in the political preferences of the Dalits and sizeable numbers of them voted for the BSP. The Congress managed to retain power in Delhi but its vote share declined compared to previous elections, and the decline in Dalit support for the party contributed to it. On the other hand, the increasing vote share of the BSP is largely credited to its increasing popularity amongst the Dalit voters. The politics of the city, which was largely bipolar, seems to have moved towards multipolarity.

It is quite evident that both the national parties–the BJP and the Congress—have suffered a loss of votes within the Dalit community. This can be attributed to the growing presence of the BSP in Delhi. With close to 2.5 million Dalit voters in Delhi, the stakes are huge. The BSP has split the Dalit vote in Delhi that traditionally used to go to the Congress. While for the Congress it is a matter of retaining a traditional vote bank that appears to be slipping away, for the BSP it is all about establishing a major presence in the national capital. The BSP has a significant following among people belonging to the Ravidas Jatav sub-caste, which is considered among the most backward. Its grip on this subcaste, which has the maximum strength in Delhi after the Valmikis, would be a cause of concern for the Congress, more so because a large number of Delhi Congress Members of Legislative Assembly (MLAs) belong to this subcaste.

The Muslim Vote

The Muslims constitute 11 per cent of the city's electorate and play an important role in the city's politics in about 7–8 Assembly constituencies. Prior to the delimitation of Assembly constituencies, the Muslim voters were in sizeable numbers in Babarpur, Seelampur, Seemapuri and Karawal Nagar Assembly constituencies in East Delhi, and Matia Mahal, Ballimaran, Minto Road and Paharganj in central Delhi region. There are also sizeable numbers of Muslim voters in Okhla and Badarpur Assembly constituencies in South Delhi. The settlement patterns of the Muslims have not changed over the years, but due to changes in the boundaries of Assembly constituencies, there is some change in the constituencies where they are numerically in large numbers. At present, the Muslims are in sizeable numbers in Chandni Chowk, Matia Mahal and Ballimaran Assembly constituencies in central Delhi, and Gandhi Nagar, Seemapuri, Seelampur, Babarpur, Mustafabad and Karawal Nagar Assembly constituencies in East Delhi. They are also in sizeable number in Kirari Assembly constituency.

Most of the Muslim-dominated constituencies have elected Muslim representatives; so over the years, various Assemblies in Delhi have had 7–8 representatives from the Muslim community. The Muslims have largely voted in favour of the Congress; some of them voted for individual candidates other than the party, though. The Muslims seem to have a favourable attitude towards the Congress, even as they have a lot of grievances against the party. Sometimes they vote for the Congress as the only option in order to keep the BJP away from power. The absence of any choice other than the BJP and the Congress has made them retain their allegiance with the Congress in Delhi over the past several elections.

The Congress was not a very popular choice amongst the Muslims during the 1993 Assembly election (Figure 2.9), but soon after that the popularity of the Congress amongst the Muslims increased. In the 1998 and 2003 Assembly elections, 53 and 68 per cent of the Muslims respectively voted for the Congress. The 2008 Assembly election witnessed a decline in the support base of the Congress amongst the Muslims, some of them voting for the BSP. Still a large majority of the Muslim voters forms a vote bank for the Congress party in Delhi.

Figure 2.9:
The Muslim Vote in Delhi: Assembly Elections, 1993–2008

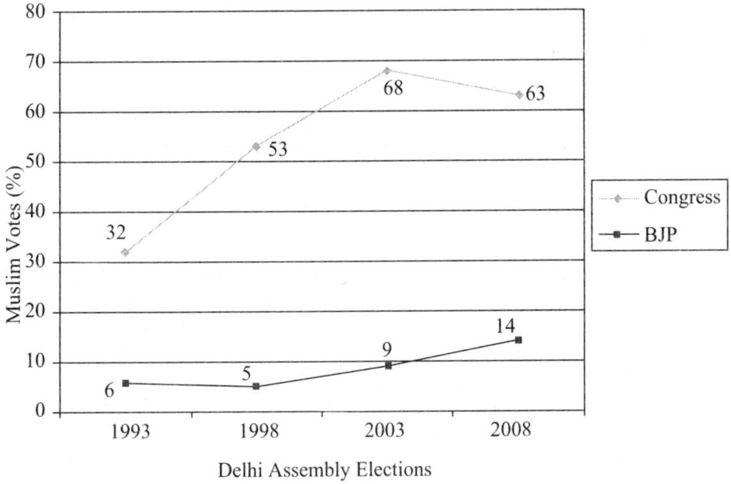

Sources: HT–CSDS Delhi Surveys, 1998 and 2003; Post-poll Survey, 2008.

The Sikh Vote

The Sikhs constitute 4 per cent of Delhi's population (Census of India 2001). In numerical terms, this is not a big number to matter in an electoral contest, but what makes the Sikh voters important in the city's politics is their concentration in a few constituencies and their influence to some extent amongst the Sikh voters in other states, mainly Punjab, where they have a huge majority.[6] Prior to the redrawing of the boundaries of Assembly constituencies in Delhi, the Sikhs were nearly one-third of the total voters in Vishnu Garden Assembly constituency, from where Ajay Maken got elected a few times to Delhi's Assembly. Apart from Vishnu Garden, there were a few other constituencies like Hari Nagar, Tilak Nagar and Rajouri Garden in West Delhi, and Kalkaji in South Delhi where Sikh voters were in sizeable numbers. Post-delimitation, the Sikhs form an important vote bank in the Assembly constituencies of Rajouri Garden, Hari Nagar and Tilak Nagar in West Delhi. The Assembly constituencies of Jangpura, Moti Nagar and Sadar Bazar too have some presence of Sikh voters.

One of the popular misconceptions regarding the voting pattern of Delhi voters is that the BJP is considered to be the first choice of Sikh voters. It is widely believed that Operation Blue Star and the anti-Sikh riots of 1984 in Delhi, leading to the massacre of Sikhs, had angered the Sikhs towards the Congress and that the Sikh voters had turned their back to the Congress. That may be true for early elections held soon after the anti-Sikh riots in Delhi, but certainly not since the state came into being in 1993.

The last one and a half decade have seen intense competition between the Congress and the BJP for the Sikh vote (Figure 2.10). Over the last four Assembly elections, nearly 90 per cent of the Sikh votes got divided between the Congress and the BJP, and except for the 1993 Assembly election, both the Congress and the BJP got more or less equal shares of the Sikh vote. During the 2009 Lok Sabha election, the voters belonging to the Sikh community were initially enraged by the Congress nominating Sajjan Kumar and Jagdish Tytler, the accused masterminds of the 1984 anti-Sikh riots, as party candidates but the Congress soon withdrew their names following protests.

Figure 2.10:
The Sikh Vote in Delhi: Assembly Elections, 1993–2008

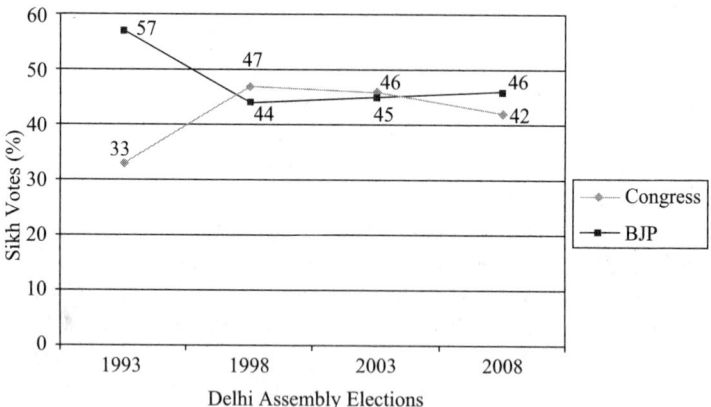

Sources: HT–CSDS Delhi Surveys, 1998 and 2003; Post-poll Survey, 2008.

Delhi continues to be a cosmopolitan city, with a mosaic of vote banks, which has witnessed a lot of competition for the seat of power. Sheila Dikshit and development have also become synonymous with Delhi's election by retaining power for a third term. The BJP, unlike the

Congress, has had a leadership crisis in Delhi. Besides caste, class, sect and religion, charismatic personality, leadership and development have also emerged as important factors among educated voters and Delhi has witnessed such a change over the years.

Notes

1. Brahmin voters constituted 20–34 per cent of the electorate in Sarojini Nagar, Hastsal, Patparganj, Mandawali, Rohtas Nagar, Seelampur and Yamuna Vihar.

2. As per estimates reported in *Navbharat Times* (September–October 2008) and *Times of India* during the Assembly election, after the new delimitation, the Brahmins are in sizeable numbers in Rithala, Palam, Patparganj, Laxmi Nagar, Krishna Nagar, Shahdara, Ghonda, Babarpur, Matiala and Najafgarh Assembly constituencies.

3. Punjabi Khatris constituted one-third of the electorate in Janakpuri, Hari Nagar and Timarpur while they comprised 20–34 per cent of the electorate in Jangpura, Kalkaji, Malviya Nagar, Tilak Nagar, Rajouri Garden, Madipur, Shakurbasti, Shalimar Bagh, Badli, Geeta Colony, Krishna Nagar, Vishwas Nagar, Shahdara, Wazirpur, Moti Nagar and Patel Nagar.

4. There are sizeable numbers of Punjabi Khatri voters in Timarpur, Rithala, Rohini, Shalimar Bagh, Shakur Basti, Trinagar, Moti Nagar, Hari Nagar, Tilak Nagar, Uttam Nagar, Jangpura, Kasturba Nagar, Malviya Nagar, R. K. Puram, Mehrauli, Laxmi Nagar, Vishwas Nagar, Krishna Nagar and Gandhi Nagar Assembly constituencies.

5. During the 2009 Lok Sabha election, Sajjan Kumar was nominated as the Congress candidate from the South Delhi seat. But sensing the anti-Sajjan mood amongst the Sikh voters and with the fear of losing a sizeable section of Sikh votes in Punjab, the party withdrew his candidature and nominated his brother Ramesh Kumar as the party candidate for that seat.

6. As per the 2001 Census, Sikhs are 59.9 per cent of the total population of Punjab.

3

The Voting Patterns: Caste or Class?

The people of Delhi have remained loyal to the Congress most of the times since Independence, as reflected in the results of the various elections held in Delhi. The Congress has performed so well not only since the 1998 Assembly election, but also during the various Lok Sabha elections, an exception being the 1977 Lok Sabha election when the Janata wave swept the entire North India. In that election, the Bharatiya Lok Dal won all the seven Lok Sabha seats in Delhi. The popularity of the Congress in Delhi was largely because it received support from all sections of society. Things changed in Delhi's politics mainly after the 1989 Lok Sabha election, when the BJP emerged as an important political player in the city's politics. The success of the BJP during that election was a result of the shift amongst the upper castes in Delhi towards the BJP. Even though in its electoral journey in Delhi, the BJP has witnessed success and failure, the upper castes have remained loyal to the BJP even when the party fared badly. On the other hand, the OBCs, the Dalits and the Muslims have remained loyal to the Congress for a long time. Caste remains one of the important considerations for voting amongst voters of Delhi, but caste polarity in voting behaviour does not present the complete picture; in recent years voters seem to be divided on class lines. This is visible more amongst the voters of Delhi compared to voters in any other state.

Politics in most of the Indian states is discussed mostly in terms of caste and ethnicity. Such analysis is so popular that we tend to believe that elections in India are only about caste and ethnic cleavages, and that economic considerations hardly play any role in voter mobilization.

The larger question at this juncture could be about the role of economic and social classes in shaping the cleavage structures of the political domain of the city.

The nature of the formation of these cleavages in any urban setting is different from the larger political compass. This is because of the demographic composition of the city, which defines itself on the basis of public consumption. An urban setting like Delhi is composed of people mainly from the working class. The extremities of the upper class and the lower class also make their appearance to a large extent, but not as significant as the middle, working class.

There is a vast and sophisticated body of literature on caste and politics in contemporary India (Srinivas 1962), including works that emphasize the unprecedented "politicization of caste" (Kothari 1970) amongst deprived groups in the recent past. This has had a dramatic impact on the landscape of regional democratic politics and, at a time of rising ascendancy and central importance of regional political configurations to coalition governments at the centre, on national democratic politics in India (Jaffrelot 2003). Understandably, the focus of much of this research has been the political articulation of numerically powerful, regionally mobilized lower caste groups that enjoy a high profile in the national domain, such as the Yadavs of UP (Michelutti 2004). Again, when it comes to backward caste groupings and the economic sphere, the focus in post-Mandal Commission India has naturally tended towards the impact of job reservations in the formal (public) sector on the employment possibilities and larger well-being of these groups (Parry 1999).

Discussion on the shifts in Indian politics will, therefore, be preoccupied with analyzing the 'immediate', because realpolitik is concerned with the immediate. It is, however, necessary to also consider the factors impacting upon the immediate. These relate to the very nature of our society. Delhi's changing demography, which has seen the *purabia*s (easterners) outnumbering the Punjabis and the Banias, has also been to Sheila Dikshit's advantage. When it comes to determining an individual's political preference during elections, which is more important—class or caste?

Caste is referred to as the most common, primordial identity of the people. There is also a shared notion that people tend to shed this primordial identity and look for a secondary identity mainly in the form of class. The emergence of class struggles has not been able to eliminate the influence of caste in these struggles. What facilitates this transformation is the level of educational mobility, occupational mobility from agrarian sector to the formal sector of occupation, and spatial mobility from village to the urban centre. The identification of the people with their acquired identity is reflected not only in their day-to-day lives but also in their political attitudes and behaviour.

Understanding Class

Class has multiple definitions and interpretations. Some sociologists refer to class in terms of 'life chances' in the economic domain (Giddens 1973; Weber 1922), some see it relating to the positions of people in a status hierarchy (Parsons 1970; Warner 1949), some give conflict more importance than any other factor and see class in terms of their positions in power structures (Dahrendorf 1959), whereas the Marxists see class in terms of positions in the social organization of production (Bukharin 1921; Lenin 1914). These varied definitions make class a confused concept and thus open multiple arenas in which the notion of class can be conceptualized. Wright writes,

> At the risk of some oversimplification, the diverse definitions of class can be analyzed in terms of three nested theoretical dimensions: (1) whether class is fundamentally understood in gradational or relational terms; (2) if class is understood in relational terms, whether the pivotal aspect of class relations is seen as located in the market or in production; (3) if class relations are primarily located within production, whether production is analyzed above all in terms of technical division of labour, authority relations, or exploitation. (Wright 1979: 4)

One way of understanding class is to conceptualize it in terms of space. It is necessary to do so while keeping in mind the geography of a particular space because of the changing meaning and dynamics of class, especially in a country like India, where caste is more widespread and its ideology more dominant, and the class relation takes different nature. There can be different reasons for that. Capitalist development in India was very much different from that of Europe or America. This was mainly because of the policies of the government post-Independence, which were more socialist than capitalist. Post-Independence, the Government of India tried to initiate affirmative action for the backward classes of the country. It was this motive of the government which led to the constituting of the Kaka Kalekar Commission during the Congress

Figure 3.1:
The Chief Approaches to Class

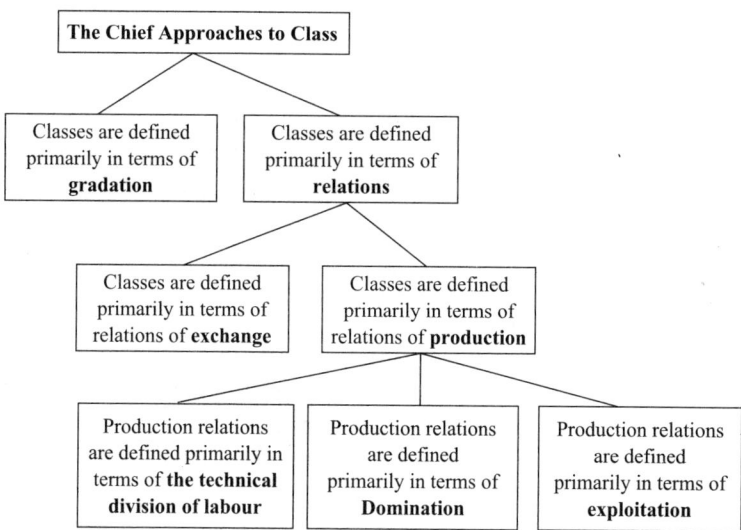

Source: Wright (1979).

government and the B. P. Mandal Commission during the Janata party regime. Kaka Kalekar recommended reservation of 25 per cent for class–I employees, 33 per cent for class–II, and 40 per cent for class–III and IV employees, for the economically backward classes. Similar commissions were established in many states for the reservation of the economically and educationally backward classes. Even the development of class differentiation in India did not strictly follow the relations of production, primarily because of the growth of the tertiary economic activities. Even after the abolishment of the zamindari system, the zamindars who had earlier formed the upper caste were still the upper class. The classes in India never transformed themselves into a 'class for itself' or create a situation of class struggle or even become a homogeneous group in itself. Thus, their affiliation to any class was the remnant of their caste identity and hence their political participation was an extension to their relation in power structures. Nevertheless it serves as a prime difference between groups on the issues of political mobilization, especially since the growth of the 'new middle class', which is a highly fluid and mobile concept. The middle class in India which largely inhabits the cities shows different colours on different issues. Its positions on the Babri

Mosque issue, the Kashmir issue, the reservation issue and nuclear disarmament have been highly problematic. This class has not been able to clear its own preferences and stand on different issues till date. This gives reason for their counterparts to stand straight, be it the upper class or the lower class. Therefore, we witness clear stand of the upper class and the lower class on different issues of interest.

Delhi, the capital of the country, witnesses class as one of the dominant forces for political mobilization and an important tool used by the political parties for voter mobilization. The voters may be divided more on class lines compared to caste lines. Class is first and foremost about differences in objective material conditions, but it is not only about those conditions. Differences in objective conditions are accompanied by a growing consciousness of those differences. Do these economic differences accompanied by differences in social consciousness get translated into differences in political behaviour? Does class override caste identity in expressing political preferences, mainly while voting at the time of election?

Class: What Does It Denote in Terms of Political Mobilization?

The caste–class dynamic in India has also changed because of the economic policies of the government, especially after the new economic policies of globalization and liberalization in the late1980s. The urban centres where the impact of the process of liberalization could be seen, saw two kinds of movement: increasing numbers of both the rich as well as the poor. The post-liberalization phase has also witnessed a change in political processes. It is interesting to note that in India one kind of classification has often been tackled by raising other kinds of classifications. Religious fervour, which threatened to tear India apart, was dealt with by gently reminding Indians about caste (1991–92), and then, too, much caste and religion were got over by groups raising the gender question (even if briefly, in the March 2013 vote in the Rajya Sabha on the women's reservation bill) and this in turn has influenced Indian politics in terms of voting behaviour as well as candidature. Post-liberalization, a 'new' India is growing up, with dreams and expectations of a much better material future. Old mores are being picked apart, for better and for worse. The political leaderships are struggling to find a framework to respond to these aspirations and frustrations.

Liberalization and democracy are moving the Indian economy and polity in opposite directions. People who are excluded by the economics of markets are included by the politics of democracy. Hence, inclusion and exclusion have become asymmetrical in politics and economics. The distribution of capabilities is also uneven in the economic and political spheres. The rich dominate the economy now more than earlier, but the poor have a strong voice in the polity more than earlier. And there is a mismatch. It is difficult for the state to mediate in the conflicts between economic development and political democracy because there is no consensus on economic reforms (Nayyar 1998). People often use elections to choose their representatives and the government but rarely can they use elections to choose policies that matter most to them (Yadav 1999). Besides, capitalist development and the changing nature of caste occupation linkages have contributed to internal economic stratification within each caste and the creation of a middle class. The new economy of the post-liberalization period has intensified these economic divisions within castes and aggravated the material crisis faced by small and marginal castes, forcing them to fall back on their caste identity for material and symbolic survival. Interestingly, along with the poor groups, the emerging middle classes from each caste too seem to invoke their caste identity in a more emphatic manner, mainly as a weapon for consolidating political power.

Class and Voting in Delhi

Delhi is the third largest metropolitan centre, with 12.79 million people. According to Census 2001, the Mumbai urban agglomeration has a population of 16.37 million, Kolkata 13.22 million and Chennai 6.42 million. Although Delhi is among the top three states or union territories in terms of per capita income, a vast portion of its population lives in slums, unplanned settlements and unauthorized colonies. The capital has turned into a major attraction for the skilled, semi-skilled and unskilled labourers because the minimum wage offered in Delhi is comparatively high.

In Delhi, even if someone belongs to the same caste, the voting patterns may not be similar. This is influenced and determined by their economic status and condition. Therefore, political parties eye the vote bank of the people more in the name of class than a particular caste. This shift in Delhi's politics became pronounced since the liberalization of the economy in the 1990s.

The Congress party's slogan '*Congress ka haath garib ke saath*' and Dikshit's politics are marked by a heavy dose of populism. The Delhi Development Goals were aimed at eradicating poverty and hunger to achieve universal elementary education, to promote gender equality and empower women, to reduce child mortality, to improve maternal health, to combat HIV/AIDS, malaria and other diseases, to ensure environmental sustainability, to strengthen Bhagidari and to improve public safety. The issue of unauthorized colonies, the policy for allotment of low-cost flats to urban poor under the Jawaharlal Nehru Urban Renewal Mission, and her gestures like personally blocking a bulldozer from razing a slum settlement and voicing concern for the JJ clusters have also helped in retaining the support of that section. The Bhagidari scheme of participatory governance has also bolstered her image among voters. Over the years, the Congress has always emphasized its record of good governance. The Congress has also made concerted efforts to look after the poor sections of the society, by also making attempts to bring more families under the cover of the public distribution system. However, slums have also been evicted forcefully as and when land has been needed for 'public use', and been mercifully shifted to resettlement sites as part of Delhi's new Master Plan 2021, writes Amitabh Kundu, and further adds that this new policy has added to the benefits of the middle class but not the slum or jhuggi dwellers who are again but vote banks.

Delhi may have a greater middle-class presence than other states, but the fact remains that Delhi is predominantly a working-class city, which also has large numbers of migrants, most of them poor. In fact the voting behaviour in Delhi is a textbook illustration of class-based voting: the poorer the voter, the higher the chances of voting for the Congress and vice versa for the BJP, though one noticed some changes in the voting pattern in the 2008 Assembly election. The Congress has got around the caste–community structure of Delhi. Sheila Dikshit has been instrumental in winning substantial Brahmin support for the Congress, while developing a small, middle-class base for the party. The party makes up for its disadvantage among the upper castes by gaining a big lead among the Dalits and the Muslims, who constitute about one-third of the electorate.

The composition of Delhi's population is diverse. Disparity in every sphere of life is very wide and the system's response—be it government, political parties or local representatives—is partisan and selective. Who votes for whom? And what separates the supporters of one party from another? These are the questions that need to be asked. While people belonging to lower socio-economic groups tend to support the Congress, the exact opposite holds true for the BJP. This became quite evident during the sealing drive launched by the Delhi government and the central government in 2008, where the BJP led a de-sealing campaign and supported the traders. In fact, the lower the status in terms of caste and class, the farther they are from the BJP. Caste hierarchies are not merely levels of social ranking; they have an economic aspect too. People belonging to higher castes are economically, professionally and socially better off. Therefore, economic variables reflect caste hierarchies and voting choices. We can, therefore, say that since the BJP draws higher support amongst the upper-caste voters, it naturally implies that the party also draws sizeable support amongst the upper-class voters. The support for the BJP largely comes from people placed higher in terms of education and occupation. On the contrary, since support for the Congress comes mainly from amongst the middle- and the lower-caste voters, it also implies that the party is more popular amongst the middle- and the lower-class voters compared to the rich. The support for the Congress comes mainly from the poorer sections of the society. The recent trend suggests that regional parties such as the BSP enjoy a definite edge over both the Congress and the BJP when it comes to attracting 'very poor' and 'poor' voters. The BJP's inability to attract voters from the lowest economic class constitutes one of its greatest weaknesses. While this is a commonly shared belief, this chapter looks into the details of the voting patterns across class, and whether class cuts across caste when it comes to voting.

Class and Voting

Though caste-based voting is an important feature in Delhi, its voters seem to be divided more on class lines than on caste lines. Sharply defining distinct economic classes is an almost impossible task, but nevertheless for the purpose of analysis of class and voting, Delhi's voters could be classified as falling under three broad economic categories—the upper class, the middle class and the lower class. All voters belonging to one economic class do not necessarily vote for one particular party, but a broad trend can clearly be traced.

One can, thus, make a fairly correct estimation of which party a voter is likely to vote for, based on the knowledge of the voter's class. Recent elections have, however, witnessed some changes. For instance, the BJP over the years had enjoyed the support of Delhi's upper-class voters, partial support from middle-class voters and negligible support of lower-class voters. The Congress, however, has shared a diametrically opposite profile in terms of its support base amongst different classes of voters; it has been very popular amongst the lower class, slightly less popular amongst the middle class and least popular amongst the upper-class voters in Delhi.

The CSDS survey findings indicate that a majority of the upper-class voters voted for the BJP in the 1998 and 2003 elections, and it was only during the 2008 Assembly election that Delhi saw a decline in the support base of the BJP amongst the upper-class voters (Figure 3.2). It is worth noting that the Congress had virtually swept the Assembly elections, both in 1998 and 2003, despite the fact that a majority of the upper-class voters voted for the BJP. The upper-class votes received by the BJP were much higher compared to its average vote share in the state during those elections. The 2008 Assembly election witnessed some decline in

Figure 3.2:
Voting Pattern of Delhi's Upper-class Voters: Assembly Elections, 1998–2008

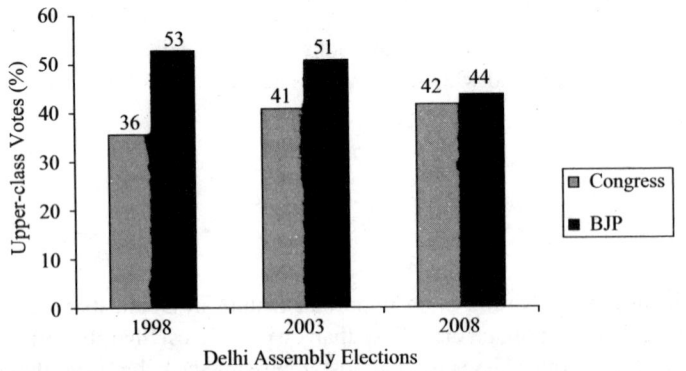

Sources: HT–CSDS Delhi Surveys, 1998 and 2003; Post-poll Survey, 2008.
Note: In the 2008 Assembly election, amongst the upper-class voters, 6 per cent voted for the BSP and another 9 per cent voted for other smaller parties and independents.

the support base of the BJP amongst the upper-class voters, yet, compared to the Congress, it managed to corner more support of the upper-class voters.

According to a World Bank study,

From the early 1990s, India has experienced one of the fastest economic growth rates in the world, averaging over 6 per cent and reaching 7–8 per cent per year since 2003. While the country still continues to face the tremendous challenge[s]... robust economic growth has already allowed millions to emerge from poverty, creating a sizeable middle class of 300 million people. (World Bank 2006: v)

Aijaz Ahmad is of the view that far from being mere 'agents' of the ruling classes or a mere 'vacillating mass', the intermediate and auxiliary classes of the periphery occupy a strategic field in the economy and politics of their countries, thus obtaining power and initiatives which make it possible for them to struggle for political dominance over other classes, including the bourgeoisie; and it will not be incorrect to state that one of the more noticeable outcomes of the recent socio-economic and political processes in India has been the emergence of the socio-economic group described as the 'middle class'. By all reasonable estimates, the strength of the middle class in India is bigger in size than the entire population of many nations.

Delhi too has a huge middle-class population. As per the estimate of the CSDS Survey, Delhi's middle class constitutes nearly 42 per cent of the city's total population. What is also important to note is that not only does the middle class constitute a sizeable proportion of Delhi's voters, but due to the expansion of the middle-class population, its share in the city's electorate is increasing year after year. The BJP formed the first government after Delhi got statehood, but the Congress defeated the BJP in the 1998 Assembly election. Besides other issues, it was the rising price of onions which had contributed to the victory of the Congress then. As such, middle-class voters' support for the Congress played a crucial role in the party's victory in the 1998 Assembly election, when 46 per cent of Delhi's middle class voted for the Congress (Figure 3.3). The popularity of the Congress party amongst the middle class continued even in the 2003 Assembly election, when 47 per cent amongst them voted for the Congress.

During the last couple of years, there has, however, been some decline in middle-class support for the Congress. This is largely because

Figure 3.3:
Voting Pattern of Delhi's Middle-class Voters: Assembly Elections, 1998–2008

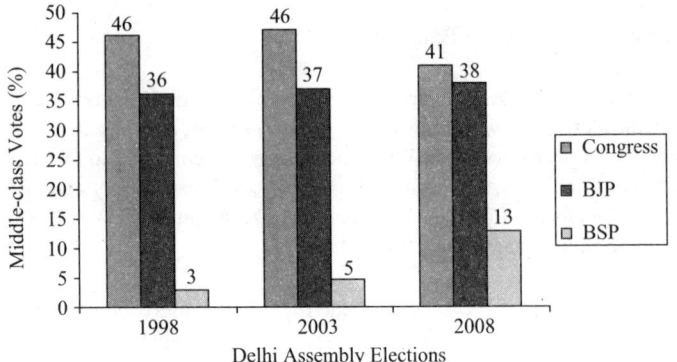

Delhi Assembly Elections

Sources: HT–CSDS Delhi Surveys, 1998 and 2003; Post-poll Survey, 2008.
Note: During the 2008 Assembly election, amongst the middle class, 8 per cent of the voters voted for other smaller parties and independents.

the BSP has been able to make its presence amongst the middle-class voters in Delhi, especially during the 2008 Assembly election; but the Lok Sabha election that followed the Assembly election did not show a similar trend.[1] The 2008 Assembly election witnessed some decline in the popularity of the Congress amongst middle-class voters, yet the party remained the first choice among them. However, the tilt of the middle-class voters towards the Congress, in no way indicates an unpopularity of the BJP amongst Delhi's middle class. Over the last few Assembly elections, sizeable proportions of middle-class voters have voted for the BJP. Voting patterns amongst the middle class suggest that the BJP has garnered a committed middle-class voting population, even though slightly smaller in size compared to what the Congress commands, but it nonetheless constitutes nearly one-third of Delhi's middle-class population.

Owing to the caste-ridden nature of Indian society, the middle class had traditionally been dominated by the higher castes. Chennai-based political analyst Cho Ramaswamy is, however, of the view that this no longer holds true. Class-based upward mobility cuts across caste distinctions. Ramaswamy says, "But they (middle class) are not going to vote en masse for one party." He further adds: "It will take a while at least for the new middle class to imbibe the values of the old middle class. The middle class right now is divided." Around 50 per cent of the households classified as middle class constitute the 'new' middle class, according to Rajesh Shukla. Delhi-based psephologist Bhaskara Rao agreeing to this view says: "The middle-class vote is not homogeneous anymore ... It will converge because issues affecting them (the old and new middle class) are the same, but it is not possible to say when. Convergence is the trend everywhere."

The emergence of the BSP in Delhi's political arena is posing a serious challenge to the Congress. Until a few years back, especially till the 2003 Assembly election, there was hardly any challenge to the Congress in terms of its popularity amongst the lower-class voters. But the scene changed during the 2008 Assembly election. The BSP emerged in the city's politics mainly at the expense of the lower-class support base of the Congress. The BSP was able to mobilize the voters from the Dalit communities, especially in constituencies with a sizeable proportion of Dalit voters. This naturally led to a marked increase in the BSP's vote share amongst the lower class, from 10 per cent in 2003 to 19 per cent in the 2008 Assembly election (Figure 3.4). The 2009 Lok Sabha election, however, saw a reversal of the trend. Since the BSP was not seen as a viable alternative to the Congress or the BJP in any Lok Sabha seat, and since the size of the constituencies were big, the BSP failed to attract the lower-class voters (mainly the Dalits) and its vote share amongst them, as such, went down to 11 per cent. The Congress managed to win back the lower-class votes, which it had lost to the BSP in the Assembly elections. While the BJP has been able to hold on to its lower-class support base, the Congress, in terms of lower-class support, suffered badly between the 2003 and 2008 elections, losing 13 percentage points. Even though the emergence of the BSP in the city's politics did damage the prospects of the Congress amongst the lower-class voters, trends from various elections seem to suggest a clear overlap between classes and voting pattern—the upper and middle classes seem to favour the BJP, while the Congress seems to be the preferred choice amongst lower-class voters. The emergence of the BSP as a new political force has seen some movement in the lower-class voters, from the Congress to the BSP; at the same time, there is some movement amongst the upper- and middle-class voters from the BJP towards the Congress due to the personal popularity of Sheila Dikshit. But this gradual shift in the voting pattern has not altered the basic trend of voting by Delhi's voters.

A study conducted by John Harriss (2005) in Delhi on political participation, representation and the urban poor describes and explains patterns of political participation, focusing on ways in which poorer social groups organize and obtain political representation and try to solve collective

Figure 3.4:
Voting Pattern of Delhi's Lower-class Voters: Assembly Elections, 1998–2008

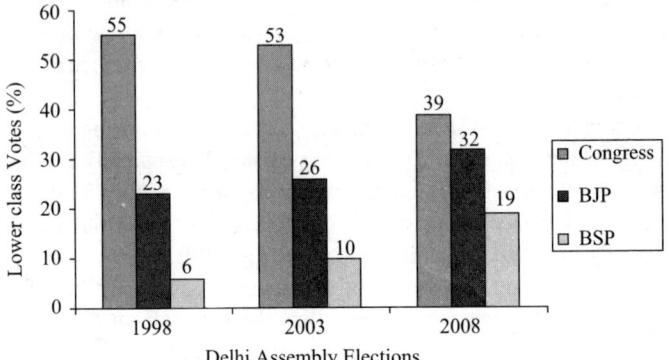

Delhi Assembly Elections

Sources: HT–CSDS Delhi Surveys, 1998 and 2003; Post-poll Survey, 2008.
Note: In the 2008 Assembly election, amongst the lower class, 10 per cent of the voters voted for other smaller parties and independents.

social problems. It appears, contrary to most expectations, that the needs and interest of poorer people are increasingly being met through the 'new politics' of social movements; that the poor seek to represent themselves and tackle their problems through political parties. The study brought about certain important findings in terms of political participation and opinion of the poor, and their attitude towards political parties. Poorer people in Delhi are likely to be supporters of the Congress, and 29 per cent of the respondents in the whole sample (36 per cent in the poorer sections) said that Congress was 'most concerned with the problems that are most important to you' (in the words of the question that was asked). This compares with 52 per cent who said that no political party was concerned with their problems (47 per cent amongst the poor) and only 13 per cent (10 per cent amongst poorer sections) who said that the BJP was most concerned with their problems. From those among the poorer sections who identified with the Congress, 72 per cent said that the party 'had done a lot' or had done 'something' to solve their problems. Indeed, detailed analysis of the data confirmed that poorer and less-educated sections of Delhi's population, as well as Muslims, younger people and men (rather than women) tend to support the Congress, while older, wealthier, better-educated people, and quite a lot of those outside the labour force are drawn towards supporting the BJP.

What is interesting to note is that this class divide among the city's voters is reflected among voters belonging to different caste communities too. Even though the Brahmins and the Punjabi Khatris voted for the BJP in big numbers, the class divide can be clearly seen amongst them—the rich were more sharply polarized in favour of the BJP, while the lower-class Brahmins and Punjabi Khatris preferred the Congress (Tables 3.1 and 3.2). During the last three Assembly elections, the upper- and middle-class Punjabi voters voted for the BJP while the lower class voted for the Congress. There was hardly any change in the trend amongst the Punjabi Khatri voters in the 2008 Assembly elections; it nonetheless witnessed some change in the voting preferences amongst the Brahmins in Delhi. There was a shift in preference from the BJP to the Congress amongst the upper-class Brahmin voters. It is also important to note that even though the Brahmins, like the Punjabi Khatris, have remained divided on class lines when it comes to voting, the divide is not as sharp amongst the former as it is in the latter.

Table 3.1:
The Class Divide among Brahmin Voters

	1998		2003		2008	
	Congress	*BJP*	*Congress*	*BJP*	*Congress*	*BJP*
Upper	30	63	35	57	47	34
Middle	42	55	45	45	32	49
Lower	50	45	46	42	36	31

Sources: HT–CSDS Delhi Surveys, 1998 and 2003; Post-poll Survey, 2008.
Note: All figures are in per cent.

Table 3.2:
The Class Divide among Punjabi Khatri Voters

	1998		2003		2008	
	Congress	*BJP*	*Congress*	*BJP*	*Congress*	*BJP*
Upper	31	67	39	58	37	53
Middle	39	59	40	49	24	67
Lower	40	55	46	49	50	17

Sources: HT–CSDS Delhi Surveys, 1998 and 2003; Post-poll Survey, 2008.
Note: All figures are in per cent.

Besides the Punjabi Khatri caste, the Jats too are inclined towards the BJP. One can see the class divide even amongst the Jats in Delhi, but that only affects the degree of support for the BJP amongst the three different classes of Jat voters. Other than a few exceptions, the Jats—irrespective of the class they belong to—had voted for the BJP in successive elections in the past (Table 3.3). Over the last few elections, however, we find that like other communities, the upper-class Jats are more inclined towards the BJP vis-à-vis the lower-class Jats; the 1998 Assembly election was as exception to that. During that election, which the BJP lost by a huge margin, the Jats, irrespective of their economic status, voted overwhelmingly for the BJP. It was mainly due to Sahib Singh Verma, whom the Jats wanted to see as Delhi's chief minister, that they voted for the party in huge numbers.

Table 3.3:
The Class Divide among Jat Voters

	1998		2003		2008	
	Congress	*BJP*	*Congress*	*BJP*	*Congress*	*BJP*
Upper	48	48	32	53	11	67
Middle	35	62	40	46	44	44
Lower	31	68	51	33	45	54

Sources: HT–CSDS Delhi Surveys, 1998 and 2003; Post-poll Survey, 2008.
Note: All figures are in per cent.

As far as the Sikh community is concerned, there is a belief that the Sikhs hardly vote for the Congress mainly due to the involvement of some Congress leaders in the anti-Sikh riots that had sparked off in Delhi as a result of the assassination of Indira Gandhi. In the Assembly election held in 1993, the first after Delhi got its statehood, a large majority of the Sikh voters voted for the BJP, but subsequent Assembly elections have seen a close contest between the Congress and the BJP for the Sikh vote in Delhi (Table 3.4). In the contest between the two parties for the Sikh vote, the upper-class Sikh voters have clearly sided with the BJP

Table 3.4:
The Class Divide among Sikh Voters

	1998		2003		2008	
	Congress	*BJP*	*Congress*	*BJP*	*Congress*	*BJP*
Upper	39	58	38	58	50	50
Middle	48	51	46	43	37	44
Lower	53	37	59	28	50	50

Sources: HT–CSDS Delhi Surveys, 1998 and 2003; Post-poll Survey, 2008.
Note: All figures are in per cent.

while a large proportion of lower-class Sikh voters have voted for the Congress. The middle-class Sikh voters seem to be more or less equally divided between the two parties. The recent election has seen some shift in preference amongst the upper-class voters towards the Congress, but largely the upper-class Sikh voters voted for the BJP.

The Dalits, cutting across economic classes, have in the past voted overwhelmingly for the Congress (Table 3.5). The BJP got only a small proportion of the Dalit vote. But the entry of the BSP in the electoral scene radically changed the nature of competition for the Dalit votes in Delhi; the BSP began to attract a large section of Dalit voters in Delhi. The recent elections have witnessed cracks opening up amongst the Dalit voters on class lines, but the competition is not between the Congress and the BJP; rather it is largely between the Congress and the BSP. With the presence of the BSP, the rules of the game seem to have somewhat changed. Cutting across caste, it is the Congress which is more popular amongst the lower class and the BJP is more popular amongst the upper class, though there may be some exceptions. But the class divide amongst the Dalit voters suggests that the lower-class Dalits are more in favour of the BSP while the upper-class Dalits seem more inclined towards the Congress. The upper-class Dalits seem to be largely divided between the Congress and the BJP. There is a movement towards the BSP even amongst the middle-class Dalit voters, though there is a slight difference in the trends of the Assembly and the Lok Sabha elections.

Table 3.5:
The Class Divide among Dalit Voters

	1998			2003			2008		
	Congress	*BJP*	*BSP*	*Congress*	*BJP*	*BSP*	*Congress*	*BJP*	*BSP*
Upper	73	23	–	66	19	6	54	39	7
Middle	59	27	10	53	19	19	37	22	37
Lower	65	21	12	53	15	26	36	25	32

Sources: HT–CSDS Delhi Surveys, 1998 and 2003; Post-poll Survey, 2008.
Note: All figures are in per cent.

Findings from various surveys clearly indicate the presence of a class divide amongst Delhi's voters, which is evident among most caste communities. It is however not true that there are no other factors that determine the voting decisions of the voters. Other factors such as level of education, locality and gender also tend to influence the voting decision, but amongst all these factors, class seems to be the most imperative. Therefore, what distinguishes Delhi's voters from voters of other states is the fact that class plays a greater role in determining voting behaviour in the city. Moreover, even though the influence of class on voting decisions has not declined over the years, recent years have seen some changes in political preferences. With the emergence of the BSP in the city's politics, there is a shift in the voting preference amongst all the three classes of voters—the upper, the middle and the lower.

An overall assessment of the scenario points to certain voting trends vis-à-vis class status in the capital. The upper-class voters cutting across castes had voted for the BJP for a long time, while the lower-class voters had voted for the Congress. But the rule of the game seems to have gradually changed. There is, on the one hand, a movement amongst the lower class away from the Congress towards the BSP; on the other hand, the Congress has been able to compensate for this loss by increasing its popularity amongst the upper-class voters. There is a close contest for the middle-class votes but they largely seem to be with the BJP. Even though the movement of the lower-class voters away from the Congress had remained largely limited amongst the Dalits, one cannot rule out this sort of change in voting preferences in future amongst the lower-class voters—a movement away from the Congress and towards the BSP. It is vital to note that the gradual rise of the BSP's popularity in Delhi is linked to its increasing support amongst the lower-class voters.

However, it is not that there is a shift only amongst the lower-class voters; there is also a shift amongst the upper-class voters from the BJP towards the Congress. Sheila Dikshit, with her clean image on the one hand, and the development work that has been carried out in Delhi on the other hand, has been able to attract the upper-class voters. Moreover, in the absence of the BJP as a vibrant opposition, the Congress is naturally seen as the most suitable party for governance. The BJP, however, still seems to be popular amongst the middle-class voters.

Note

1. The BSP performed well in the 2008 Assembly election but not in the 2009 Lok Sabha election. The support for the BSP amongst the lower-class voters too declined—smaller proportion of lower-class voters voted for the BSP in the 2009 Lok Sabha election compared to the 2008 Assembly election.

4

The Electoral Verdict

The Rise of BSP as a Third Force in Delhi Politics

The shift in the voting behaviour of the people of Delhi is important for the fact that the state is the national capital of India too, with its Assembly having a sizeable number of people's representatives. The city, which has got the status of a state, has witnessed four Assembly elections since it got statehood in 1992, but it had been electing members to the Parliament since the first Lok Sabha election, which took place in 1952. Like in many states, the politics in the city of Delhi had been dominated by a strong presence of the Congress, with the Bhartiya Jana Sangh (BJS) being the main opposition party till 1971. While the Congress managed to continue its position as one of the dominant political parties in Delhi, the political space vacated by the BJS was occupied by the Bharatiya Lok Dal (BLD) during the 1977 Lok Sabha election. It is important to note that the 1977 Lok Sabha election brought a change in the national government and Delhi played an important role when all the seven Lok Sabha seats were won by the BLD. After the failed Janata experiment, the space created by the BLD was filled by the Congress in the next two Lok Sabha elections (held in 1980 and 1984), but since the 1989 Lok Sabha election, the dominance of the Congress in Delhi politics had been challenged by the BJP. The BJP initially came into power during the 1990s when Madan Lal Khurana was the leader of the BJP. The BJP posed a serious challenge for the Congress in Delhi and managed to win a sizeable number of seats in the various Lok Sabha elections held between 1989 and 1999, but the 2004 Lok Sabha election resulted in a reversal of fortune for the Congress and the party won six of the seven Lok Sabha seats. In the 2009 Lok Sabha election, the Congress improved upon its performance and managed to win all the seven Lok Sabha seats and polled 57.1 per cent votes (Table 4.1). In the long journey of electoral politics, the city mainly witnessed a bipolar political contest. In this, bipolar contest, while the Congress stood at one pole, its counterpart kept changing at different points of time in different elections.

Table 4.1:
Party Performance in Delhi: Lok Sabha Elections, 1952–2009

		Congress		BJP*		BSP		Independents/ Others	
Year	*Turnout*	*Seat*	*Vote*	*Seat*	*Vote*	*Seat*	*Vote*	*Seat*	*Vote*
1952	57.92	3	49.43	–	25.92	–	–	1	24.65
1957	57.29	5	54.33	–	19.71	–	–	–	25.96
1962	68.75	5	50.68	–	32.66	–	–	–	16.66
1967	69.49	1	38.79	6	46.72	–		–	14.49
1971	65.19	7	64.39	–	29.57	–	–	–	6.04
1977	71.31	–	30.15	7	68.15	–	–	–	1.70
1980	64.89	6	50.40	1	37.90	–	–	–	1
1984	64.48	7	68.72	–	18.85	–	–	–	12.43
1989	54.30	2	43.41	4	26.19	–	3.65	1	26.75
1991	48.52	2	39.57	5	40.21	–	0.92	–	19.30
1996	50.62	2	37.29	5	49.62	–	–	–	13.09
1998	51.29	1	42.64	6	50.73	–	2.34	–	4.29
1999	43.54	–	41.96	7	51.75	–	2.24	–	4.05
2004	47.09	6	54.81	1	40.67	–	2.48	–	2.04
2009	51.84	7	57.11	–	35.23	–	5.34	–	2.32

Source: CSDS Data Unit.
Notes: * BJS (1952–71), BLD (1977), JNP (1980) and BJP (1984 onwards).

Challenging Bipolarity: Assembly Elections and the Third Pole

The politics of this city seems to have witnessed a continuous shift since the city voted for its first Assembly election in 1993. Even though the first two Assembly elections (held in 1993 and 1998) did not witness any substantial change in the nature of political contest or in the nature of electoral outcomes, they indicated a possible change in the city's politics. A significant proportion of the voters who voted for parties other than the two main contenders, the Congress and the BJP, in the first two Assembly elections indicated the possibility of emergence of a third political force in the city's politics.

The Assembly election held in 1993, the first after the creation of the state, witnessed a bipolar contest between the BJP and the Congress. The BJP formed the government, winning 49 of the 70 Assembly seats and polling 42.8 per cent votes (Table 4.2). The Congress emerged a poor second by managing to win only 14 Assembly seats and polling 34.5 per cent votes. Though largely a bipolar contest, it should be noted that a significant proportion of the city's voters preferred voting for parties and candidates who belonged neither to the Congress nor the BJP. The results of the 1993 Assembly election indicates that 20.8 per cent of Delhi's voters voted for those who contested either as independent candidates, or as candidates of other smaller political parties. The sizeable support for the non-Congress, non-BJP candidates resulted in the victory of seven candidates who did not belong to either of the two dominant political forces.[1] Apart from these seven constituencies, which elected the candidates from the non-dominant political parties, there was sizeable support for such candidates from non-dominant political parties in another 10 Assembly constituencies, where a non-Congress, non-BJP candidate got more than 20 per cent of the votes polled.[2] During the 1993 Assembly election, the place of the third force in the city's politics was largely occupied by the Janata Dal, as in 9 out of these 10 Assembly constituencies the Janata Dal candidates could garner more than one-fifth of the votes polled; also, an independent candidate won a seat.

Table 4.2:
Party Performance in Delhi: Assembly Elections, 1993–2008

Year	Turnout	Congress		BJP/BJS		BSP		Independents/ Others		Effective No. of Party
		Seat	Vote	Seat	Vote	Seat	Vote	Seat	Vote	
1993	61.8	14	34.5	49	42.8	0	1.9	7	20.8	3.1
1998	49.0	52	47.8	15	34.0	0	3.1	3	15.1	2.9
2003	53.4	47	48.1	20	35.2	0	5.8	3	10.9	2.8
2008	57.6	43	40.3	23	36.3	2	14.1	2	9.3	3.2

Source: CSDS Data Unit.

Five years later, the Assembly election of 1998 not only saw a complete reversal in the political preference of Delhi's voters, it also witnessed the downfall of the third pole, or rather a beginning of the clash for the third pole. The other smaller political parties and independents (combined) managed to win only three Assembly seats and poll 15.1 per cent votes.[3] The 1998 Assembly election witnessed the emergence of the BSP in Delhi politics, though as a minor political force. The BSP polled 3.1 per cent votes and there was a corresponding decline in the combined vote share of the other smaller parties and independents. Riding on the wave against the BJP on the issue of the rising price of onion, the Congress registered an impressive victory winning 52 Assembly seats and polling 47.8 per cent votes. The BJP managed to win only 15 Assembly seats and poll only 34 per cent votes.

The third Assembly election since Delhi got statehood was held in 2003. There was hardly any change in the city's politics with regard to the two dominant political players, the Congress and the BJP. The Congress almost repeated its performance of the 1998 Assembly election. The party managed to win 47 Assembly seats (5 seats fewer compared to the 1998 Assembly election) and to increase its vote share, though marginally. The BJP added five more seats to its tally of 15 Assembly seats in 1998 and also marginally increased its vote share. The BSP could not open its account in terms of seats, but the vote share of the party increased by nearly 2.6 percentage points (5.8 per cent in 2003 compared to 3.1 per cent in the 1998 Assembly election). The increase in the vote shares of all the three political parties—the Congress, the BJP and the BSP—was largely at the cost of the other smaller parties and the independents, whose combined vote share declined from 15.1 per cent in the 1998 Assembly election to 10.9 per cent in the 2003 Assembly election. In spite of this decline, the other smaller parties and independents (combined) managed to win only three Assembly seats.[4]

The results for the 2008 Assembly election indicated hardly any change for the two major political players in the state. The Congress registered its third successive victory under the leadership of Sheila Dikshit. Though the vote share of the Congress declined by nearly 8 percentage points (40.3 per cent compared to 48.1 per cent in the 2003 Assembly election), it did not result in the loss of too many seats. The party managed to win 43 Assembly seats, four fewer than in the previous Assembly election (47 seats in 2003), but had a comfortable majority needed for forming the government. On the other hand, the vote share of the BJP increased by just 1 per cent (36.3 per cent compared to

35.2 per cent in the 2003 Assembly election), but the party improved its tally of seats from 20 in the 2003 Assembly election to 23 in the 2008 Assembly election. The BSP opened its account by winning two Assembly seats. Lok Jan Shakti Party candidate Shoaib Iqbal won from Matia Mahal while an independent Bharat Singh won from Nazafgarh constituency.[5]

And Slowly the Elephant Stands

Since the 1993 Assembly election, it seems that the Janata Dal made the strongest pole among the smaller parties in Delhi, with its winning record in almost all the elections. In the 1993 election the Janata Dal largely filled the gap of the third force in the city's politics by winning nine seats; this was also the election when the BSP began its political journey in Delhi politics by putting up its candidates in 55 Assembly constituencies. The party began its journey but it polled only 1.9 per cent votes, which went unnoticed in city's political circle. But one must note that the votes that were cast in favour of the BSP came from the constituencies with sizeable and concentrated Dalit population. The pattern of support which the party got was an indication for the possibility of the rise of the third force in the form of the BSP since Delhi has a sizeable Dalit population. In the early 1990s, the BSP built a strong base in UP, from where it spread to a number of states in North India. This was possible because of the rapid decline of the broad dominant party system in UP, providing room for narrower political formations. In this situation, the BSP organized a Dalit movement in UP by mobilizing on the basis of identity and created a strong Dalit-based party. Both the Congress and the BJP came to be identified as upper-caste formations. These developments gave Dalit politics a seminal position, both in UP and national politics.

The 1998 Assembly election marked the beginning of the consolidation of the BSP even though it failed to open its account. The increase in the vote share for the BSP was a clear indication of the increasing support base of the party. The party polled 3.1 per cent votes, with more than 10 per cent votes in constituencies reserved for the Dalits—like Mangolpuri (12.6 per cent), Trilokpuri (18 per cent) and Nand Nagri (12 per cent)—which was a clear indication of the BSP's increasing popularity amongst the Dalit population. Besides these three Assembly constituencies, there were 12 other Assembly constituencies where the BSP managed to poll between 5 to 10 per cent votes.[6]

There was a marginal increase in the vote share of the BSP in the 2003 Assembly election compared to the 1998 Assembly election. The BSP again could not win even one Assembly seat but it is important to note that in the Assembly constituencies of Mangolpuri, Nand Nagri and Ghonda, the BSP candidates (Megh Singh, Satish Kumar and Rohtash Kumar respectively) were runners-up. In another 13 Assembly constituencies, the BSP polled more than 10 per cent votes.[7] There were a few other Assembly constituencies where the BSP managed to garner reasonable support, reflected in terms of the votes polled by the party.[8] Most of these initial gains for the BSP during the 2003 Assembly election came from East Delhi, which accounted for 20 Assembly seats prior to the redrawing of boundaries of Assembly constituencies. Many of these Assembly constituencies share their geographical boundaries with UP, and a number of migrants from Bihar and adjoining UP constitute a large proportion of the voters in these constituencies.

The writing on the wall was clear: with sizeable Dalit voters and a large proportion of migrants, mainly poor, there was scope for the rise of a new third force in the city's politics. The BSP was emerging as the party to fill this gap.

After the initial success in Delhi in the 2003 Assembly election and also in the municipal election later, the BSP was serious about expanding its presence in the city's politics. The victory for the party in UP in the Assembly election held there in 2007 gave an impetus to the rank and file within the BSP leadership. Much before the 2008 Assembly election in Delhi, the BSP had geared itself to make its presence felt in the election. The party announced the candidates well before the dates for the Assembly election were announced, and the BSP supremo Mayawati addressed several rallies and campaigned extensively in various parts of the city.

The 2008 Assembly election witnessed the emergence of the BSP on the political map of Delhi in a significant way. With its first success in the 2008 Assembly election, the BSP seems to have finally made its presence in the city's politics. The BSP managed to increase its vote share from 5.7 per cent votes in the 2003 Assembly election to 14.1 per cent vote in the 2008 Assembly election. It also managed to win two Assembly seats in the most recent Assembly elections held in 2008. The BSP won the Gokalpur reserved Assembly seat by a decent margin of over three thousand votes and in the Badarpur general Assembly seat, the BSP candidate Ram Singh Netaji defeated a stalwart of Delhi politics (Ram Singh Bidhuri of the Congress) by a huge margin of over

13,000 votes. Apart from that, the BSP was also runner-up in another five Assembly constituencies—Narela, Badali, Deoli, Tughkalabad and Badarpur. In all these constituencies the BSP polled a sizeable proportion of the votes. Apart from these seven Assembly constituencies where the BSP either emerged victorious or was runner-up, there were another eight Assembly constituencies where the BSP polled more than 20 per cent of the votes.[9] There were various other Assembly constituencies where the BSP polled marginally less than 20 per cent of the votes. It polled 31 per cent votes in Baburpur, 17.5 per cent in Ambedkar Nagar, a whopping 47.3 per cent in Badarpur, 26 per cent in Badli, 19 per cent in Bijwasan, 30 per cent in Chhatarpur, 26 per cent in Deoli, 29 per cent in Gokalpur and as much as 31 per cent in Narela, narrowly missing a victory in this constituency.

It was quite apparent in Delhi's municipal corporation election as well as in the Assembly elections in UP that the BSP's appeal was growing and was confined not merely to the Dalits. The party has tried to woo the voters of other castes and communities, with Mayavati's policy of social engineering gaining momentum. However, it was quite obvious that the emergence of the BSP in Delhi would definitely hamper the prospects of the Congress more than that of the BJP, as both the Congress and the BSP bank upon a common support base.

In the 2009 Lok Sabha election, the BSP did not do as well as its performance in the 2008 Assembly election, but it marginally improved its performance compared to the 2004 Lok Sabha election. The BSP managed to expand its political support base amongst the lower- and middle-class voters of Delhi. The findings of the CSDS Survey indicate that during the 2009 Lok Sabha election, the BSP managed to increase its support base amongst Delhi's middle class by nearly 6 percentage points compared to the 2004 Lok Sabha election.

What Changed for the BSP between 2003 and 2008?

A comparison between the 2003 and 2008 poll results indicates that the BSP has been able to expand its political base in Delhi substantially in these five years, which is proved by the stark increase in its vote share. This proliferation in votes was possible only because the party was able to expand its base not just geographically but also demographically. To better comprehend the change in the voting scene, let us first look at the regions where the BSP has been able to make its electoral presence felt substantially. In geographical terms, even though the BSP has not been able to radically expand its support base in the heart of the city, its support base increased in constituencies which are located on the periphery of the city and also in the constituencies which are in the Trans Yamuna localities.[10] The periphery of the city accounts for 16 Assembly constituencies. There is an equal number of Assembly constituencies in the Trans Yamuna locality. The BSP performed better in these 32 Assembly constituencies compared to the rest of Delhi. In the constituencies on the periphery of the city, the BSP polled 20 per cent votes and won one Assembly seat, while in the constituencies in the Trans Yamuna localities, it polled 15.5 per cent votes and managed to win one Assembly seat (Table 4.3).

Table 4.3:
Region-wise Vote Shares of Political Parties in Delhi: Assembly Election, 2008

			Congress		BJP		BSP		Others	
Region	*Seats*	*Turnout (%)*	*Seats*	*Vote (%)*	*Seats*	*Vote (%)*	*Seats*	*Vote (%)*	*Seats*	*Vote (%)*
Trans Yamuna	16	59.0	10	42.2	5	35.6	1	15.5	0	6.7
Periphery	16	55.7	8	33.5	6	30.9	1	20.0	1	15.6
North-West	17	59.6	9	41.1	8	40.8	0	11.0	0	7.1
City North	11	59.1	8	44.1	2	39.5	0	8.6	1	7.8
City South	10	53.7	8	44.6	2	36.4	0	11.4	0	7.6
Total	70	57.6	43	40.3	23	36.3	2	14.0	2	9.3

Source: CSDS Data Unit.

The BSP's expansion in these two localities is, however, not a mere coincidence; rather it is related to the settlement pattern of the migrants from Bihar and UP. The periphery of Delhi and the Trans Yamuna localities are typically inhabited by lower-middle-class residents, and unlike the northern and southern parts of the city, which are inhabited by relatively richer and upper-class residents. The periphery and the Trans Yamuna localities also have a large concentration of jhuggis and slums. Poor migrants from Bihar and UP in sizeable numbers, live along with the Dalits in these localities. After the delimitation of constituency boundaries in the capital, 12 Assembly seats are reserved exclusively for the Dalits. There are, however, a few more constituencies with considerable Dalit and migrant population, which form the backbone of the

BSP's support base in Delhi. As per a rough classification, there are 16 Assembly constituencies where these migrants play a decisive role and many among them have shown a positive tendency of voting for the BSP.[1] It is important to note that in the constituencies dominated by the migrants, the BSP polled 19 per cent votes, 5 percentage points more than its average vote in the city. Both the seats which BSP won had a sizeable migrant population. The BSP had been popular among migrants even in the 2003 Assembly elections and had polled 7.5 per cent votes in constituencies where they were present in sizeable numbers, but the support base of the BSP increased enormously among the migrant voters after 2003, marking a dent in the support for the Congress. In constituencies dominated by the migrants, the Congress polled 36 per cent votes, 4 per cent less than its average vote in this particular election.

Delhi's politics is largely discussed in terms of the 'Jat vote' or the 'Punjabi vote', but there is hardly any discussion about the 'Dalit vote' even though the Dalits constitute nearly 17 per cent of Delhi's voters. Also, over the last few decades, rapid migration in Delhi has changed the nature of the electorate—migrants from Bihar and UP constitute a large proportion of the population in a number of Assembly constituencies (see Table 4.4). To add to the changing nature of the electorate is the new delimitation which has resulted in a change in the nature of the electorate geographically. For instance, Chandni Chowk, which was traditionally considered to be a Muslim-dominated constituency, now has a Muslim population of 14 per cent, compared to 40 per cent in the past, with

Table 4.4:
Vote Shares of Political Parties in Different Types of Constituencies

Community Type	Seats	Turnout (%)	Congress		BJP		BSP		Others	
			Won	Vote (%)	Won	Vote (%)	Won	Vote (%)	Won	Vote (%)
UP–Bihar migrants	16	58.0	8	36.1	6	33.9	2	18.9	0	11.1
Punjabi-dominated	16	58.0	10	43.3	6	41.1	0	8.6	0	7.0
Peasant community	11	55.8	7	34.7	3	31.8	0	17.7	1	15.8
Rest	27	58.1	18	43.9	8	37.2	0	12.4	1	6.5
Total	70	57.6	43	40.3	23	36.3	2	14.0	2	9.3

Source: CSDS Data Unit.

only two of its eight Assembly segments (Ballimaran and Matia Mahal) actually having a Muslim majority. The dominant caste presence next to that of the SCs and OBCs is that of the Punjabis and the Vaishyas, with areas like Shakur Basti having 31 per cent Punjabi presence. Northeast Delhi, on the other hand, is now the new Chandni Chowk with its 21 per cent Muslim presence. The Brahmin domination of erstwhile East Delhi Lok Sabha constituency has been replaced by a plethora of unauthorized colonies in Burari, Karawal Nagar, Mustafabad, Gokalpur, Seemapuri and Ghonda, and the substantial SC–OBC presence. Brahmins now constitute a poor third at 12 per cent, marginally worse off than in East Delhi where their proportion is now down to 11 per cent.

Amongst the various Dalit castes in Delhi, the Jatavs constitute the largest number and they have largely voted for the BSP. The Jatav vote for the BSP in Delhi is not as concentrated as it is in UP, yet 37 per cent amongst them voted for the BSP in the 2008 Assembly election in Delhi. Moreover, since 2003 there has been hardly any shift among the Jatavs' support for the BSP. But in the same period (2003–8), there has been a shift in the non-Jatav Dalit votes in favour of the BSP. In the 2008 Assembly election, 22 per cent of the non-Jatav Dalits voted for the BSP, compared to a meagre 8 per cent that voted for it in previous Assembly elections. Subsequently, the Congress lost its sizeable support base among these voters between 2003 and 2008. The BJP was also affected to some extent. The BSP, thus, managed to increase its vote share, which inevitably had a negative impact on the vote shares of both the Congress and the BJP. Amongst those who voted for the BSP in the 2008 Assembly election, 55 per cent were those voters who had voted for the BSP in the previous Assembly election held in 2003; at the same time, the BSP snatched 28 per cent of its votes from the Congress and 12 per cent votes from the BJP. It has to be noted that the BSP did particularly well in the rural areas in the 2008 Assembly election—its candidates received votes in sizeable numbers, (very close to that of the winning candidates) in Narela, Badli, Okhla and Baburpur.

But the success of the BSP did not depend only upon the Dalit vote. The popularity of the party has also gradually extended to the voters of other communities, owing to its strategy of distributing tickets to non-Dalits, that is, from 'Bahujan to Sarvajan'. In the 2008 Assembly election, 17 per cent of the voters from the Gujjar and Yadav communities voted for the BSP, compared to a mere 4 per cent in the previous Assembly election. The party was also able to increase its support base among voters belonging to the OBC. Amongst the OBC, 18 per cent voted for the BSP in the last election compared to only 5 per cent of them voting for the BSP in the previous ones. Furthermore, the BJP lost sizeable support amongst the Gujjars and the Yadavs. There is also a noticeable shift among the Muslim voters in favour of the BSP. How enduring is this shift in favour of the BSP among the non-Dalits cannot be known at this point in time, but it is clear that the rise of the BSP has adversely affected both the Congress and the BJP in electoral terms and dented the biparty nature of political competition in Delhi.

Even now, the BSP's presence in Delhi's politics remains limited, but recent voting trends in the capital clearly indicate that the BSP is gradually emerging as a potential player in the city's politics. The factors that had enabled the BSP to make its presence felt in Delhi's politics would also ultimately help the party in consolidating its position and keeping its increasing popularity intact.

There were broadly two factors which made the emergence of the BSP in the city's politics possible—first, a sizeable Dalit population (17 per cent as per 2001 Census), and second, a sizeable migrant population (about 40 per cent of Delhi's population). These two communities share one common characteristic: a large number of them belong to the lower economic strata and a vast majority of them live in jhuggis, unauthorized colonies and similar locations. Even though the migrants belong to various caste communities, it is their lower economic status that cuts across other identities. Their relatively low economic status forms the basis of their common identity which consequently binds them together. Thus, the BSP has also tried to woo this section of voters on class lines.

The city of Delhi faced large-scale migration in the past few decades, which led to a change in the social composition of the city's population, from a predominantly upper-class city to a city which encompasses people broadly from three different classes—the upper, the middle and the lower. The class identity of the people is seen to override all other primordial identities. Unlike many other states, where political behaviour is determined primarily by one's caste affiliation, the political behaviour of the people in Delhi is largely guided by their class identity. The voters belonging to different classes show different political choices: while the upper-class voters are seen to be more inclined towards the BJP, the lower-class voters favour the Congress. The situation has, however, changed gradually in recent elections. The BSP has been able to attract the voters belonging to the lower class in its favour. Even though there has been some shift in preference amongst the middle-class voters towards the Congress, a large proportion of the upper-class voters largely remains with the BJP. The huge and ever increasing lower-class population—as a result of rapid migration and successful mobilization by the BSP—has paved the way for the rise of the BSP in the city's political arena, ultimately leading to the city's politics taking a turn from bipolarity to a three-cornered contest.

Notes

1. The Janata Dal candidates got elected from Okhla (Parvej Hasami), Badarpur (Ramvir Singh Bidhuri), Seelampur (Matin Ahmed) and Matia Mahal (Shoaib Iqbal) Assembly constituencies, while independent candidates got elected from Najafgarh (Suraj Prasad), Tughlakabad (Shish Pal) and Bhalswa Jahangirpuri (Jitendra Kumar) Assembly constituencies.
2. The constituencies where a non-Congress, non-BJP candidate polled 20 per cent or more votes were Bawana (SC), Sultanpur Mazara (SC), Vishnu Garden, Palam, Mahipalpur, Saket, Trilok Puri (SC), Patparganj (SC), Nand Nagri (SC) and Paharganj.
3. The three Assembly seats which the combined force of other political parties and independents managed to win were Matia Mahal (Shoaib Iqbal of Janata Dal), Seelampur (Martin Ahmed, a Congress rebel) and Badarpur (Ram Singh, a Congress rebel).
4. The Assembly seats which the combined force of other political parties and independents managed to win were Matia Mahal (Sohaib Iqbal of Janta Dal [United]), Badarpur (Ram Vir Singh Bidhuri of Nationalist Congress Party) and Najafgarh (Ramvir Singh, an independent).
5. Matia Mahal (Soahib Iqbal of Lok Jan Shakti Party) and Najafgarh (Bharat Singh, an independent) won.
6. The BSP polled between 5–10 per cent votes in Sahibabad Daulatpur (5.1 per cent), Sultanpur Mazara (5.1 per cent), Mahipalpur (7.7 per cent), Saket (5 per cent), Ambedkar Nagar (6.4 per cent), Badarpur (5.7 per cent), Patparganj (7.6 per cent), Mandawali (5.3 per cent), Rohtas Nagar (6.6 per cent), Ghonda (5.2 per cent), Adarsh Nagar (5.9 per cent) and Baljeet Nagar (7 per cent).
7. In the 2003 Assembly election, the BSP polled more than 10 per cent votes in Sultanpur Mazara (15.6 per cent), Badarpur (14.3 per cent), Trilokpuri (21 per cent), Patparganj (16.4 per cent), Mandawali (15.2 per cent), Shahdara (13 per cent), Seemapuri (11 per cent), Rohtas Nagar (10.5 per cent), Karawal Nagar (19.1 per cent), Wazirpur (10 per cent), Narela (10.6 per cent), Bhalswa Jahangirpuri (13.2 per cent) and Adarsh Nagar (13.3 per cent).

8. In the 2003 Assembly election, the BSP polled 6.9 per cent votes in Kasturba Nagar, 7 per cent in Sahibabad Daulatpur, 9 per cent in Mahipalpur, 7.6 per cent in Ambedkar Nagar and 8.9 per cent in Tughlakabad.

9. The eight constituencies were Sultanpur Mazara (22.6 per cent), Mangolpuri (21.5 per cent), Palam (22.8 per cent), Chhatarpur (29.3 per cent), Okhla (21.5 per cent), Trilokpuri (23.5 per cent), Kondli (24.6 per cent) and Ghonda (23.7 per cent).

10. As per the regional classification of Delhi by the CSDS Data Unit, Delhi can be divided into five broad regions—the Periphery, the region of North-West, Trans Yamuna region, City South and City North. The Periphery has 16 Assembly constituencies (Narela, Burari, Bawana, Mundka, Kirari, Vikaspuri, Matiala, Najafgarh, Bijaswan, Mehrauli, Chhatarpur, Deoli, Ambedkar Nagar, Sangam Vihar, Tughlakabad and Badarpur). The region of Trans Yamuna consists of 16 Assembly constituencies (Trilokpuri, Kondli, Patparganj, Laxmi Nagar, Vishwas Nagar, Krishna Nagar, Gandhi Nagar, Shahdara, Seempuri, Rohtas Nagar, Seelampur, Ghonda, Babarpur, Gokalpuri, Mustafabad and Karawal Nagar). The region of North-West Delhi consists of 17 Assembly constituencies (Adarsh Nagar, Badali, Rithala, Sultanpur Mazara, Nangloi Jat, Mangolpuri, Rohini, Shalimar Bagh, Shakur Basti, Madipur, Rajouri Garden, Hari Nagar, Tilak Nagar, Janakpuri and Palam). The City North consists of 11 Assembly constitutes (Tri Nagar, Wazirpur, Model Town, Sadar Bazar, Chandni Chowk, Matia Mahal, Ballimaran, Karol Bagh, Patel Nagar, Moti Nagar and Timarpur). The region City South consists of 10 Assembly constituencies (Delhi Cantonment, Rajinder Nagar, New Delhi, Jangpura, Kasturba Nagar, Malviya Nagar, R. K. Puram, Greater Kailash, Kalkaji and Okhla).

11. There are 16 Assembly constituencies where migrants from Bihar and UP are in sizeable numbers and play a decisive role in elections. These constituencies are Burari, Adarsh Nagar, Wazirpur, Uttam Nagar, Dwarka, Palam, Ambedkar Nagar, Sangam Vihar, Tughlakabad, Badarpur, Trilokpuri, Kondli, Seemapuri, Gokalpuri, Mustafabad and Karawal Nagar. Similarly, there are 17 Assembly constituencies where voters of the Punjabi community are in sizeable numbers. These constituencies are Timarpur, Badali, Shalimar Bagh, Shakur Basti, Wazirpur, Patel Nagar, Madipur, Rajouri Garden, Tilak Nagar, Hari Nagar, Janakpuri, Jangpura, Malviya Nagar, Kalkaji, Vishwas Nagar, Krishna Nagar and Shahdara.

5

Popular Perception about Leaders and Parties

The issue of leadership has contributed to the rise of the Congress in Delhi and the simultaneous decline of the BJP during the last one decade. Even though there have been challenges to the leadership of Sheila Dikshit from time to time, her second successive victory in the 2008 Assembly election and the impressive performance during the 2009 Lok Sabha election have virtually silenced all her critics. She stands tall today as a leader who has created a record of sorts by becoming the first Congress chief minister to retain power for a third term. But on the other hand, after the exit of Madan Lal Khurana from the BJP, the party has always faced a leadership crisis in Delhi; the party has tried several leaders for leading the party in Delhi. The BJP tried hard to play on the 'magic' of Sheila Dikshit—to try to comprehend the phenomenon associated with her leadership—but have not been able to succeed till date. The recent debacle of the BJP, both in the Assembly and the Lok Sabha elections, is largely seen as the failure on the part of the BJP to put up a formidable leadership. So, on the one hand, the Congress had the advantage of having a strong leader as Sheila Dikshit, and on the other, the BJP is facing a serious handicap on the issue of leadership.

This is not a new phenomenon for the Congress. The party, since the day it was formed, has relied and followed on its strong leaders. Sheila Dikshit became another face in the chain of leaders with her success stories in the national capital.

What Is Political Leadership All About?

Political leadership is different from the notions of leadership we have in respect to group dynamics or management phenomena. Most of these views put sole emphasis on the individuals who occupy managerial position and bring about change in organizations or systems.

For instance, some leadership theorists identify leadership as the focus of group processes (Bass 1990). From this perspective, the leader is the centre of the group change and activity, and embodies the will of the group.

In his book *Leading Minds: An Anatomy of Leadership*, Howard Gardner, an American psychologist, defined a leader as "an individual (or, rarely, a set of individuals) who significantly affects the thoughts, feelings, and/or behaviours of a significant number of people" (Gardner 1996: ix).

In the 1970s and 1980s, a genre of leadership theory, alternatively referred to as 'charismatic', 'transformational', 'visionary', or 'inspirational', emerged in the organizational literature (Bass 1985). These theories focused on exceptional leaders who have extraordinary effects on their followers and eventually on social systems.

But leadership in the party system in a democracy like India means something very different. The multiplicity of the range of leaders in the country makes it very difficult to tag any leader as being charismatic and attributing to them any party's victory at any level of election. For example, many people vote for the local leaders irrespective of the parties they belong to—such as Shoaib Iqbal from Matia Mahal, who has been winning that seat despite changing his allegiance to different parties. On the other hand there are voters who vote for the Congress not because of Sheila Dikshit but because of the popularity of Sonia Gandhi or Rahul Gandhi (or Manmohan Singh for that matter). But the importance of leadership cannot be denied at any level in electoral politics.

Leadership: Is Delhi's Politics Different from National Politics?

There is no reason to expect Delhi's politics to be different from national politics or politics in other states, with respect to the role of leadership. Leadership does matter and did matter in the city's politics in the last few elections. After coming to power in Delhi in the 1998 Assembly election, the Congress was able to consolidate its position mainly due to the leadership of Shelia Dikshit, whereas the leadership crisis within the BJP contributed to the decline of the BJP party in the city's politics. Empirical evidence from the surveys conducted by the CSDS indicates that Dikshit's popularity increased election after election (Table 5.1), but the BJP kept making wrong choices regarding leadership. Sheila Dikshit has always shared a connection with all age groups, especially the youth and the women. She has made a certain bond with the people of Delhi and her ability to speak with considerable conviction over issues is indeed a personality trait. None of various leaders chosen by the BJP, after Madan Lal Khurana, seemed to be popular with the average *Delhiwala*. The Congress reaped the benefit of Dikshit's increasing popularity due to her charismatic personality and her developmental work in the city. Over the years, more and more people in Delhi preferred her, to be the chief minister of Delhi, compared to any other leader. During the 2003 Assembly election, despite a pro-BJP wave across North India, (especially in Madhya Pradesh, Rajasthan and Chhattisgarh) the saffron brigade failed to cut ice in the national capital. Prominent Congress leaders like Digvijay Singh, Ashok Gehlot and Ajit Jogi were defeated in their states but Sheila Dikshit stood her ground. The landslide victory of the Congress in the capital in the following Lok Sabha election could also be attributed to Mrs Dikshit and the cultural change ushered in by her in terms of the large numbers of English-speaking party workers who effectively managed the counting centre of the Gole Market Assembly constituency.

Table 5.1:
Increasing Popularity of Sheila Dikshit, 1998–2009

Leader	1998	2003	2008	2009
Sheila Dikshit	3	30	32	49
Madan Lal Khurana	11	17	2	–
Sahib Singh Verma	7	1	–	–
Sushma Swaraj or Vijay Kumar Malhotra	3	–	13	2
Any Congress leader	16	4	1	–
Any BJP leader	6	2	3	1

Sources: HT–CSDS Delhi Surveys, 1998 and 2003; Post-poll Survey, 2008; National Election Study 2009.
Note: All figures are in per cent.

How important the issue of leadership is could be gauged from the fact that within a year of suffering a major defeat in Delhi's Assembly election in 1998, when the party had been led by Sushma Swaraj, the BJP bounced back in the 1999 Lok Sabha election by winning all the seven Lok Sabha seats. Since this was a national election, and Atal Bihari Vajpayee was leading the BJP, a large number of voters supported the BJP and voted for its candidates due to the effective leadership of the party.

While the leadership of the party at the national and state levels matter, what is also important is the candidate. In the Delhi parliamentary election of 2004, candidates mattered in the final outcome. While the BJP fielded all its sitting members of Parliament, the Congress presented a blend of old and new faces, which worked in its favour. The party fielded two new and young candidates—Ajay Maken in New Delhi (against Jagmohan, a minister in the Vajpayee government) and Sandeep Dikshit in East Delhi (against Lal Bihari Tiwari). In December 2001, Maken was made the Transport, Power and Tourism Minister in the cabinet of Sheila Dikshit. Having a good track record, he was projected as a young and upcoming leader with whom the middle class could identify (Raj 2004). With Sheila Dikshit as his mother, Sandeep Dikshit earned an easy victory.

What Went Wrong with the BJP

Leadership has played a crucial role in the political journey of the two national parties, the Congress and the BJP. Most of the credit for the revival of the BJP in Delhi after its humiliating defeat in the 1984 Lok Sabha election should go to its leader Madan Lal Khurana, who raised the demand for statehood to Delhi; it helped the Sangh Parivar in elevating their political ambitions in Delhi. The Constitution (69th Amendment) Act, 1991, declared the union territory of Delhi to be formally known as National Capital Territory of Delhi. The Act gave Delhi its own Legislative Assembly, with limited powers, though. The semi-statehood for Delhi that came out of this tussle in 1993 brought the BJP to power with a Congress government at the Centre. It was the revival efforts of Madan Lal Khurana which earned him the title *Dilli Ka Sher* (Lion of Delhi).

The decline of the BJP in Delhi began with the resignation of Madan Lal Khurana as chief minister of Delhi in 1996. Despite being a BJP heavyweight, Khurana was removed from the post of chief minister of Delhi after the Central Bureau of Investigation decided to press charges against him in the Hawala case in 1997. It has widely come to be accepted that Khurana's fall from grace was orchestrated by the RSS.

Khurana was replaced by late Sahib Singh Verma, who enjoyed significant clout among the powerful Jat community in Delhi. Soon, charges against Khurana were dismissed and pressure started building within the BJP to reinstate Khurana and replace Sahib Singh Verma as the chief minister. This led to an intense factionalism between Khurana supporters and Sahib Singh Verma supporters within Delhi's BJP. Even when it was evident that Verma may not be able to ensure victory for the BJP, the RSS avoided any attempts to unseat him. Since the RSS was opposed to Khurana, it was keen on neutralizing the effect of the powerful Punjabi lobby that supported him. If Khurana had returned as the chief minister of Delhi, he would have inevitably become too powerful for the Sangh Parivar. The situation led to a compromise in which Sushma Swaraj replaced Sahib Singh Verma as the chief minister of Delhi and led the party during the 1998 Assembly election with the hope of salvaging its sinking fortunes, which ultimately did not go in favour of the BJP.

Since Madan Lal Khurana's exit from Delhi politics, BJP could not bring up a suitable leader popular with the masses, and lead the party towards victory. The party tried various leaders like Sushma Swaraj, Vijay Kumar Malhotra and Sahib Singh Verma, but none of them seemed to be popular among Delhi's voters. The findings of the CSDS surveys indicated that after the exit of Madan Lal Khurana, none of the BJP leaders has been popular enough to revive the party in Delhi by their own charisma. An average voter preferred Madan Lal Khurana over any other BJP leader as a suitable candidate for the chief minister. During the survey conducted before the 1998 Assembly election, 11 per cent of the voters preferred Khurana as the next chief minister, while 7 per cent believed that Sahib Singh Verma could be a better chief minister. The incumbent Chief Minister Sushma Swaraj was a poor third in the race; only 3 per cent of the voters believed that she was best suited to lead the state as chief minister.

It was surprising to find that in the next five years (1998–2003), the popularity of Madan Lal Khurana went up within the Delhi BJP, despite him being sidelined by the BJP from the core affairs of the party (Table 5.2). According to a CSDS survey conducted in 1998, 48 per cent of the respondents felt that the law and order situation had deteriorated during the five years of BJP rule. Approximately 50 per cent were not happy about the supply of drinking water, and 58 per cent felt the same way about the supply of electricity. About 35 per cent of the respondents said that transport facilities had worsened in those five years. Even among BJP supporters, 32 per cent of those who voted for the party in the 1998 Lok Sabha election were dissatisfied with the government's performance. Above all this, a whopping 64 per cent of the respondents considered price rise the biggest problem.

Table 5.2:
Popularity of Madan Lal Khurana

	1998	*2003*	*2008*
All voters	11	17	2
BJP voters	23	49	3

Sources: HT–CSDS Delhi Surveys, 1998 and 2003; Post-poll Survey, 2008.
Note: All figures are in per cent.

During the 2003 Assembly election, 17 per cent of the voters in Delhi believed that Khurana would make the best chief minister, an increase by 7 percentage points in his popularity compared to five years earlier. During the 2008 Assembly election, the BJP declared Vijay Kumar Malhotra as their chief ministerial candidate, despite him being not a popular choice of the people. Some believed that Vijay Goel would have been a better choice for the BJP and being a young leader and a new face, he (compared to Malhotra) could have attracted more voters to the BJP (see Table 5.3).

After Khurana none of the BJP leaders had an extensive popular appeal. It was because of the fact that they remained tagged by their identities—Sahib Singh Verma being a Jat leader, Vijay Kumar Malhotra being a Punjabi and Sushma Swaraj always seen as someone who did not belong to this city. This hardly helped in motivating not only the voters, but even the party workers. We may tend to believe that Vijay Goel could have helped the BJP, but many believed that Goel could not have helped the party since he was young, a relatively new face, and still had to learn the art of leading the party in the polls. The findings of the CSDS survey also indicated that his personal popularity was low and that he could have hardly helped in the revival of the BJP in Delhi's politics (see Table 5.4).

Table 5.3:
Malhotra's Popularity (Caste-wise), Election 2008

Caste/community	Popularity
All voters	13
Brahmins	19
Punjabi Khatris	23
Rajputs	23
Vaishyas	24
OBCs	13
Gujjars	7
Dalits	5
Muslims	1

Source: Post-poll Survey, 2008.
Note: All figures are in per cent.

Table 5.4:
BJP Leaders' Popularity (Class-wise), 1998–2008

Leader popularity	All voters	Upper class	Middle class	Lower class
Vijay Kumar Malhotra in 2008	13	18	15	9
Madan Lal Khurana in 2003	17	25	18	12
Sushma Swaraj in 1998	3	5	4	1
Sahib Singh Verma's in 1998	7	6	8	5

Sources: HT–CSDS Delhi Surveys, 1998 and 2003; Post-poll Survey, 2008.
Note: All figures are in per cent.

With a severe loss in the 2008 and 2009 elections, all of the BJP's electoral strategies failed. The party's power in Delhi was centred on Madan Lal Khurana, Jagdish Mukhi, Vijay Kumar Malhotra, Kedar Nath Sahani and Sahib Singh Verma for too long. This now included Vijay Goel. After the loss, Malhotra said, "We have reports of anti-party activities by some rebels and we will soon decide what action needs to be taken against them." If within a party there is no formal machinery to challenge well-established hierarchies and regulate conflicts within them, then it is to be expected that they will fragment. The BJP too was bogged down with factionalism between Khurana, Verma, Vijay Goel and Mange Ram. The party did not have any major issue to pin down the ruling Congress party.

In putting the blame on anti-party activities for the defeat of the BJP during the 2008 Assembly election, Malhotra might have been correct. But the long-term decline of the BJP in Delhi has largely been due to the untimely exit of Khurana, successive mistakes in choosing a leader to lead the party in polls, and the growing popularity of Sheila Dikshit as chief minister of the state. Even though Vijay Kumar Malhotra remained the most popular choice for chief Minister among the BJP voters, his popularity did not seem to cut across all BJP voters. Even among the BJP voters, only 31 per cent preferred him as the chief minister while 9 per cent wanted Sheila Dikshit to be the chief minister.

Sheila Dikshit Adds Strength to the Congress

Sheila Dikshit made a slow, but steady start in Delhi politics. During the 1998 Assembly election, when the Congress did not announce its chief ministerial candidate, only 3 per cent of the voters mentioned the name of Sheila Dikshit as the chief minister. But her popularity increased election after election, as is evident from the findings of the CSDS surveys. In the most recent Assembly election held in 2008, 32 per cent of the voters mentioned her name as the most suitable chief minister for Delhi (Table 5.5). After her victory in 2008, her popularity again witnessed an upward swing, with more voters expressing faith in her as the most suitable Delhi chief minister. With the Congress being popular generally among lower-class voters and her personal popularity among middle- and upper-class voters (apart from the lower-class sections of voters) added strength for the Congress in the city's politics.

Table 5.5:
Sheila Dikshit's Popularity (Class-wise), 1998–2009

Economic class	1998	2003	2008	2009
All	3	30	32	40
Upper class	2	31	34	50
Middle class	3	31	32	50
Lower class	2	28	30	46

Sources: HT–CSDS Delhi Surveys, 1998 and 2003; Post-poll Survey, 2008; National Election Study, 2009.
Note: All figures are in per cent.

The Congress regained power by winning the Legislative Assembly election in 1998, and under the leadership of Sheila Dikshit, it retained power after the results of the 2003 and 2008 elections. By turning the incumbency factor in her favour, she joined the elite club of chief ministers—such as Mohanlal Sukhadia of Rajasthan, Jyoti Basu of West Bengal and Narendra Modi of Gujarat—who won elections using their personality, charisma and performance record. Sheila Dikshit is one of the few Congress leaders who have managed to write a success story for her party, even though she is only the second woman to become the chief minister of Delhi. The *India Today* 'Mood of the Nation' too rated Sheila Dikshit as the second best chief minister amongst all other chief ministers in different states.

Before the 2008 Assembly election, there was a widespread belief that the people of Delhi would vote against Sheila Dikshit as the urban, middle class were concerned about security after the Mumbai terror attack. But the findings of the CSDS survey indicated that Dikshit's charisma appealed to a section of the educated, middle class and helped to attract the young voters. She was able to win the voters' confidence with her clean and untainted image, good governance and work ethic. Once labelled as an 'outsider' by some sections of her own party, Sheila Dikshit showed her capabilities and popularity by leading the Congress back to power for a consecutive third term in Delhi. Riding on the double plank of development and governance, she almost single-handedly led the party to victory in Delhi, dismissing all the attacks on her from outside and within the Congress (see Table 5.6).

Table 5.6:
Sheila Dikshit's Popularity (Caste-wise), 2003–09

Caste/community	2003	2008	2009
Brahmins	27	29	50
Punjabi Khatris	25	28	64
Rajputs	27	32	43
Vaishyas	23	21	42
Jats	29	28	53
Gujjars	29	32	57
Other Backward Classes	25	25	52
Dalits	27	33	43
Muslims	34	46	52

Sources: HT–CSDS Delhi Survey, 2003; Post-poll Survey, 2008; National Election Study, 2009.
Note: All figures are in per cent.

She was able to unite the Congress, which was once divided between various factions led by Chaudhry Prem Singh, Sajjan Kumar, J. P. Agarwal and Jagdish Tytler. She decided to create a second line of leadership which stood independent of these fiefdoms.

But the Congress in Delhi has had to deal with political dissidence against Sheila Dikshit from various quarters within the party. At one time, the powerful Delhi trio of Jagdish Tytler, Subhash Chopra and Sajjan Kumar (with the tacit blessings of Kamal Nath) constantly attempted to get rid of her. At least 28 of the party's 53 members of the Legislative Assembly wanted her replaced by Ambika Soni. The crisis blew over after Sonia Gandhi's intervention. The All-India Congress Committee reshuffle, orchestrated by Sonia Gandhi, sent out a loud and clear message to party rebels—who had been trying to topple her for years—that Sheila Dikshit was here to stay. In 2003, Sonia Gandhi replaced the dissident-friendly Kamal Nath with Ahmed Patel as general secretary in charge of Delhi. She also brokered peace between Sheila Dishit and her long-time detractor (Congress Committee chief) Rambabu Sharma. In doing so, Sonia blew the hopes of the anti-Sheila segment of the party, which was led by Jagdish Tytler. Due to the controversy surrounding their involvement in the 1984 anti-Sikh riots, the Congress party dropped both Jagdish Tytler and Sajjan Kumar as Congress candidates for the Lok Sabha 2009 election. Tytler blamed his 'enemies' within the Congress party for scuttling his nomination.

Leadership involves influence. It is concerned with how the leader influences the followers. Influence is the sine qua non of leadership. Without influence, leadership does not exist. If on the one hand, Sheila Dikshit managed to consolidate her position with the tacit support of the central Congress leadership, dissidence against Sheila Dikshit within the Congress ranks was quickly and effectively clamped down under the guidance of Sonia Gandhi. Much of Dikshit's popularity is founded on some skilful, image construction and sustained developmental work. She incorporates liberal sensitivity to middle-class concerns with grassroots populism aimed mainly at the welfare of people living in Delhi's slums and resettlement colonies. Even though the Congress has been extremely popular amongst the poor voters living in resettlement colonies, slums and unauthorized colonies, Sheila Dikshit has managed to make inroads into the BJP's political turf: Delhi's middle-class population. Her gestures like personally blocking a bulldozer from razing a slum settlement and voicing concern for the JJ clusters have also helped in retaining support of the poor class. The Bhagidari scheme of participatory governance also bolstered her image among voters. Patwant Singh, a writer-architect and Delhiite of long standing, puts it, "She has given a sort of coherence to urban development, unlike other politicians who only want to regularize irregular things. She's also accessible, receptive to complaints, puts in a full day's work and seems clean" (Kang 2003).

On the other hand, the BJP failed to tackle rebellion within its Delhi leadership successfully. The tug-of-war between L. K. Advani and Rajnath Singh continued unabated. After the Jinnah episode, the leadership within its own national ranks was in jeopardy. In such a scenario, BJP's national leadership failed to unite its Delhi State Executive, leading to disintegration.

Leadership is an important issue in politics. A dynamic leader pushes the support base of the party upward while lack of leadership dissuades even those voters who may have voted for the party. The BJP has failed to find a dynamic leader after the exit of Madan Lal Khurana. The party put various leaders—like Sushma Swaraj, Vijay Kumar Malhotra and Sahib Singh Verma—in command, election after election to lead the party, but none of them could match the stature of Madan Lal Khurana. On the other hand, Sheila Dikshit has successfully led the Congress in Delhi during the last 15 years. She has presented herself as the tallest leader of the Congress in the Delhi political scene.

6

Unheard Voices

The diversity of Delhi is reflected not only in geography but also in religion, language, caste and class. These diversities tend to impact the thought processes as well as the choices people make, which they express at regular intervals during elections. This is what results in the change in the fortune of various political parties, both during the national as well as state elections.

There is another kind of diversity among people, which attracts less attention—the differences between people who exercise their political rights and those who do not enjoy such political rights. In simple terms, those who vote and those who do not. A finer distinction could be between those who do not vote as a matter of choice and those who do not vote because they do not have voting rights, that is, they are not enrolled as voters. Whether they wanted to be enrolled is a completely different question and remains unanswered. In a nutshell, the broad classification of people could be between those who do not exercise political rights as a matter of personal choice and those who are unable to do so due to impinging constraints and impediments. The former category may be described as the 'de facto' citizens while the latter could be called the 'dormant' or marginal citizens of a democracy. The category 'dormant citizens' stands excluded from the democratic and participatory process of the state. This is not due to a matter of choice but largely due to the existential preoccupations of bare survival. The state in such situations has remained a mere spectator and has hardly tried to intervene. The people, in this context, are actually the marginal citizens who hardly enjoy any political rights in this city. The very concept of citizenship in

India gives rise to a lot of debates. Does one become a citizen merely by being able to exercise the 'right to franchise', which is considered a right in any democracy? As Subrata Mitra (2010) points out, trying to pin citizenship down to visible symbols like a dress code, race, ethnicity, religion or language had led to a lot of debates and controversies in the Constituent Assembly of India (1947–49) that framed the main Articles (5–11) on citizenship. The Constitution abjured racial purity in favour of birth and residence on the soil of India. Political attempts at giving a concrete meaning to citizenship, as one can easily gather from a brief perusal of Indian politics over the past two decades, have been divisive and become entangled with larger and darker debates on identity, political, social and economic exclusion, collective memory and violent inter-community conflict. However, citizenship comes with certain benefits, which in turn put certain obligations on the citizen; it cannot be understood in black and white.

The Conceptual Framework

Industrialization brought two kinds of problems in the housing sector. One, there was a large number of people that turned homeless in the urban areas after leaving their homes and migrating to cities in search of jobs. Some of them got places to stay in very deteriorating civic situations while others found no place except streets and old, wrecked buildings and shops to stay. This problem attracted the attention of many economic and social theorists since the early days of industrialization, both in the developed countries and the underdeveloped countries. Engels (1936) wrote descriptively against the housing conditions created in England. His book *The Condition of the Working Class in England in 1844* gives an account of Manchester. He writes that

> the couple of hundred houses, which belong to old Manchester, have been long since abandoned by their original inhabitants; the industrial epoch alone has crammed into them the swarms of workers whom they now shelter; the industrial epoch alone has built up every spot between these old houses to win a covering for the masses whom it has conjured from the agricultural districts and from Ireland; the industrial epoch alone enables the owners of these cattle-sheds to rent them for high prices to human beings, to plunder the poverty of workers, to undermine the health of thousands, in order that they alone, the owners, may grow rich. In the

industrial epoch alone has it become possible that the worker scarcely freed from feudal servitude could be used as mere material, a mere chattel; that he must let himself be crowded into a dwelling too bad for every other, which he for his hard earned wages buys the right to let go utterly to ruin. (Engels 1936)

On similar lines, Lewis Mumford wrote a book called *The City in History* (1961) in which he argued how the industries became the centre of the city and everything else was surrounded near the factory, thus leading to deteriorating conditions in all aspects of life.

As for housing itself, the alternatives were simple. In the industrial town that grew up on older foundations, the workers were first accommodated by turning old, one-family houses into rent barracks. In these made-over houses, each separate room would now enclose a whole family: from Dublin and Glasgow to Bombay, the standard of one room per family long held. Bed overcrowding, with three to eight people of different ages sleeping on the same pallet, often aggravated room overcrowding in such human sites. (Mumford 1961)

Carrying forward the issue, Charles Abrams' book titled *Men's Struggle for Shelter in an Urbanizing World* deals with the issues of housing in not just America or Europe but other cities in the underdeveloped nations too.

Most of the studies done on this subject have addressed it as a problem of policy framework and considered the people inhabiting such housing conditions as a homogeneous group. There have been studies on the politics of the government on the housing issue but little has been written on the politics of the houseless and the slum dwellers. This chapter will deal both with government policies as well as the politics of the houseless.

Being Houseless, Being without Identity

Daly (1996) writes that homelessness is the result of recent economic changes which made it almost impossible for the low-income household to afford a shelter in the cities. For him, the home is not just a roof but something that offers physical security, a source of stability and hence shapes the identity of people. Quoting Vaclav Havel, he writes that "all people must have room to realize themselves freely as human beings, to exercise their identities. Our homes are an inseparable element of our human identity. Deprived of all the aspects of his home, man would be deprived of himself, of his identity" (Daly 1996: 149).

The Election Commission, the agency responsible for enrolling people as voters, fails to do so since large numbers of these people do not have a place to live. One of the most determining criteria for being included in the rolls remains a proof of residence. "Not having an address disentitles people from ration/identity cards which deprives them from eligibility to elementary food security and social protection, and from establishing savings accounts. In turn, this capability deprivation threatens the physical security of their savings" (Harriss-White 2003).

In an unpublished survey carried out by the Indo-Global Social Service Society, it was reported that the homeless remain on the fringes of society, without even being considered relevant for political reasons as they do not form a 'vote bank' unlike slum dwellers.

Apart from that, homelessness constitutes an infraction of such fundamental human rights and dignities as the right to security of the person, the right to be free from cruel, inhumane or degrading treatment or punishment, the right to freedom from discrimination, the right to privacy, the right to freedom of expression, the right to freedom of association, the right to vote, the right to social security, the right to health and, of course, the right to adequate housing (Lynch and Cole 2003). The new census estimates that there are 13 million homeless people in India. Not only that, each of them has at least 5–6 members dependent on them, which means, that a huge section of India does not have accommodation. It has to be noted here that India still does not have a national policy on homelessness. Being homeless in a metro city comes with its own set of advantages and disadvantages from the kind of treatment that is meted out to these people. The large-scale migration into Delhi results in increasing numbers of such people in the capital, who are not enrolled on the voter lists and do not exercise their political rights. There are people who are not enrolled as voters in their respective constituencies simply because they keep changing their residence from one locality to another. But there are also large numbers of people whose names do not figure as voters of Delhi, since they are homeless and live on footpaths. Such people do not have an address which they can mention as their home. With large numbers of people migrating to Delhi in search of gainful employment from relatively poorer states like Bihar and UP, the number of homeless in this city has increased manifold. Friedrich Engels had said that the housing problem arose only after the industrial revolution.

Truly, there are 'few' homeless people in countryside India. It is an urban problem. People do not have access to home for various reasons and poverty is one of them. People do migrate from poor regions to cities and here they do not find any shelter. Most often they leave their 'home' and become homeless once they enter the cities.

Though the existential disparities are apparent during daytime, they take an extreme form at odd hours. If one goes around the city during the late evenings, or say midnight, one witnesses a very different Delhi. While on the one hand one can see a large number of people enjoying ice cream even at midnight in the chilly winds of December, one can also see large numbers of people sleeping on the roadside, mostly on pavements, and trying to cover their body with small pieces of cloth which they have. According to reports in the media, in 2002 the police found 3,040 corpses during winter. Of these, no fewer than four hundred (corpses) were those of people who had died in a single cold wave (Zaidi 2005). A homeless person without a secure place of residence is especially vulnerable to random attacks of violence threatening both the security of the person and, potentially, the right to life (Lynch and Cole 2003). Very often people express sympathy as they pass these pavement dwellers. But this 'fragmented concern' serves no purpose for the down-trodden. It needs to be conglomerated and executed as a social response by the state. The homeless lead an even more precarious life and are deprived of even the basic minimum amenities like access to education, health care, risk of violence and general discrimination. Most of the homeless are not only deprived of the right to vote but are also denied a ration card, pension, and other government welfare schemes and services on account of not having an address proof; hence, they are dispossessed of their 'identity'. From the discussion it follows that the state is wanting in fulfilling its obligations on many counts.

Number of Houseless in Delhi: An Assessment

The census of India uses the notion of 'houseless population', defined as persons who are not living in 'census houses', the latter referring to a 'structure with roof'. Census enumerators are instructed to take note of the possible places where the houseless population is likely to live such as on the roadsides and pavements, in Hume pipes, under staircases, or in the open: temples, mandaps, platforms and the like (Census of India 2001). By the aforementioned procedure, Census 2001 brought out a figure of 13 million 'houseless households', each household accounting for 5–6 members, and the total population of such houseless (or shelter-less) being at least 60.5 million in the country (Kanth n.d.). Women make up 7–10 per cent of Delhi's homeless. The only year-round shelter for women in the capital was closed down in June 2007, leaving them with no safe place to sleep. When the shelter was closed, these women were forced into living on the streets again, leaving them more vulner-able to violence and sexual abuse. Children and adolescents are also an extremely vulnerable category. They huddle together on railway plat-forms, around temples and other places of worship where they feel safe with fellow women. More shelters with specific provisions for women and children would mean fewer rapes and assaults on Delhi's streets. While one can find houseless people in various cities, their concentra-tion is more in big cities, Delhi being one of them. A study, done by the Indo-Global Social Service Society in Delhi, on homelessness further brought out that more than 50 per cent of the homeless population are unskilled and manual workers below 50 years of age, and 20 per cent are children. Rickshaw-pullers and casual workers form the major-ity. Children mostly engage in rag-picking, begging and vending. The homeless are mostly illiterate, but 7 per cent are graduates, and con-sumption of drugs and other psychoactive substances is rampant among all age groups and sexes. In terms of homes and shelters provided, the Municipal Corporation of Delhi (MCD) runs 17 permanent shelters for the homeless, and is setting up another six. However, all of these are for men, and none exclusively for women, who are more vulnerable. One shelter for women that opened in 2004 was shut in just 10 months, and used for storing building material for construction in the city centre. The official reason for the lack of shelter homes for women is that the women do not usually want to stay in these shelter homes, and when they do, they bring all their belongings and begin to settle down, least realizing that the shelter is provided for only one night. Therefore, thousands of women continue to huddle together near temples or railway stations.

The methodology of the census, however, remains faulty and devoid of the sensitivity it deserves. The enumerators are instructed to go to the mentioned places in the course of one night and enumerate the people sleeping there. More often than not, the enumerators indulge in falsi-fying data, verbally and physically abusing the houseless, and without reasonably attempting to make sure that the majority of the houseless persons are included in the census (Singh 2001).

Zaidi (2005) wrote, "According to a report based on the consultation 'Space for the Homeless and Marginalised in Delhi', organized by ActionAid India and the Slum and Resettlement Wing of the MCD in July 2003, the total homeless population in India was found to be 78 million (based on the 2001 Census)." In Delhi, the capital of the country, there are an estimated over 150,000 houseless including children, women and old who experience harsh winter nights. Lokayan's (a Delhi-based non-governmental organization [NGO]) study of rickshaw-pullers indicated that 22 per cent of the 400,000 rickshaw-pullers in Delhi were houseless. Even the Delhi Development Authority (DDA) admits that at least 1 per cent of the capital's population is houseless, that is, 140,000 at present (Consultation Report 2003, Action Aid and MCD). A Delhi-based NGO, Ashray Adhikar Abhiyan, counted 52,765 people sleeping in the open in June 2000, excluding those sleeping in night shelters (Aashray Adhikar Abhiyan 2001). This means that no fewer than 140,000 people live on the streets of Delhi. This figure does not include those who sleep in carts or rickshaws or under flimsy plastic-sheet roofs. Moreover, large numbers of people remain occupied in loading and unloading one or the other time of the night, and therefore remained unaccounted.

The estimates about the actual number of houseless people in Delhi may vary, but there is no disagreement about the fact that this city has large numbers of houseless people. Though the city may never have been free from houseless people since Independence, it is undoubted that the number of such houseless people has increased enormously during the last 10 years. Various factors can be accounted for this steady rise in homeless population, rapid migration being one of them. Most of the homeless people come to this city looking for jobs, while some others are brought to this city by their relatives. There are also those homeless who are brought to this city by their friends or fellow villagers. Most of them choose the streets because paying rent would mean no savings, and therefore no money could be sent back home; hence the street is the only option for these people. These shelterless people are invisible during the day, but at night one spots them everywhere, especially on footpaths, parks and under the overbridges spanning the length and width of the city, especially around old Delhi, the commercial hub of the capital, which is the address of more than 30 per cent of Delhi's houseless people. They are there in rain and winter, facing the vagaries of the weather and perhaps begging without the least notice of the democratic state, of which, they are legitimate citizens. In a study of homeless population by the United Nations Development Programme, homeless men, women and children in four cities reported that they were beaten by the police at night and driven away from their makeshift homes and shelters.

How People Become Houseless

Looking at the people sleeping on the roadside, even in chilly winters, one would think that all these people are houseless since they are unemployed and have no money to rent a house. This may be true of some pavement dwellers, but not all. Most of the houseless people sleep under the open sky not because they do not have any income but mainly because the money they earn is not sufficient to rent a room. There are also some who are habitual sleepers on roadsides. Some of these homeless do not sleep on pavements all the time, but they spend a few nights on the roadside so that they can get some company of people to rent a room together, which would be much cheaper compared to renting a room on their own. But the most important reason for sleeping on the roadsides is that these people want to save their hard-earned money, which can be sent back home.

But this does not mean that a large number of people are houseless as a matter of choice. There are various reasons for people being houseless in Delhi. The economic misery of marginal farmers in the Indian villages—mainly due to landlessness, indebtedness and regular failure of the crop—forces them to rush to the cities. More than that, lack of employment opportunities also forces the people to migrate to urban centres. When they come to the cities, they get gainfully employed more easily compared to their village, but even in these cities, the economic competition is no less intense. Once in the city, the struggle for survival takes priority over accommodation, which remains deferred primarily due to economic constraints. Moreover these people also want to save money for family members back in their native villages and also for their rainy days and do not want to rent a house. This is what adds to the increasing numbers of the houseless in Delhi.

Apart from that, many people become houseless in Delhi because of the government's drive to clear the hutments on the banks of the Yamuna River, and various such places. The demolition of slums as part of the city's beautification drive of the government, without making an alternate arrangement for oustees' relocation, also adds to the increasing numbers of houseless in this city. Moreover, many homes have been closed down by the MCD, including one Palika Hostel for women and the government is yet to open spaces for the rehabilitation of the homeless. An NGO working on rehabilitation of the homeless in Delhi reported that at least 100,000 jhuggis were demolished since 2000. In Yamuna Pushta alone, around 50,000 people have been rendered homeless whereas only 30,000 were rehabilitated. The narratives of a few of such people explain how demolition of slums adds to the numbers of the houseless year after year. For a few others, living like pavement dwellers is a compulsion for saving money on transportation, since the slum where the family lives is far off from the place of work. They would prefer to sleep on roadside every night than spend sizeable money on going back home and coming for work every day. There are instances when in order to save money, one would also be forced to live on the streets as a houseless pavement dweller (as one narrative elaborates), like the poor 'fractured family', leaving children and wife back home.

He said his name is Ram Prasad. He guessed he was born in 1942. It is 12.30 at night and he is awake on the veranda of the lane housing the Delhi Stock Exchange, at Asif Ali Road, Darayganj—the hub of bustling commercial part of the capital during the day. He is awake as he is asthmatic. He does not know when he came to Delhi, but has heard about Emergency. He was in Delhi when people talked about it. As we talk, two stout, lathi-wielding policemen yell and shoo away a few of the sleeping people. They suddenly get up and fold their sheets on which they are sleeping. However they remain sitting at the same place. As the policemen walk past, the men again spread their sheets and go to sleep. Ram Prasad is not addressed or disturbed. "They recognize me," he said.

I came to Delhi maybe 30 years ago. Yes, Emergency. I remember Emergency. Everybody said it is there. I never saw it. I lived near Patna Bihar in Khajuri village. I came to Delhi because I had nothing to do at the village. I left my wife and child behind. I began to pull rickshaw. It was on hire. I always pulled a hired rickshaw. I went to my village once in a year. But my wife died. The child also died. For 10–15 years I have not gone there. For 5–6 years now, I am unable to pull rickshaw because I have contacted this *saans kee beemari* (asthma). I have become useless because of it. There is a dhaba nearby. I cut the vegetables or help in other work during the day there. I eat there in lieu of that. I have kept my *saaman* (personal belongings) also there. It is safe there. I use this place for sleeping only. I either sleep here or over there. I have been sleeping here for many years. These policemen do not disturb me. They somewhat recognize me. They know I am harmless. They are harsh to the strangers. After all it is their duty to check the people. It is not right that we are sleeping here. It is wrong; it is illegal.

Sadhu Rajwala wakes up suddenly as the lathi of the policeman stirs him from his deep slumber. He wakes up like a frightened cat and immediately folds his sheet while protesting meekly, *"marte kayo ho"* (Why do you beat). To this he gets another blow from the policemen who pass ahead nonchalantly as they mechanically stroke another pavement sleeper out of sleep. Sadhu Rajwala feels strongly insulted and curses his poverty and fate as he lights a bidi to smoke. He seems a defeated man as was evident from his tone and content of what he told us. He is around 45, works in a *gutta* (cardboard) factory at Sadar Bazaar and lives at a slum in Gaziabad, a neighbouring district of Delhi, with his wife and three school-going children.

Nobody likes to sleep like this. I also wish to go home. But I do not. It costs 25 rupees to reach there. And when I come to work I will spend 25 more. That is too much for me. I only get Rs 2,700 in the factory. A few extra hours daily add 500–600 more. Tell me how I will feed my family if I go home daily. Half of the money will be spent in transportation. I have three children and wife. How will they survive? Once in a week I go there. I wash my clothes and then take a bath. My job is steady. That is why I am sticking to it. About a year before, I used to sleep near my factory. But one or two drunkards began creating problem there. For over six months I sleep here. It is peaceful here except these mean policemen. Look how they treat everyone. They see nothing but thieves and terrorists. Poor man is every one's victim. It is not their fault. My poverty is my problem.

Deva, 14, is lean and thin, tanned, undernourished and tall for his age. He narrated his story thus:

I ran away from my house at Dakshin Puri (an urban slum in South Delhi) six years ago. I did not know how to go back. I loitered around for a day and two and then I worked for a *chaiwala* (roadside tea vendor) who gave me food in lieu of work, but no cash. I did not like the work for long. He made me work for long in the night. I met some other boys of my age too. They became friends. Later I worked for the parties (employed by the tent contractors for the wedding arrangements). Even now I do party *ka kaam*. When there is no wedding season I do rag-picking. I collect plastic, empty water bottles, *addha*s and *pauaa*s (quarter and half denominators of the wine bottles). On an average I make 30–40 rupees a day. I have a saving of 80 rupees that I have deposited with the *bhaiya* (caretaker of the night shelter, an employee of the NGO that is looking after it). I have two shirts and two pairs of trousers that are in a bag in storeroom. I have lots of friends. Everybody is everybody's friend here. I like kite-flying and cricket.

Janak Mahto was living like many at Yamuna Pushta till a year back. But he became not only houseless but also familyless. Lived on the pavement near Zakir Hussain College and did the job of occupying seats in the general compartment of certain trains for a few rupees!

I was living *arram se* (without hassles). I repaired punctures on roadside. I lived in a rented jhuggi with my wife and a four-year-old child. I paid Rs 400 for rent. I earned about Rs 2,500. It was not big money but we did not starve. We managed. If things remained all right I could buy a jhuggi in a year or so. Because of committee (the demolition squad) everything collapsed (*barbad ho gaya*). Area was cleaned off. We had come to Delhi because of flood in Orissa. How did I know that there would be trouble here too? I have sent her back. How could she survive on the street with the child? I am managing with so much of difficulty. There is no guarantee I shall be able to sleep continuously for two hours. Rail's job is full of tension. There is no certainty. I am looking for a job of party (catering work in a wedding). (Aashray Adhikar Abhiyan 2001)

'Nobody goes hungry in Delhi', meaning everyone gets some work here, is an impression that most people carry regarding the city, attracting a large number of unemployed to the city. Unemployment (58 per cent) and family problems (15 per cent) constitute major reasons for this 'distress migration' (Aashray Adhikar Abhiyan 2001). Work opportunities being the major lure for migration, it is not surprising that the states with low level of economic development, namely UP and Bihar, in the last decade-and-half account for a large number of people who come to Delhi in search of employment and are forced to be shelterless. While nearly 42 per cent of the houseless are from UP, about 32 per cent are natives of Bihar. Nearly 3 to 5 per cent amongst the houseless had come from states like Rajasthan, Madhya Pradesh or West Bengal. There were very few among the houseless who were natives of Delhi.

State's Sensitivity to the Houseless: Is Government Doing Enough?

The Responsibility of the State

So what does the right to housing ultimately mean for the people on the streets, the tribals, the Dalits and slum dwellers, the marginalized communities, women and children who are being evicted arbitrarily and forcefully every day? Is this right, as we believe, a distinct, enforceable, justiciable human right which citizens can demand from the state if not fulfilled? Or are we to continue to depend on the whims and fancies of our esteemed judges to interpret this right sensitively?

The Universal Declaration of Human Rights (UDHR), 1948, to which India is a party, states,

> Everybody has the right to a standard of living adequate for the health and well being of himself and of his family, including food, clothing, housing, medical care and necessary social services, and the right to security in the event of unemployment, sickness, disability, widowhood, old age or lack of livelihood in circumstances beyond his control. (Article 25)

Internationally, the right to housing has a significant place in several instruments. On the basis of the provisions established in the UDHR, the right to adequate housing occupies a significant place in the International Covenant on Economic, Social and Cultural Rights, 1966 (ICESCR). Article 11.1 of the Covenant states,

> The States Parties to the present Covenant recognize the right of everyone to an adequate standard of living for himself and his family, including adequate food, clothing and housing, and to the continuous improvement of living conditions. The States Parties will take appropriate steps to ensure the realization of this right, recognizing to this effect the essential importance of international cooperation based on free consent.

The right to adequate housing is also recognized internationally in several other instruments that have focused on the need to protect rights of particular groups, such as the Committee on the Elimination of Discrimination against Women, the Committee on Rights of the Child and the Committee on the Elimination of Racial Discrimination; there are even a few General Comments specifically on housing as a fundamental human right (Kothari 2002).

The United Nations Human Rights Commission (UNHRC) lays down certain rules and provisions for the parties to follow with respect to provision of voting rights. These rules (UNHRC 2001) entitle adult citizens of countries to the right to vote, irrespective of income, caste or class. It has also been stated that "residency requirements must not be imposed or applied in such a way as to exclude the homeless from the right to vote." Therefore, it becomes very important for nations which follow the Human Rights Charter to not exclude the 'homeless' from their electoral rolls. The human right to vote is an essential right recognized in Article 25 of the International Covenant on Civil and Political Rights.[1] The United Nations Office of the High Commissioner for Human Rights (OHCHR) has also talked about the important relationship between homelessness and the right to vote. It says,

> Lack of political rights is both a cause and a consequence of poverty. Socially and politically excluded people are more likely to become poor, and the poor are more vulnerable to social exclusion and political marginalization.... Active participation in political decision-making processes plays a role in expanding political freedoms and empowering people, which in turn contributes towards combating social exclusion and political marginalization. (UNOHCHR 2002: 48)

India is a party to the ICESCR. Article 51 of the Constitution of India states that "the state shall endeavour to ... foster respect for international law and treaty obligations in the dealings of organized people with one another." The Supreme Court too has concurred that this provision enjoins the state to meet its international obligations.

Besides, article 21 of the constitution of India provides for the fundamental right to life that encompasses the right to live with human dignity. Giving meaning to the same, the Supreme Court in *Francis Coralie Mullin vs* The Administrator, Union Territory of Delhi has ruled:

> The fundamental right to life, which is the most precious human right and which forms the arc of all other human rights, must be interpreted ... (to) enhance the dignity of the individual and the worth of a human person ... we may think that the right to life includes the right to live with human dignity and all that goes also with it, namely, the bare necessities of life such as adequate nutrition, clothing and shelter. (SCR 1981)

Government Policies

National Housing and Habitat Policy, 1998

The first national housing policy draft was introduced in January 1987. The second national housing and habitat policy (NHHP) was formulated in 1998. The policy was laid before the Parliament on 29 July 1998. It opened with a very radical assessment and a target of construction of 2 million houses (out of which 1.3 million were to be for rural areas and 0.7 million for urban areas) every year with the emphasis on the poor and deprived. It was resolved in the draft policy that for this purpose all impediments would be cleared. But, on the contrary, the government in 1998 repealed the Urban Land (Ceiling and Regulation) Act (ULCRA), 1976. The ULCRA had a ceiling to the amount of land that could lie vacant with private agencies in urban areas—a limit of 500 m had been set for Mumbai and Delhi. Any vacant land in excess of the ceiling was to be acquired by the state governments for public housing purposes. This law, if properly implemented, could have greatly reduced the housing deficit (Combat Law). But on the contrary, the government repealed the said law with the result that when it comes to building of night shelter or providing other facilities for the houseless, one of the pleas that the government forcefully forwards is that there is no land available for the purpose (*Times of India*, 6 October 2004).

Apart from the National Agenda for Governance, and the NHHP 1998, there are several much talked-about pro-poor policies and programmes. They include the National Slum Development Programme, the Indira Awaas Yojana, the 10th Plan Approach for the Urban Poor and the Marginalized, the Swarna Jayanti Shahari Rozgar Yojana, Valmiki Ambedkar Awas Yojana, Nirmal Bharat Abhiyan and last, but not least, the half-hearted Housing and Urban Development Corporation's (HUDCO) scheme of Shelter and Sanitation Facilities for the Footpath Dwellers in Urban Areas. It may be seen that except for the HUDCO's scheme (it itself having very limited coverage), there is hardly anything for the shelterless under the government's programme for these poorest among the poor. One finds in the same context that the international commitments, such as Habitat Agenda, 1996 and the Istanbul Declaration have not been put into action, even though ratified.

The 11th Five-Year Plan and the National Urban Housing/Habitat Policy 2007 have set up a national goal of 'affordable housing for all'. At the end of the 10th Five-Year Plan, the housing shortage was estimated to be 24.7 million for 67.4 million households, 99 per cent of them being from Economically Weaker Sections or Lower Income Groups. Among the poor and the weaker sections, the urban homeless deserve to be given special attention, which is not happening.

Night Shelter for Urban Shelterless, 1988–89

This scheme for the houseless stipulates that 50 per cent subsidy is to be provided by HUDCO and the remaining has to be arranged by the state government or implementing agency. But an analysis of the execution of the scheme shows a lack of commitment to the housing needs of the most vulnerable. Out of 35 states and union territories (28 states and 7 union territories) only 7 states attempted to create night shelters for the houseless. Out of the 47 shelters' intents that came up, Maharashtra had the lion's share of 28; the rest six put together 19 in all. While Madhya Pradesh constructed 7, Chhattisgarh 5, Andhra Pradesh 3, the remaining ones—West Bengal, Karnataka, Odisha and Rajasthan—constructed one each. Delhi, UP, Bihar and others did not attempt even one (Singh 2004).

Also, an important factor remains the lack of coordination between the MCD, the New Delhi Municipal Council (NDMC) and the departments of social welfare and revenue of the Government of Delhi, which results in no agency claiming responsibility, with each one passing the buck to the other.[2] Tragically, it is the homeless who suffer from this unfortunate bureaucratic mess.

According to Miloon Kothari (2007), former UN Special Rapporteur on adequate housing,

> The government needs to be held accountable for the persistent human rights violations against the homeless. There is an urgent need for a combined human rights and humanitarian approach to uphold the rights of men, women, youth and children to adequate housing, security of the person, water, health, food and work. Failure to take these steps indicates a clear violation of India's commitments under constitutional and international law.

He elaborated that a human rights approach to addressing homelessness would involve dealing with the structural causes of homelessness— including the lack of an effective comprehensive policy to address the housing rights of Delhi's poor, non-existence of low-cost and public housing options; large-scale eviction drives and slum demolitions without

adequate livelihood-based rehabilitation; shift in land use towards inten-
sive infrastructure development; and taking immediate measures to
ensure that all city inhabitants are able to live in homes that are safe and
secure and adequately serviced. The severe winter, however, calls for an
immediate and focused humanitarian response in the form of adequate,
warm, and clean shelters that provide all basic services and are located
close to people's sources of livelihoods. The city, tragically, has failed
on this front as well. From 46 shelters in 2008–09 in Delhi, the number
of homeless shelters in 2009–10 fell to 24 (16 temporary), despite an
increase in the number of homeless people.

In Delhi in 2002, there were only 14 night shelters providing floors
and sleeping benches for 5.6 per cent of the city's homeless (Harriss-
White 2003). The number then increased to 46 night shelters, of which
17 were permanent and 29 temporary. But the numbers of such shelters keep changing. As per a recent estimate, there are only 33 shelters,
of which 17 are permanent while 16 are temporary. The government
instead of opening more has been closing them on one pretext or another.
In fact, the only female shelter for women that was being run with the aid
of an NGO in an NDMC building was forcibly ordered to be shut down
by the Corporation in October 2004 (*Times of India*, 13 October 2004).

The MCD charges six rupees for night shelter per person, in the name
of providing certain basic facilities. But those who make use of them
complained of several problems, including dirty blankets and lack of
water there. Although the MCD is required to clean blankets every 15
days, this is rarely done. Moreover, more often than not, there is a shortage of blankets in winter. The lack of toilets was identified as another
problem. In many shelters toilets are not functional due to lack of water
and maintenance. In one night shelter (Nehru Place) there was no toilet
at all and in another shelter (Lahori Gate) there were three toilets for as
many as 240 inmates. There were no storage facilities inside the night
shelters, and in some of these night shelters pick-pockets were identified
as a problem. Another problem is that of timings in the night shelters.
The watchman forces inmates to wake up and leave the shelter before
the official closing time of 7 A.M. This becomes a difficult proposition
for old and infirm inmates, especially during winter. The watchman uses
a stick to wake them up, which many of them consider inhumane and
insulting. There are no educational, recreational or medical facilities for
these inmates. The MCD runs 260 mobile dispensaries but none of them
visits the night shelters. The pavement dwellers therefore do not have
incentives to spend the night in the government night shelters even if

they were adequate in number to house them (ibid.). While on the one hand, the houseless are not supported either by the state, on the other hand they are quite often harassed by the police and the local strongmen (*dada*s and goondas). The demolition on 22 December 2009 of the Pusa Road night shelter reflects not just an abrogation of legal obligations of the MCD but the link to the government's policy to further marginalize and criminalize the city's poor and homeless (Shahri Adhikar Manch 2009). According to the same report, there were only 24 night shelters for the Delhi's over 100,000 homeless and only one night shelter for the city's 10,000 homeless women.

Life on the Street: Far from the State and Government

Being houseless is a problem, which cannot be tackled overnight. No government policy, however well designed, can provide shelter to all those who do not have a roof. But this is not to say that the government cannot and should not think about these houseless people. There is a need for greater government intervention for resolving the problems of these houseless people. If on the one hand, there is need for more night shelters for the houseless, it is also necessary that the existing night shelters should be maintained in such a way that those who wish to spend their night there can do so happily. What is needed is a more humane approach from the state as well as from the government.

The houseless people are also the citizens of this country. Though they live on pavements, the law makes it very clear that they should not be discriminated against in matters of political rights. The houseless people have the right to be enrolled as voters in the constituency where they live. They are entitled for more or less equal political rights like any other citizens living in this country. The law favours them to be included in the voters' list thereby ensuring that they develop a sense of belonging to the city, besides acquiring an identity.

A person is said to be ordinarily resident in a place if he uses that place for sleeping. He need not be eating in that place and may be eating from a place outside.... Mere ownership or possession of a building or other immovable property will not bestow on the owner, the residential qualification. On the other hand, even persons living in sheds, and persons living on pavements without any roof are eligible for enrolment provided they are ordinarily resident in the sheds or on pavements in particular area, do not change the place of residence and are otherwise identifiable (*Census of India* 1991).

The law, in black and white, may guarantee equal political rights for the houseless but the practice is far from reality. Only a handful of the houseless are enrolled as voters in this city. There are no official records but the estimates of the PUCL–CSDS Survey of the Homeless in Delhi indicate that only 9 per cent amongst these houseless people have been enrolled as voters in Delhi. No wonder a vast majority of these houseless people are deprived of their basic political rights. The number of houseless who possess a photo identity card is much lower. Only 5 per cent mentioned have the photo identity card, while 95 per cent do not have the photo identity card.

It is not that only a few of these houseless are enrolled as voters; the majority of them also do not enjoy other facilities. Very few amongst them possess a ration card. It is not that they do not wish to have a ration card, but large numbers of them have not been issued the ration card even though they have applied for the ration card. The study indicated that while 22 per cent of the houseless applied for the ration card, only, 6 per cent actually posses the ration card. For large numbers of the houseless, a 'democratic India' is still a dream.

It is reasonable to believe that most of the houseless people are unaware of their political rights. Large numbers of them do not know that no law in this country debars them from being included in the voters' list of one or the other constituency. One would expect the officials to be popularizing among these houseless people their voting rights. But in most instances, these officials are unmindful of their duty. Not only that, they also create various hassles for the people when they want to be enrolled as voters. Even with all the supporting documents required for getting enrolled as voters, that is, address proof, it is not easy for an average citizen to get his name included in the voters' list, if left out at the time of electoral roll revision. One would imagine how difficult it could be for the houseless to get their names included in the voters' list, without any address proof.

The fact that the houseless people live without an address renders them identityless—they lose not only their individual worth but also their sense of belonging to the city, society or the nation. Without an address they cannot open a bank account, procure any government-sponsored subsidy or enjoy any other social security benefit. Though 90 per cent of them are able-bodied working people, they acquire broken self-consciousness that leaves them timid, lonely and silent.

But more than providing the material benefits, efforts should be made for the integration of these houseless people into the mainstream of the democratic process. The right to vote is one political right which, in a way, empowers the common people. This gives the people a sense of their worth for the country and their importance in the democratic process of the country. Since the law does not debar the houseless people from being enrolled as voters, government officials should make efforts to empower more of these houseless people, by simply enrolling them as voters in constituencies where they live. This one political right can bring greater change in the lives of these houseless people in Delhi much more than what different welfare policies of the government can do. Some beginning has been made. There were reports that about 50 houseless people actually voted for the election to the 14th Lok Sabha (*The Hindu*, 18 May 2004). During the 2009 Lok Sabha election, the NGO Aashray Adhikar Abhiyan managed to get about 2,000 enrolled as voters in Delhi and 500 of them got their voter identity cards. Most of these homeless who got their voter identity card also voted during the 2009 Lok Sabha election and many of them were filled with a lot of excitement and joy.

"I voted!" said an excited 70-year-old Prithvi Chand after he cast his vote in the Ramnagar polling booth in Paharganj in Central Delhi." He was happy because he had voted for the first time in his life. Chand also said, "It is a different world for me today. I hope that change will happen for the good and that the politicians would highlight our issues. I am thankful to the NGO for letting me use my franchise." Santosh, a part-time painter was also a first-time voter. Standing at the Ramnagar polling booth he said, "Although I could have earned some money in the time that I spent in commuting till here, I choose to spend money to come back here and vote." Forty-year-old Mansoor was another first-time voter, who waiting for his turn to cast his vote in Jhandewalan said, "It's great that now even we can vote. I have been waiting to vote for quite some time now."

But these are only a handful—amongst hundreds of thousands of houseless—who managed to vote during the 2009 Lok Sabha election or on previous occasions. Also it is important to note that these lucky ones were those who were living in camps run by the NGO, but those who sleep at night were not lucky. Even though there has been a beginning with regard to granting political rights to the houseless, this is just a beginning; there is a long way to go. Very little attention has been paid to the houseless by political parties cutting across ideologies since the houseless are largely non-voters. They do not have a permanent address, and without a permanent address one cannot have a voter identity card or any other card, making them ineligible to vote even if they managed to get enrolled as voters. This allows candidates and political parties to neglect the houseless people from electoral considerations. They remain the uncounted as voters in Delhi and their voices remain unheard in the democratic process of this city.

The Indian government is bound by constitutional and international human rights law to respect, protect and fulfil all human rights. The UN Committee on Economic, Social and Cultural Rights in 2008 also called upon India to address the issue of rising homelessness, including the need for disaggregated data on the homeless. There is a critical need for all government departments to consolidate efforts and take urgent measures to protect the rights of Delhi's homeless. Continued failure to take the required measures is nothing short of negligence of Delhi's poor and the dereliction of duty of elected and appointed officials at all levels of government.

The politics of the houseless and slum dwellers get translated in the way they show their allegiances to any political party in the elections and their interests on different issues. Sometimes it becomes the deciding factor in the city as a significant population of the city lives in these situations. One very clear example from the national capital is the growing popularity of the BSP, which we discussed in Chapter 4. The other political preferences of the houseless and the slum dwellers will be discussed in the next chapter.

Notes

1. Voting as a human right: enfranchising people experiencing homelessness and imprisonment, Homeless Persons Legal Clinic, Submission to the Parliament of Victoria Electoral Matters Committee into Voter Participation and Informal Voting, July 2008. Retrieved from http://www.parliament.vic.gov.au.
2. In an NDMC building, an NGO operated two shelters—one for women and children, and another for young boys up to the age of 18. A week later, the NDMC evicted the inmates of both the shelters on the ground that it was NDMC's land; it required the premise to build staff quarters and that to run a shelter for the houseless was the job of the state government.

7

The New Definition of Delhi

Most Indian cities, like life in India, have a dualistic, 'schizoid' character. Traditional values are put to test in a struggle with the contemporary global forces of change. Layer upon layer of distinctive culture in the time zone overlap, merge, interact and assimilate fusing into a continuum of inexplicable complexity and so has been the case with the ancient historical city of Delhi (Kapadia 2006).

The whole notion of this city has changed in recent years. People of an earlier generation used to talk of 'New Delhi' and 'Old Delhi'. In the 1980s, the vocabulary changed to 'Yamuna Paar' and the rest, with 'Yamuna Paar' used for referring to those belonging to the lower-income group. This has changed dramatically during the past two decades. Delhi can no more be divided into Yamuna Paar and the rest.

The city of Delhi needs a new definition. The way this city has expanded both geographically and demographically over the last few decades, it seems that Delhi hardly remains as one city. It would be more appropriate to say that the city of Delhi represents three cities merged into one city. These three cities are identified with their geographical divisions, in terms of the class character or in terms of political outcomes. The three cities of Delhi in terms of geographical divisions are the city of the Periphery, Yamuna Paar and the Central City. If seen in terms of class, the three cities of Delhi can be seen as the city of the lower class, the middle class and the upper class. The city that the British built had a special purpose. The British needed an image of lasting stability and that was provided by Edwin Lutyens and Herbert Baker at an estimated cost of Rs 760 million (pound sterling 9.5 million in 1935). New Delhi did not deviate at all from the feudal principles governing Indian life. In fact, with all the British prejudices at his command, Edwin Lutyens evolved a working model of a city structure that not only projected the British might but at the same time legitimized the concepts of exclusiveness—space segregated on the basis of social and political hierarchies. This concept of spatial segregation based on class was also the central theme of the different types of layouts propagated in the *Shilpa Shastras*. It appealed very much to the Indian psyche and has been with us ever since. While there is no neat division of the geographical divisions into the three class divisions, still there is some overlap between the two. One can identify the Periphery with the lower-class city, the Yamuna Paar with the city of the middle class and the Central City with the upper-class city. In terms of political outcome, the three cities could be identified as the stronghold of the BSP, the stronghold of the Congress and a sizeable presence of the BJP. All these three categories overlap each other.

The plight of Delhi as we know it today goes back to the troubled times of the partition of the country into India and Pakistan in 1947. Political turmoil saw floods of immigrants pouring into the city. It is estimated that the population of Delhi in the decade 1941–51 went up by 90 per cent (the population of Delhi in 1951 was 1,744,072). Huge rehabilitation colonies—Lajpat Nagar, Kingsway Camp, Karol Bagh and Lodhi Colony—came up almost overnight. As time went by, the refugee residents of these colonies tried their best to recreate the areas in Pakistan that they had left behind. Much later, as their economic condition was to improve with time, these residents became the pioneers in opening up new frontiers, in the then far-flung locations of Delhi, which are today known as the exclusive abode of the rich. In this context, it is important to note that development in Delhi is linked to four different periods. These periods are precolonial (before 1911), pre-Independence (1911–47), post-Independence (1947–61) and Master Plan period (1961–81). During each of these periods, migration to Delhi was circumstantial.

We may believe that Delhi is a city of the upper class and rich but large-scale migration to this city in recent times, especially from other parts of the country, in search of better opportunities, has changed the social profile of Delhi's population. Less than one-fifth of the city's population belong to the upper class, while a little more than one-third of the city's population belong to the lower-income group who could be classified as belonging to the lower or poor class. There is a big middle class estimated to be anything between 45–50 per cent of the city's population. This middle class is also growing with the expansion in white collar jobs.

Even though it is difficult to imagine a neat settlement pattern of people from these three different classes, a large proportion of the upper-class people live in the heart of the city referred to as 'City' and only a few of them live in the Trans Yamuna colonies, which are largely seen as localities inhabited by the middle and lower classes. Till a few decades back, the Trans Yamuna localities were seen as habitations with a large proportion of lower-income class or poor-class people; that has changed with the coming up of various housing societies in the Trans Yamuna localities, namely in Patparganj and Mayur Vihar. There is a small proportion of upper-class people amongst those living in Trans Yamuna localities, but in these localities the middle-class people are more or less in equal proportion as in the City. A little less than half of the people living both in the City and Trans Yamuna belong to the middle class compared to only one-third in the Periphery. There is a large concentration of lower-class people in the region classified as the Periphery. Half of the population living in the Periphery belong to the lower class, only 14 per cent of the people in this locality belong to the upper-income group, and the rest are middle class. People from the three broad income groups—upper, middle and lower—are spread across the city, but in different proportions. We can, however, divide this city into three broad categories—the City (which may represent upper-class people), the Trans Yamuna (which represents middle-class people) and the Periphery (which represent lower-class people).

Rapid urbanization has led to one distinct feature in Delhi: different types of settlements. The types of settlements in Delhi are categorized in terms of civic infrastructure, types of houses, and authorized vs unauthorized settlements. The types of settlements are listed below:

- Jhuggi and jhopri resettlement colonies
- Slum resettlement colonies
- Refugee resettlement colonies
- Approved/planned colonies
- Unauthorized–regularized colonies
- Urbanized colonies
- Urbanized villages
- Jhuggi and jhopri clusters
- Notified slum areas/Walled City
- Rural villages

Delhi is clearly a place held hostage by different interest groups. An unprecedented economic boom has revealed the unpleasant side of sociocultural identity of this city. The cultural conditioning of the population makes this city one of the most difficult to govern. It is said of Delhi that there are no 'residents' of Delhi. The entire population is in transition. This belief springs from the fact that Delhi being the seat of power, with numerous offices and headquarters located here, has had its share of immigrant residents needed to handle the scores of government jobs and other key installations over the years. Several of these migrants decided to settle in Delhi after retirement. One major factor that has contributed to socio-economic inequality, and hence a plethora of cultural conflicts, has undoubtedly been the aspect of land in the matters of land ownership, land pricing, land use and land planning, and even the quick and abundant profit to be made from land dealings.

As stated in Chapter 3, over the years the voting pattern in Delhi has shown a strong correlation with two broad categories of stratification—class and caste. Both these forms of stratification have been subject to considerable sociological analysis and evaluation. In analyzing class location, sociologists have traditionally relied on conventional indicators of class location such as market position, relations to the means of production and occupation. However, one can evaluate an individual's class location not only in terms of economics and employment, but also in relation to cultural factors such as lifestyle and consumption patterns. Accordingly, it can be said that our current age is one in which symbols and markers related to consumption are playing an ever greater role in daily life. Individual identities are structured to a greater extent around lifestyle choices. Owing to such factors, a substantial overlap between voting preference and class status also seems to be inevitable. However, since class stratification often tends to be more ambiguous than other identities such as caste, a clear demarcation and categorization is difficult to arrive at.

The French sociologist Pierre Bourdieu, however, sees class groups as identifiable according to their varying levels of cultural and economic capital (Bourdieu 1986). The possession of 'capital' tends to influence not just the choice of lifestyle but also attitude towards and opinion on various aspects of society. Hence, a person's class position not just determines one's access to resources but also disposes him to a particular mode of thinking. Shared cognition also stems from what has been referred to as 'class consciousness'. According to Lukács (1922) class consciousness is what people, as occupants of a particular location within the production process, would feel and believe if they were rational. Further, others have conceptualized class consciousness as a particular aspect of the concrete subjectivity of human individuals. When it figures in macro-social explanations, it does so by virtue of the ways it helps to explain individual choices and actions (Wright 1985: 243). Thus, one's sociocultural background and heritage, along with a class-centred ideology, tend to influence the way one thinks and the way in which social issues are approached.

The sharp divide between the three classes of people—upper, middle and lower—is not limited to only their views regarding issues related to privatization of services which affect them directly, but goes beyond that. It is clearly reflected from their views on various issues concerning politics and society, and also on issues concerning the day-to-day lives of the people.

Opinions of People on Different Issues

Privatization

There is a trend of privatization of various services in this city, from transport to education, and also in the area of health. If we try and divide the degree of support for privatization into four, starting from totally opposed to privatization, neutral to the issue of privatization, partial support to privatization, to those who fully support privatization, the people in Delhi seem to be divided as follows: nearly one-third are completely opposed to privatization, about one-quarter are mildly in support of privatization, 12 per cent are in complete agreement to the issue of privatization, while a little more than a quarter of people are neutral on this issue. There is some degree of support for privatization amongst the upper and the middle classes, but not amongst the lower-class people. Amongst upper-class people, the majority are in support of privatization in varying degrees, one-fifth are fully opposed to privatization and a little more than one-quarter are neutral on this issue (Figure 7.1). Compared to this, amongst the lower class, only one-quarter are in support of privatization in varying degrees, nearly the majority are completely opposed to privatization while one-quarter are neutral on the issue. The middle class seems to be more evenly divided with one-third completely against privatization, a little less than that neutral while a little more than one-third support privatization policies in varying degrees. There are many reasons for the current state of affairs.

Figure 7.1:
Attitude of Delhi's Voters towards Privatization

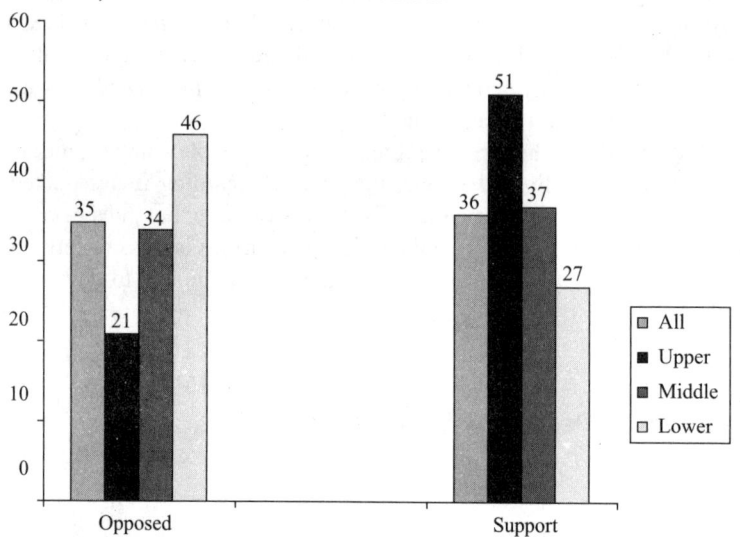

Source: HT–CSDS Delhi Survey, 2003.

There has been strong public resistance to privatization worldwide. The extent of this opposition is much greater and more widespread than is usually acknowledged, involving a general rejection of privatization across the economy that is not limited to utilities or traditional public services. A 2002 survey concluded that "privatization remains widely and increasingly unpopular, largely because of the perception that it is fundamentally unfair, both in conception and execution" (Birdsall and Nellis 2002). The pattern of habitation by people of different income groups is further reinforced by sharply divided opinions.

This division can be seen amongst the three classes of people on services which have either been privatized or the government is contemplating to privatize, completely or partially.

Transportation

The Delhi Transport Corporation (DTC) was the only public transport available to the people of Delhi till Metro rail came into operation. Once called the Delhi Transport Undertaking and fully owned by the government, there have been many changes in the administrative structure in the DTC. No bus was allowed to carry more than its seating capacity and 12 standing passengers. At the moment, the government-owned fleet of buses provide facility of public transport to the people, but there are also private buses plying on Delhi roads as a means of public transport. These are popularly known as 'Blue Line' buses.[1] While it is true that a large number of people feel dissatisfied with the bus services provided by the DTC, it is surprising to note that they are not in favour of privatization of the public transport system. Also, DTC has always been focused on achieving a high level of operational efficiency. It has developed around 3,000 buses in the NCR. Delhi buses cover numerous routes all over the NCR and the bus fare is very reasonable. Thus, even masses belonging to the lower-income strata can afford to travel by buses in the city.

Nearly two-thirds of them want government to take up the responsibility of providing public transport while only 19 per cent prefer privatization of the public transport system (Table 7.1). But opinion on this seems to be sharply divided on class lines. Compared to the lower-class people, the upper class are more in favour of privatization of DTC services. This may be because many amongst the upper class do not use this mode of public transport; so a smaller proportion of people amongst the upper class would like the government to take up the responsibility of providing this service, which hardly bring any profit for the government or adds to economic development. The opposition to privatization of the DTC is more amongst the lower class that actually uses it for commuting, compared to those who own a car and hardly use the DTC service for commuting. Also, some felt that this would be a failure of the government to provide the people with basic facilities. The class division amongst Delhi's citizens can be clearly seen when it comes to expressing their view on how the DTC should be run in Delhi as a means of public transport.

Table 7.1:
Public Opinion on Privatization of DTC (Class-wise)

	All	*Upper*	*Middle*	*Lower*
DTC should be privatized	19	30	20	13
DTC should be a government undertaking.	64	55	66	67

Source: HT–CSDS Delhi Survey, 2003.
Note: All figures are in per cent. No difference = 5 per cent; No opinion = 12 per cent.

In 2010, IBM's first 'commuter pain study' found Delhi among the 10 cities in the world worst hit by traffic congestion. Beijing and Moscow topped the list. A good majority of the people in Delhi then felt that the traffic scenario had worsened in the past three years. It is the world's fifth worst place for commuters. New Delhi also scores badly in terms of stop–start traffic. As for a reduction in travel stress, 36 per cent of the respondents said that improved public transportation would help.

Another aspect to be highlighted here is that traffic jams in the city cost Delhiites Rs 100 million and the government exchequer Rs 10.5 million per day, revealed a survey by the Centre for Transforming India (CTI). With nearly 1,000 new vehicles being added to Delhi roads every day and the capacity of roads already stretched, experts feel that the only way to bring down congestion levels is to develop a sound public transport system that commuters can shift to. The traffic assessment study revealed that on any given day, one-third of the six million vehicles registered in the city are on the roads. Each of these, on average, wastes 1.6 litres (2.5 litres for cars and 0.75 litres for two-wheelers), which works out to a total wastage of 3 million litres of fuel (*Times of India*, 15 October 2009). According to the CTI report, there has been a drastic decrease in the number of people using public transport, and experts say that that is one of the biggest reasons for the traffic problems. "Till 2001, 62 per cent of people used public transport; it has now fallen to 46 per cent", an expert said (*Indian Express*, 15 October 2009).

What needs to be questioned is why, despite there being seven types of public transport in Delhi—the highest in any Indian city—people still prefer private modes. The chief minister of Delhi suggested that mere expansion of roads and building of flyovers were not the solutions to the problem and that the people of Delhi have to join hands with the government to evolve a solution to this problem. It is time those driving private vehicles switched to using the public transport system for their daily use. The extensive use of various types of vehicles has also made it imperative that the drivers are fully trained and well versed with the traffic rules so as to prevent accidents resulting in thousands of deaths every year.

To ease the congestion on Delhi's roads, the government had thought of various policies which in the past created controversies. Even though the Delhi government has been successful in controlling the commercial traffic coming frequently to this city from adjoining cities, the government is still to think of polices to effectively control the flow of private traffic, mainly cars which come to Delhi every morning in huge numbers.

Some time back the government thought of levying an additional tax on private vehicles registered outside Delhi but which enter Delhi city every day. There had been a few other suggestions as well. While the government thinks of these policies in desperation to control the enormously increasing traffic, most of the policy initiatives suggested by the Delhi government are seen as anti-democratic and are opposed by the public at large. When the people of Delhi were asked to respond to the issue of whether there should be some restriction on buying a new car, a lot of people agreed to this as a suggestion, but there were also people who opposed this idea. One is not sure if those who are supporting the idea of putting restriction on purchase of car would actually support it if it were implemented; those who oppose the idea of having any such policy would certainly oppose such a policy. Nearly 16 per cent of the people support the idea that people living in Delhi should have the right to buy and drive a new car and that there should be no intervention from the government (Figure 7.2). This view is shared more amongst upper-class people, compared to lower-class people. The class division is quite evident on this issue of freedom to buy and drive a car on the city's roads.

Figure 7.2:
Public Support for the Right to Buy and Drive a Car in Delhi

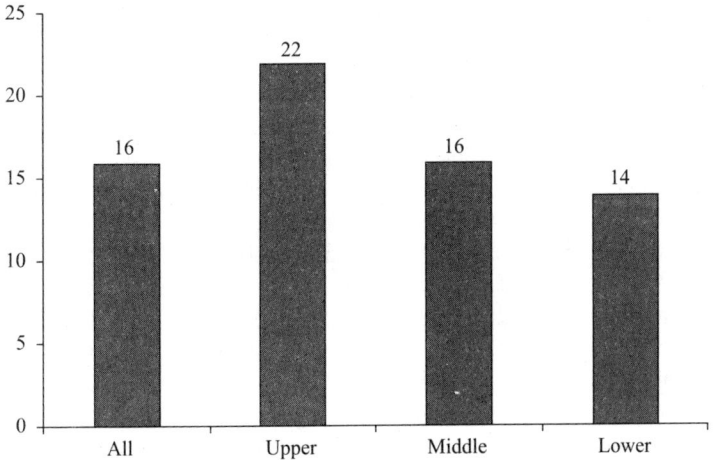

Source: HT–CSDS Delhi Survey, 2003.
Note: All figures are in per cent. The figures represented here are for those who support the idea that people in Delhi should have the right to buy and drive a car, and that government should not restrict.

However, with the expansion of the Delhi Metro, there has been a diversion. According to a survey conducted by the Central Road Research Institute (CRRI) among Metro users, 23.27 per cent of the respondents cited traffic jams as the main reason for their shifting to the Metro. For the rest, making the transition from private to public transport was a consequence of endless parking problems, safety, time and comfort. With the number of commuters on the Delhi Metro rising, the environmental and social benefits gained by the city because of the mass transport system will help recover the full cost of Phase I two years earlier than anticipated by the CRRI, said a senior Delhi Metro Rail Corporation official. The advancement of the break-even point by two years is mainly because of the increasing ridership of the Metro, which was 500,345 per day in 2007 and went up to 850,170 in 2009 when CRRI conducted the fresh review study. These benefits could be assessed as passenger time saved, fuel cost saved, reduction in capital and operating costs of vehicles, reduction in environmental damage, accidents prevented, and time saving and less maintenance cost on infrastructure. The survey indicated that the number of two-wheeler users who had the option of shifting to the Metro and did so had more than doubled from 32.81 per cent in 2007 to 66.3 per cent in 2009. The number of car owners who had the option of shifting to the Metro and did so had increased from 52.35 per cent to 62.29 per cent in the two years. One-fourth of all Metro commuters (about 24.8 per cent) were two-wheeler owners and almost one-fifth (18.11 per cent) were car owners.

The CRRI survey said that the number of vehicles taken off the road with the introduction and expansion of the Metro had shown a progressive reduction in daily vehicle demand. In 2009, the Metro was expected to take the daily share of 57,953 vehicles for all other modes of travel such as cars, buses, two-wheelers and autorickshaws, the survey claimed.

The survey claimed that the Metro had also substantially helped reduce the rate of accidents on the roads. The Metro would help avoid a total of 255 accidents, including 51 fatalities, in 2009. In 2007, the respective figures were 196 and 21. The accident-cost saving was expected to be Rs 90 million in 2009 as against Rs 60.28 million in 2007.

With the metro fast expanding, the removal of 'Blue Line' buses from the roads and the introduction of fleets of Volvo and air-conditioned buses by the government, traffic scenario is presumed to get better, but it is a question of time.

The Bus Rapid Transit (BRT) system is part of a multimodal transportation policy that envisions a strong integrated public transportation system consisting of a network of Metro, monorail, light railway and BRT services. The first BRT corridor in Delhi was opened in April 2008. The 14.5 km bus lane is in the middle of a road. A motorized vehicle lane is located on the side of the bus lane and separate lanes are available for non-motorized vehicles and pedestrians. Half of the corridor is currently under a trial run. Traffic volume on the BRT corridor is very high, with buses carrying 55–60 per cent of the total commuters. What has irritated the Delhi's upper-class people is that now they have less wide roads to navigate their cars on. Of course, there is a point here. Delhi was known for its freewheeling wide roads and, suddenly, narrower roads for cars in the BRT corridor do seem irritating. Thus the BRT has come under heavy criticism with a lot of people even wanting the Delhi chief minister to quit due to this so-called disastrous experiment. With the BRT in place now, the buses are moving rapidly in the corridors which are traffic-free. Bus commuters feel like kings and queens, while car owners, being more in number, wait in relatively much longer queues to reach each traffic signal and go beyond. Most of the bus stops are near traffic signals; so, even though the bus corridor is between the roads, people use the zebra crossing regularly to reach a bus stop, which has led to a decline in the number of accidents and road mishaps. And on the other front, car owners are being forced to stop before the zebra crossings, which is a good practice.

Recently the transport department suggested to the government that another 34 km be added to the BRT in the city, with seven of the 18 proposed stretches—including Central Secretariat to Vasant Kunj, Badarpur to IGI and Dhaula Kuan to Dabri—slated for Phase III (*Times of India*, 28 October 2010). As of now, the proposal is a part of a RITES report on the future of public transport and awaits the government's nod. The report recommended 18 new corridors in all, the alignments for which are yet to be decided. Interestingly, the first BRT corridor, which got buried in tremendous public opposition, is yet to run its full stretch between Ambedkar Nagar and Delhi Gate. The outcry was so huge that the government opted for mere line-demarcated lanes between Moolchand and Delhi Gate, rather than the earlier physical division. Even now, there is little enforcement on the second stretch, even as travelling time in the first part remains much higher than it was before the BRT came into being. Reports have pointed out that the BRT remains the best available option for viable public transport and the concept should be encouraged.

The divide between people belonging to three different classes is reflected in the opinions they have expressed on some of the current policies or initiatives of the government. When the BRT corridor became operational, it led to huge traffic jams, leading to hue and cry. The way the media reported the news, it looked as if a vast majority of people living in Delhi were opposed to the BRT corridor. But the study revealed that the opinion of the people living in Delhi was divided on the issue of the BRT corridor. Contrary to what seemed like an uproar against the BRT corridor, less than one-third of the people living in Delhi believed that the traffic situation had deteriorated due to the BRT corridor (Table 7.2), while a little more than one-third (36 per cent) shared the view that the BRT may be inconvenient for those using their own car, but it is much more convenient for those using public transport, that is, bus (since the dedicated lane for the bus resulted in faster movement of the traffic on the bus lane). Even on this issue, the opinions of the *Delhiwala* is divided on class lines—the criticism of the BRT corridor is much more sharper amongst the upper and middle classes, compared to the lower class.

Table 7.2:
Public Opinion on the BRT Corridor (Class-wise)

Economic Class	*Traffic Deteriorated Due to BRT*
All	30
Upper class	31
Middle class	38
Lower class	22

Source: Post-poll Survey, 2009.
Note: All figures are in per cent. Figures represent those who believe that overall traffic situation has deteriorated due to the BRT corridor.

Housing

Till 2001, as per estimates of the Delhi Urban Environment and Infrastructure Improvement Project, 76 per cent of the city's population were residing in sub-standard settlements. In the last five years, there has been large-scale relocation of 'informal settlements' from various parts of the city to its periphery. Along with polluting industries, informal settlements have also been pushed out of the city, all in the name of city 'cleaning' and 'beautification'. Those who have been primarily involved in building the city and its economy are being vehemently excluded from its services and other benefits. The MCD is pressing ahead with its relocation programme, often without consulting the slum dwellers.

Since 2000, 11 new resettlement colonies have been created, many of them with thousands of plots waiting to be filled.

Slum resettlement in Delhi is the responsibility of the slum and JJ department of the MCD. It has undertaken a three-pronged strategy, comprising relocation of slum clusters, in situ upgradation of slum clusters and informal shelters, and the extension of minimum basic civic amenities for community use. The strategy was adopted with effect from 1990, which means that encroachers on public land prior to 1990 are not entitled to resettlement at all. According to the 2002 report of the Government of the National Capital Territory of Delhi, the three-pronged strategy has so far been a failure. "The number of JJ [jhuggi jhopri] clusters had increased from 929 in 1990 to 1,100 in 2001," states the report. The most heart-rending aspect of resettlement is the loss of livelihood. The sites being located on the outskirts means no jobs in the vicinity and people tend to hold on to their older jobs, forcing them to travel long distances (at times, 10–13 km at a stretch), and thus incur heavy expenditure on transport. Resettlement colonies are all situated around the border of the city, displaced right from the heart of the urban centre.

Such an act of displacement is no less than a human rights violation. Article 21 of the Constitution grants each and every citizen the right to life, which is being violated by the government through this act of displacement. The right to life essentially has no meaning without the right to shelter and livelihood that these slum dwellers have been denied as a result of the demolition of the shanty structures that were their homes.

The main difference between slums and JJ clusters is that while slums are legal the JJ clusters are illegal. JJ clusters being illegal, they are not entitled to any public services. Nor did the Slum Areas Act, 1956—the Act that governed the approach of the government towards notified slums—apply to them. Under the Slum Areas Act, 1956, the government dealt with slums in the following ways: (*a*) clearance/relocation; (*b*) in situ upgradation; or (*c*) environmental improvement schemes. Since the Act did not apply to JJ clusters, the attitude towards dealing with them was basically clearance.

There have been various changes in the allocation of departments for the purpose of JJ evacuation and clearance since the 1960s. After 1986, at the end of the Sixth Five-Year Plan, the policy of clearance and relocation was stopped. With focus on in situ upgradation, no major clearance was carried out until a Revised Resettlement Policy was brought out in

1992 by the DDA. The slum and JJ department is at present back with the MCD.

The class divide amongst the people is more evident when it comes to expressing their views or suggesting policies which clearly affect one class of people much more than the other class of people. Even though we tend to believe that Delhi is a city of rich people living in big houses and flats, in reality a very large portion of the population of Delhi lives in jhuggis.[2] Most of the people living in Middle-income Group (MIG) flats, Low-income Group (LIG) flats or in big houses popularly known as *kothi*s depend upon the people living in jhuggis for various household services, but a large number of them see these jhuggis as a nuisance and like them to be removed from the city as soon as possible. While the majority of the people living in Delhi are in favour of removal of the jhuggis from Delhi (Figure 7.3), even on this issue the opinion is divided on class lines—the upper class is more in favour of removal of jhuggis while there is little support for the removal of jhuggis from Delhi amongst lower-class people. Amongst the upper class, nearly two-thirds are in favour of the removal of all jhuggis, but amongst the lower class only 39 per cent share this view. The view also draws sizeable support amongst the middle-class people of Delhi.

Figure 7.3:
Public Opinion on Jhuggis in Delhi (Class-wise)

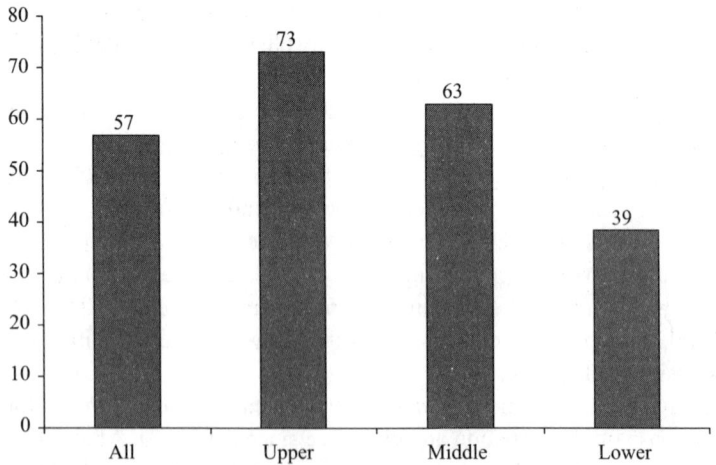

Source: HT–CSDS Delhi Survey, 2003.
Note: All figures are in per cent. The figures represented here are for those who support the idea that jhuggis should be completely eliminated from Delhi.

Opinion is divided also on the issue of regularization of jhuggis in Delhi. One-third of the people living in Delhi share the view that unauthorized jhuggis are regularized as a result of the vote-bank politics of political parties. This opinion is shared more amongst the upper-class people compared to the lower-class people. Amongst the upper-class people, 42 per cent believe that jhuggis are regularized as a result of vote-bank politics of political parties, but amongst the lower-class people, this view is shared only amongst 24 per cent of the people. It is the lower-class people who benefit most from regularization of these colonies and it is obvious that the support for regularization of jhuggis would come from those living in these jhuggis, compared to those living in *kothi*s or flats.

Figure 7.4:
Public Opinion on Regularization of Unauthorized Colonies (Class-wise)

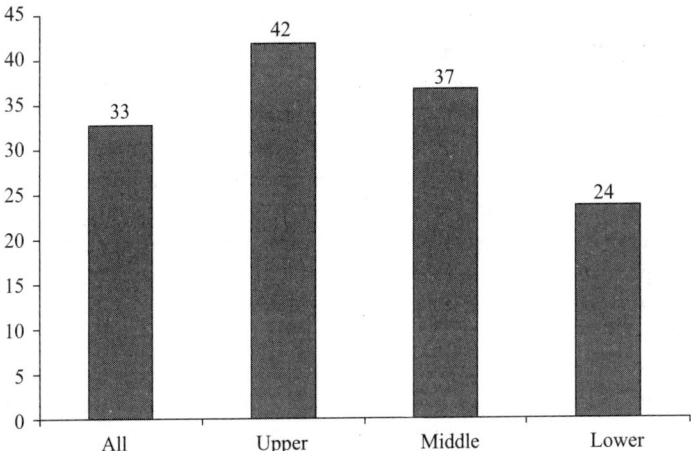

Source: HT–CSDS Delhi Survey, 2003.
Note: All figures are in per cent. The figures represented here are for those who believe that regularization of unauthorized colonies is a result of vote-bank politics by different parties.

Beggary

Beggary was first made a crime in Mumbai in 1959 through the Bombay Prevention of Begging Act, a law that has subsequently been adopted by 18 more states, including Delhi.

The issue of beggars and the homeless in Delhi was taken up with utmost seriousness before the dawn of the 2010 Commonwealth Games. This was manifest in the decision taken by the authorities to banish them from the city as part of the vast clean up for the city in order to drag Delhi to the 21st century. Mobile courts, in the back of vans and operated by a police task force, were introduced to speed up convictions for begging. Officials suggested a biometric database to identify repeat offenders so that they could be locked up or expelled from the city. By law, beggars are allowed to be sent to a special home for a year. Habitual offenders can be jailed for 10 years. The Commonwealth Games witnessed various plans to push this problem under the carpet or rather thrust it. The Delhi government's social welfare department decided to resolve this 'menace' by constituting 12 flying squads to travel across the city and collect beggars from traffic signals and pavements. Each squad was assisted by the area policemen and taken to two mobile courts, one of which was set up in Lajpat Nagar. They were then charged according to the Bombay Prevention of Beggars Act, 1959, which is also applicable in Delhi. Those charged for the same 'offence' repeatedly were sent to the government-run beggar house.

Since a majority of the beggars are migrants, discussions and dialogue were initiated with other state governments to repatriate them and resolve the growing 'menace'. The escalating number of beggars and their influx into the capital is a socio-economic problem. Their deplorable state is primarily due to large inequalities prevalent in the social fabric of the society as well as lack of opportunities.

The drive against beggars on the eve of the Commonwealth Games was merely a temporary solution. In the light of the magnitude of the issue, such a drive only allays and does not resolve the problem. If the government is seriously inclined to address this issue, it has to examine the root cause and take concrete steps.

To curb the practice of begging, the government could work on building beggar houses with basic facilities, impart training and skills to them, and ensure that the vagrants get employment opportunities. In the long run, not mere repatriation but responsibly rehabilitating the beggars could eradicate this 'menace'.

Beggars are not welcome in any city. The people of Delhi are a step ahead of that. A large proportion of the people in Delhi wants the state to deal with these beggars strictly. They see police as an active agent of the state and want this to be enforced by the police. According to statistics released by the Delhi government, there are approximately 60,000 beggars in the capital and nearly 90 per cent of them are immigrants. A little more than two-thirds of the people of Delhi want the police to deal with the beggars strictly (Figure 7.5), rather many have asked for a comprehensive strategy to deal with this problem. The upper-class people seem to be annoyed more with them compared to the lower-class people, who show some degree of sympathy for the beggars. Amongst the upper-class people, three-fourth want the police to deal strictly with the beggars, while amongst the lower-class only a little more than the majority share that view. The majority of the people, cutting across class, seem to be in favour of strict action against the beggars, but even on this issue, we witness the class divide. These beggars hardly harm anyone but they are seen as indecent elements on Delhi's streets and other public places.

Figure 7.5:
Public Opinion on How Police Should Deal with Beggars (Class-wise)

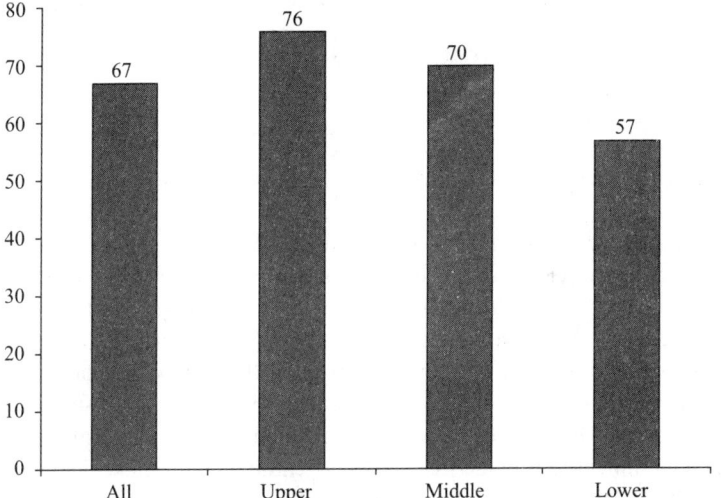

Source: HT–CSDS Delhi Survey, 2003.
Note: All figures are in per cent. The figures represented here are for those who support the idea of the police dealing strictly with the beggars in Delhi.

Other Basic Facilities

The people of Delhi seem to be equally divided on the issue of whether privatization of electricity has benefited the people or not. A majority of the people living in Delhi believe that privatization of electricity has increased problems rather than benefiting the people. While 54 per cent believed that privatization had worsened the problem for the people, only 31 per cent shared a different view. There were a few others who did not express any opinion on this issue.

The class divide in Delhi is evident even on this issue of privatization of electricity. Approval of the privatization of electricity is more amongst the upper class compared to the middle or lower classes (Table 7.3). But even amongst the upper class, the privatization of electricity is supported by less than the majority. On the contrary, the opposition to the privatization of electricity in Delhi comes more from the lower-class people, compared to the upper class. The middle class is equally opposed to the idea of privatization of electricity in Delhi.

Table 7.3:
Public Opinion on Privatization of Electricity in Delhi (Class-wise)

	All	*Upper*	*Middle*	*Lower*
Privatization of electricity has benefited people	31	45	31	22
Privatization of electricity has increased problems for people	54	40	55	59

Source: HT–CSDS Delhi Survey, 2003.
Note: All figures are in per cent. No difference = 9 per cent; No opinion = 6 per cent.

An average *Delhiwala* knows the situation of government hospitals and facilities at public health centres in Delhi. The government hospitals are in bad shape and large numbers of people go to private hospitals when in need. Even though a large number of people go to private hospitals, their expectation from the government regarding taking responsibility for providing public health facilities is very high. Nearly two-thirds of the people in Delhi are of the view that it should be the responsibility of the government to provide free medical treatment to all those who need it (Table 7.4), while 30 per cent seemed to be in support of improving the

Table 7.4:
Public Opinion on Government Hospitals (Class-wise)

	All	*Upper*	*Middle*	*Lower*
Willing to pay more for good treatment in government hospitals	30	40	32	21
Treatment should be free in government hospitals	61	51	60	69

Source: HT–CSDS Delhi Survey, 2003.
Note: All figures are in per cent. No difference = 4 per cent; No opinion = 5 per cent.

condition of government hospitals and public health facilities, for which they were also willing to pay more. There is a huge expectation from the government to deliver on the front of public health, and there are lots of people who think it should be the duty of the government.

But even on this issue, the class divide amongst the people is quite evident. While cutting across class there is demand for increasing the role of the government in delivering public health facilities, the demand for free medical health facilities comes more from the lower-class people compared to the upper-class people. Amongst those belonging to the lower class, 69 per cent believed that the treatment in government should be free; this view was expressed by a slightly lesser number (51 per cent) amongst the upper-class people. Amongst the middle class, 60 per cent believed that the treatment in government hospital should be free. On the contrary, amongst the lower class, only 21 per cent were willing to pay more for better treatment in government hospitals, while amongst the upper class, 40 per cent were willing to pay more for better medical facilities in government hospitals.

Report of the National Commission on Urbanisation, GoI, 1988, (Report, vol. II, Government of India, New Delhi) noted that if the water supply system is unequal and unjust, being highly biased in favour of the rich, the sewerage system is even more unjust. About one-third of the total urban population is not served by any drainage system and in 12 urban centres, 50 per cent or even more waste is not collected. In some small towns, even a rudimentary hygienic waste disposal system does not exist. The acute gap in provision and poor quality of basic services and amenities in these settlements result in poor environmental sanitation conditions that have the potential of resulting in an urban disaster.

There is a wide gap between the demand and supply of basic services and facilities including water supply, sanitation, solid waste management and electricity. The norms for provision of basic amenities are different for formal and informal housing (Table 7.5). What is even more lamentable is the actual level of provision in informal communities, which is far below any acceptable standards and norms. While the norm for provision of water supply to informal settlements is 40 lpcd, the actual provision is much lower at 30 lpcd. The same is the case with provision for sanitation facilities, while the prescribed norm is one community toilet seat for 25 people, there are more than hundred people dependent on one toilet seat and there are innumerable settlements where even this rudimentary facility isn't available and communities have to resort to defecation in the open.

Table 7.5:
Inequitable Provision of Basic Services in Delhi

Basic Service	Norms for Formal Housing	Norms for Informal Housing	Actual Provision in Informal Settlements
Water	363 lpcd Individual Supply	40 lpcd; 1 community stand post for 150 persons	30 lpcd
Sanitation	Individual toilets connected to city-level sewerage system	Community toilets 1 seat for 25 persons	1 seat for 111 persons; 75 per cent with sewerage cover
Solid Waste Management	Household-level collection	Deposit at nearest garbage point	44 per cent gap for all city
Electricity	Individual metered connections 150 units per individual per day	Street light and some individual metered connections through group contractor 12 units per individual per day	30 per cent gap Complete coverage with unmetered connections 8 units per individual per day

Sources: *Report of a Convention*, Sajha Manch, June 1999; *Delhi Fact File*, National Capital Region Planning Board, 1999.

There is an increasing demand for reforms in the Indian electoral system. One of the important demands being raised is that there should be some prescription of educational attainment as a prerequisite for being able to vote. About one-quarter of the people living in Delhi believes that the illiterate should not have the right to vote in elections (Figure 7.6). This opinion is shared more amongst the upper-class people compared to the lower class. There is a clear divide on this issue amongst the upper and lower classes, primarily because the proportion of educated people is more amongst the upper-class people compared to the lower class. Amongst the lower-class people, large numbers are uneducated and they would not like to sacrifice their right to vote, and hence lower support for the idea of denial of voting rights to the uneducated. The shared belief is that the uneducated people possibly cannot take a decision about their voting rights and they end up voting for the party or the candidate, which they should not have voted. Many associate this as one of the biggest ills of Indian democracy. The view is shared more amongst the urban educated class compared to those living in villages and those who are uneducated.

Figure 7.6:
Public Opinion on the Right to Vote (Class-wise)

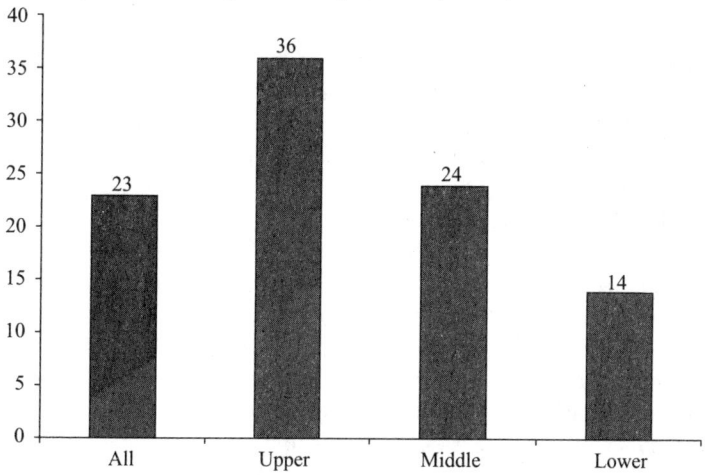

Source: HT–CSDS Delhi Survey, 2003.
Note: All figures are in per cent. The figures represented here are for those who support the idea that an illiterate should not have the right to vote in elections.

Conclusion

While territorially Delhi still represents one city, in terms of the people who live in this city, we can safely divide the city into three cities—city of the upper class, city of the middle class and city of the lower or poor—merged into one city. These do not represent any geographical division. These represent sharp divisions of opinion on socio-economic and political issues, and differences in political behaviour of the people belonging to the three classes. Even though the three classes of people do not represent clearly demarcated geographical locations, broadly they are also proxy for three different types of localities where people live in Delhi. The city of the poor can be mainly seen in the JJ clusters and resettlement colonies. The city of the middle class is represented by the localities with a large number of LIG and MIG flats (both of private builders and those built by the DDA), small houses built on small plots and similar such housing dwellers. The city of the rich is represented by the localities with High-income Group flats and big houses popularly called *kothi*s. Broadly, these three different kinds of localities represent different kinds of problems. The concerns of the people living in these three localities are also different. Under such circumstances, it may be incorrect on the part of the government to formulate a uniform policy for solving the problems of this city. It may be more appropriate to have policies aimed at addressing specific problems of specific localities. This in turn would result in addressing specific problems faced by specific people. This is what may be appropriate as a policy of the government oriented towards solving the problems of a mega city.

It is important to note that while there are problems which concern the common citizens, there are variations in terms of how people from different economic strata of society perceive different problems. It appears that the time has come for the residents to realize that all the physical attributes of a beautiful city are present in Delhi. What is missing are the human and behavioural inputs. Slow and painful as it may be, these inputs will ensure that Delhi is back to its past historic glory. Law and order is a concern more of the rich compared to the poor. Even on other issues, there are variations in how people perceive these problems. If people living in a locality feel the need for drinking water more than safety and security, there is no point in government putting emphasis on improving the law and order problem in this 'city of the poor'. But then the question arises whom will the government listen to? The powerful upper class or the middle class or the homeless people?

Note

1. These buses were earlier known as Red Line buses. Due to frequent accidents, and hue and cry of the people over such accidents, the Delhi High Court directed the Delhi government to phase out Blue Line buses in Delhi. The government responded by saying that while it was committed to phasing out Blue Line buses, this may not be possible by the deadline fed by the Delhi High Court.

Appendix 1:
Detailed Results of
Delhi Assembly Election, 2008

Constituency: Narela – 1

Candidate name	Turnout (%): 56.83	Party	Actual Vote	Vote (%)
Jaswant Singh		INC	34,662	31.66
Sharad Kumar		BSP	33,827	30.90
Ajit Singh		BJP	29,752	27.17
Raj Singh Khatri		Independent	5,041	4.60
Amit Kumar		LJP	1,704	1.56
Rest (All Other Candidates)		Others	4,503	4.11

Constituency: Burari – 2

Candidate name	Turnout (%): 55.93	Party	Actual Vote	Vote (%)
Shri Krishan		BJP	32,006	30.10
Deepak Tyagi		INC	27,016	25.40
Vinod Nagar		LJP	17,777	16.72
Anand Mohan Joshi		BSP	12,753	11.99
Ram Kishore Tyagi		NCP	4,695	4.41
Rest (All Other Candidates)		Others	12,099	11.38

Constituency: Timarpur – 3

Candidate name	Turnout (%): 59.35	Party	Actual Vote	Vote (%)
Surinder Pal Singh		INC	39,997	44.14
Surya Prakash Khatri		BJP	37,584	41.48
Sanjeev Kumar		BSP	9,491	10.47
Apramay Mishra		SP	775	0.86
Shyam Gopal		ABHM	706	0.78
Rest (All Other Candidates)		Others	2,060	2.27

Constituency: Adarsh Nagar – 4

Candidate name	Turnout (%): 59.12	Party	Actual Vote	Vote (%)
Mangat Ram		INC	36,445	44.84
Ravinder Singh (Khurana)		BJP	31,933	39.29
Sanajy Nagpal		BSP	9,990	12.29
Sudhir Pathak		Independent	753	0.93
Ram Saran Ram		CPI	654	0.80
Rest (All Other Candidates)		Others	1,500	1.85

Constituency: Badli – 5

Candidate name	Turnout (%): 57.08	Party	Actual Vote	Vote (%)
Devender Yadav		INC	39,215	39.86
Ajesh Yadav		BSP	25,611	26.03
Rajesh Yadav		BJP	18,745	19.05
Jitender Kumar		NCP	11,242	11.43
Parwinder Singh		RJD	1,165	1.18
Rest (All Other Candidates)		Others	2,403	2.45

Constituency: Rithala – 6

Candidate Name	Turnout (%): 63.43	Party	Actual Vote	Vote (%)
Kulwant Rana		BJP	64,474	55.56
Shambhu Dayal Sharma		INC	38,128	32.86
Ranbir Singh		BSP	11,203	9.65
Vidya Pati		Independent	697	0.60
Rajesh Kumar		LJP	365	0.31
Rest (All Other Candidates)		Others	1,177	1.02

Constituency: Bawana (SC) – 7

Candidate Name	Turnout (%): 52.65	Party	Actual Vote	Vote (%)
Surender Kumar		INC	60,544	48.33
Chand Ram		BJP	43,402	34.65
Ramchander		BSP	17,848	14.25
Phool Kumar		LJP	1,597	1.27
Harbir Singh		Independent	1,363	1.09
Rest (All Other Candidates)		Others	516	0.41

Constituency: Mundka – 8

Candidate Name	Turnout (%): 55.07	Party	Actual Vote	Vote (%)
Manoj Kumar		BJP	47,355	45.83
Prem Chander Kaushik		INC	32,458	31.41
Jasbir		BSP	12,382	11.98
Chandi Ram		NCP	6,909	6.69
Bhagwan Singh		Independent	858	0.83
Rest (All Other Candidates)		Others	3,367	3.26

Constituency: Kirari – 9

Candidate Name	Turnout (%): 57.94	Party	Actual Vote	Vote (%)
Anil Jha		BJP	30,005	32.73
Pushpraj		NCP	20,481	22.34
Shabnam		INC	15,472	16.88
Ram Pal Singh		BSP	10,633	11.60
Raj Pal		Independent	4,981	5.43
Rest (All Other Candidates)		Others	10,097	11.02

Constituency: Sultanpur Majra (SC) – 10

Candidate Name	Turnout (%): 61.95	Party	Actual Vote	Vote (%)
Jai Kishan		INC	39,542	48.19
Nand Ram Bagri		BJP	20,867	25.43
Satya Pal Singh		BSP	18,559	22.62
Mehar Singh		ABSP	737	0.90
Sonu		Independent	729	0.89
Rest (All Other Candidates)		Others	1,613	1.97

Constituency: Nangloi Jat – 11

Candidate Name	Turnout (%): 55.17	Party	Actual Vote	Vote (%)
Bijender Singh		INC	48,009	50.65
Raj Singh		BJP	30,449	32.12
Naresh Goel		BSP	13,568	14.31
Sunil Kumar		Independent	657	0.69
Uday Veer Singh		LJP	608	0.64
Rest (All Other Candidates)		Others	1,493	1.59

Constituency: Mangol Puri (SC) – 12

Candidate Name	Turnout (%): 64.78	Party	Actual Vote	Vote (%)
Raj Kumar Chauhan		INC	50,448	54.41
Yogesh Aatray		BJP	20,585	22.20
Mukesh Kumar Ahlawat		BSP	19,971	21.54
Sanjay Bharti		Independent	818	0.88
Nand Kumar Paswan		Independent	622	0.67
Rest (All Other Candidates)		Others	268	0.30

Constituency: Rohini – 13

Candidate Name	Turnout (%): 58.72	Party	Actual Vote	Vote (%)
Jai Bhagwan Aggarwal		BJP	55,793	62.56
Vijender Jindal		INC	30,019	33.66
O.P.Malhotra		BSP	2,293	2.57
Labhu Ram Garg		Independent	402	0.45
Jhankar Priye Chaturvedi		SHS	332	0.37
Rest (All Other Candidates)		Others	350	0.39

Constituency: Shalimar Bagh – 14

Candidate Name	Turnout (%): 58.60	Party	Actual Vote	Vote (%)
Ravinder Nath Bansal		BJP	49,976	57.63
Ram Kailash Gupta		INC	30,044	34.65
Mukesh Rajore		BSP	5,102	5.88
Savita		Independent	456	0.53
Vinod Dukhiya		ABHM	309	0.36
Rest (All Other Candidates)		Others	832	0.95

Constituency: Shakur Basti – 15

Candidate Name	Turnout (%): 58.27	Party	Actual Vote	Vote (%)
Shyam Lal Garg		BJP	40,444	50.20
S. C. Vats		INC	36,444	45.23
Jaideep Dass Gupta		BSP	2,683	3.33
Smarti Goel		Independent	497	0.62
Sansar Chand		Independent	275	0.34
Rest (All Other Candidates)		Others	224	0.28

Constituency: Tri Nagar – 16

Candidate Name	Turnout (%): 63.37	Party	Actual Vote	Vote (%)
Anil Bhardwaj		INC	41,891	46.26
Nand Kishore Garg		BJP	39,922	44.09
Puran Mal Goel		BSP	5,075	5.60
Lalit Kumar Sharma		SP	1,547	1.71
Sunder Singh Khari		BJSH	461	0.51
Rest (All Other Candidates)		Others	1,651	1.83

Constituency: Wazirpur – 17

Candidate Name	Turnout (%): 56.69	Party	Actual Vote	Vote (%)
Hari Shanker Gupta		INC	39,977	45.07
Mange Ram Garg		BJP	36,837	41.53
Janesh Kumar Bhadana		BSP	9,199	10.37
Inderjeet Yadav		RJD	860	0.97
Sunil Kumar		Independent	668	0.75
Rest (All Other Candidates)		Others	1,166	1.31

Constituency: Model Town – 18

Candidate Name	Turnout (%): 58.53	Party	Actual Vote	Vote (%)
Kanwar Karan Singh		INC	39,935	46.87
Bhola Nath Vij		BJP	36,938	43.36
Solomon George		BSP	6,388	7.50
Sahansar Pal		Independent	586	0.69
Satya Narayain Yadav		SP	333	0.39
Rest (All Other Candidates)		Others	1,017	1.19

Constituency: Sadar Bazar – 19

Candidate Name	Turnout (%): 60.15	Party	Actual Vote	Vote (%)
Rajesh Jain		INC	47,508	53.44
Jai Prakash		BJP	33,419	37.59
Rajendra Kumar Prajapti		BSP	5,004	5.63
Ganga Singh		SP	776	0.87
Raj Kumar		NCP	454	0.51
Rest (All Other Candidates)		Others	1,734	1.96

Constituency: Chandni Chowk – 20

Candidate Name	Turnout (%): 57.32	Party	Actual Vote	Vote (%)
Parlad Singh Sawhney		INC	28,208	45.61
Praveen Khandelwal		BJP	20,188	32.64
Khurrum Iqbal		LJP	9,967	16.12
Mohd Mushtaq Khan		BSP	2,055	3.32
Sunil Kumar		Independent	211	0.34
Rest (All Other Candidates)		Others	1,217	1.97

Constituency: Matia Mahal – 21

Candidate Name	Turnout (%): 56.39	Party	Actual Vote	Vote (%)
Shoaib Iqbal		LJP	25,474	39.56
Mehmood Zia		INC	17,870	27.75
Abhey Singh Yadav		BSP	11,714	18.19
Talat Sultana		BJP	6,015	9.34
Mohd Shafiq		Independent	814	1.26
Rest (All Other Candidates)		Others	2,502	3.90

Constituency: Ballimaran – 22

Candidate Name	Turnout (%): 59.60	Party	Actual Vote	Vote (%)
Haroon Yasuf		INC	34,660	42.08
Moti Lal Sodhi		BJP	28,423	34.51
Mushrafin		BSP	10,331	12.54
Ubead Iqbal		LJP	6,490	7.88
Mohd Sabauddin		RJTD	810	0.98
Rest (All Other Candidates)		Others	1,650	2.01

Constituency: Karol Bagh (SC) – 23

Candidate Name	Turnout (%): 59.65	Party	Actual Vote	Vote (%)
Surender Pal Ratawal		BJP	38,746	45.71
Madan Khorwal		INC	35,338	41.69
Veena Singh		BSP	7,555	8.91
Nathu Spare Prasad		CPM	1,496	1.77
Ram Babu		Independent	429	0.51
Rest (All Other Candidates)		Others	1,192	1.41

Constituency: Patel Nagar (SC) – 24

Candidate Name	Turnout (%): 56.57	Party	Actual Vote	Vote (%)
Rajesh Lilothia		INC	44,022	50.43
Anita Arya		BJP	34,516	39.54
Madan Lal		BSP	6,846	7.84
Sunil Pawar		Independent	665	0.76
Ghanshyam Morwal		DBP	487	0.56
Rest (All Other Candidates)		Others	754	0.87

Constituency: Moti Nagar – 25

Candidate Name	Turnout (%): 61.60	Party	Actual Vote	Vote (%)
Subhash Sachdeva		BJP	46,616	54.49
Anjali Rai		INC	31,619	36.96
Virender Kumar Mahajan		BSP	4,823	5.64
Lal Babu Pandey		SP	512	0.60
Abdul Waheed		LJP	460	0.54
Rest (All Other Candidates)		Others	1,516	1.77

Constituency: Madipur (SC) – 26

Candidate Name	Turnout (%): 58.47	Party	Actual Vote	Vote (%)
Mala Ram Gangwal		INC	40,698	48.75
Kailash Sankla		BJP	32,166	38.53
Mohan Lal		BSP	9,337	11.18
Mala Ram		Independent	649	0.78
Nirmala		Independent	392	0.47
Rest (All Other Candidates)		Others	241	0.29

Constituency: Rajouri Garden – 27

Candidate Name	Turnout (%): 62.06	Party	Actual Vote	Vote (%)
A Daya Nand Chandela A		INC	31,130	37.58
Avtar Singh Hit		SAD(M)	31,084	37.53
Duli Chand		NCP	15,434	18.63
Shamsher Singh Mehendi		BSP	1,563	1.89
Vinod Sharma		Independent	1,469	1.77
Rest (All Other Candidates)		Others	2,153	2.60

Constituency: Hari Nagar – 28

Candidate Name	Turnout (%): 57.27	Party	Actual Vote	Vote (%)
Harsharan Singh Balli		BJP	51,364	62.67
Ramesh Lamba		INC	22,606	27.58
Prem Sharma		BSP	6,464	7.89
Sumit Chugh		Independent	401	0.49
Feroz Khan		JD(U)	287	0.35
Rest (All Other Candidates)		Others	832	1.02

Constituency: Tilak Nagar – 29

Candidate Name	Turnout (%): 53.50	Party	Actual Vote	Vote (%)
O. P. Babbar		BJP	38,320	52.33
Dr Anita Babbar		INC	26,202	35.78
Ajit Singh Chadha		Independent	4,031	5.50
Arvinder Singh Maken		BSP	2,580	3.52
Herry Gulati		Independent	486	0.66
Rest (All Other Candidates)		Others	1,613	2.21

Constituency: Janakpuri – 30

Candidate Name	Turnout (%): 61.29	Party	Actual Vote	Vote (%)
Prof. Jagdish Mukhi		BJP	50,655	57.15
Deepak Arora		INC	33,203	37.46
Prem Chand Deswal		BSP	2,857	3.22
Shiv Kumar		Independent	522	0.59
Bharat Prasad		Independent	454	0.51
Rest (All Other Candidates)		Others	950	1.07

Constituency: Vikaspuri – 31

Candidate Name	Turnout (%): 55.65	Party	Actual Vote	Vote (%)
Nand Kishore		INC	47,819	34.96
Krishan Gahlot		BJP	46,876	34.27
Ashok Kumar Lakra		BSP	16,765	12.26
Sanjay Singh		Independent	9,634	7.04
Ravinder Singh		Independent	7,158	5.23
Rest (All Other Candidates)		Others	8,522	6.24

Constituency: Uttam Nagar – 32

Candidate Name	Turnout (%): 62.38	Party	Actual Vote	Vote (%)
Mukesh Sharma		INC	46,765	46.03
Pawan Sharma		BJP	39,582	38.96
Rajender Bhardwaj		NCP	8,064	7.94
Om Prakash Jain		BSP	5,071	4.99
Raj Bala		Independent	524	0.52
Rest (All Other Candidates)		Others	1,596	1.56

Constituency: Dwarka – 33

Candidate Name	Turnout (%): 62.50	Party	Actual Vote	Vote (%)
Mahabal Mishra		INC	43,608	52.33
Parduymn Rajput		BJP	29,627	35.56
Babu Ram		BSP	7,806	9.37
Mukesh Kumar Chaudhary		CPM	553	0.66
Subhash Kumar Chaudhary		Independent	400	0.48
Rest (All Other Candidates)		Others	1,331	1.60

Constituency: Matiala – 34

Candidate Name	Turnout (%): 58.55	Party	Actual Vote	Vote (%)
Sumesh		INC	52,411	40.14
Kamal Jeet		BJP	45,782	35.06
Manoj Bhardwaj		BSP	19,442	14.89
Rao Satvir Singh		Independent	8,883	6.80
Nidhi Mahajan		BRSP	1,224	0.94
Rest (All Other Candidates)		Others	2,827	2.17

Constituency: Najafgarh – 35

Candidate Name	Turnout (%): 59.14	Party	Actual Vote	Vote (%)
Bharat Singh		Independent	34,028	33.25
Kanwal Singh Yadav		INC	22,575	22.06
Bijander Dutt		BSP	18,164	17.75
Rajesh Sharma		BJP	13,576	13.27
Ranbir Singh Kharb		Independent	11,620	11.36
Rest (All Other Candidates)		Others	2,365	2.31

Constituency: Bijwasan – 36

Candidate Name	Turnout (%): 59.15	Party	Actual Vote	Vote (%)
Sat Prakash Rana		BJP	27,427	41.33
Vijay Singh Lochav		INC	25,422	38.31
Vinod Kumar Yadav		BSP	12,506	18.84
Harvinder Rana		Independent	642	0.97
Suresh Chand		LJP	370	0.55
Rest (All Other Candidates)		Others	–	–

Constituency: Palam – 37

Candidate Name	Turnout (%): 58.80	Party	Actual Vote	Vote (%)
Dharam Dev Solanki		BJP	40,712	44.12
Mahender Yadav		INC	28,119	30.47
Madan Mohan		BSP	21,014	22.77
Bhairav Dutt Dhyani		CPI	659	0.71
Mahesh Kumar		Independent	600	0.65
Rest (All Other Candidates)		Others	1,173	1.28

Constituency: Delhi Cantt – 38

Candidate Name	Turnout (%): 56.60	Party	Actual Vote	Vote (%)
Karan Singh Tanwar		BJP	23,696	55.58
Ashok Ahuja		INC	16,435	38.55
Shrichand Chauhan		BSP	1,492	3.50
Sandeep		Independent	278	0.65
Sanjay Mangal		Independent	136	0.32
Rest (All Other Candidates)		Others	596	1.40

Constituency: Rajinder Nagar – 39

Candidate Name	Turnout (%): 52.35	Party	Actual Vote	Vote (%)
Rama Kant Goswami		INC	29,394	40.78
Asha Yogi		BJP	23,988	33.28
Trilok Chand Sharma		BSP	15,871	22.02
Bhagwan Das		NCP	1,344	1.86
Sanjay Sehrawat		Independent	540	0.75
Rest (All Other Candidates)		Others	940	1.31

Constituency: New Delhi – 40

Candidate Name	Turnout (%): 56.22	Party	Actual Vote	Vote (%)
Sheila Dikshit		INC	39,778	52.20
Vijay Jolly		BJP	25,796	33.85
Rajiv Singh		BSP	6,179	8.11
Brij Mohan Upreti		Independent	879	1.15
Ramanand Madhwal		Independent	666	0.87
Rest (All Other Candidates)		Others	2,905	3.82

Constituency: Jangpura – 41

Candidate Name	Turnout (%): 59.69	Party	Actual Vote	Vote (%)
Tarvinder Singh Marwah		INC	37,261	57.00
Manjinder Singh Sirsa		BJP	23,310	35.66
Gaje Singh		BSP	3,192	4.88
Haseen Ahmed Siddiqi		LJP	559	0.86
Praveen Kumar Jain		Independent	394	0.60
Rest (All Other Candidates)		Others	658	1.00

Constituency: Kasturba Nagar – 42

Candidate Name	Turnout (%): 53.27	Party	Actual Vote	Vote (%)
Neeraj Basoya		INC	33,807	44.40
Sushil Choudhary		BJP	31,323	41.13
Satish Basoya		BSP	9,775	12.84
Prem Babbar		SP	339	0.45
Suresh		Independent	337	0.44
Rest (All Other Candidates)		Others	568	0.74

Constituency: Malviya Nagar – 43

Candidate Name	Turnout (%): 55.92	Party	Actual Vote	Vote (%)
Kiran Walia		INC	31,283	46.55
Ram Bhaj		BJP	27,551	41.00
Shri Pal Saini		BSP	6,832	10.17
Javed Farooqui		LJP	352	0.52
Rafik		Independent	309	0.46
Rest (All Other Candidates)		Others	874	1.30

Constituency: R. K. Puram – 44

Candidate Name	Turnout (%): 52.86	Party	Actual Vote	Vote (%)
Barkha Singh		INC	35,878	53.50
Radhey Shyam Sharma		BJP	26,561	39.60
Kulbir Singh		BSP	3,298	4.92
Raja Ram		LJP	364	0.54
G. Sivasankaran		Independent	334	0.50
Rest (All Other Candidates)		Others	631	0.94

Constituency: Mehrauli – 45

Candidate Name	Turnout (%): 45.91	Party	Actual Vote	Vote (%)
Dr Yoganand Shastri		INC	21,740	32.83
Sher Singh Dagar		BJP	20,632	31.15
Satbir Singh		Independent	14,954	22.58
Ved Parkash		BSP	5,697	8.60
Jagdish Singh Lohia		NCP	1,892	2.86
Rest (All Other Candidates)		Others	1,309	1.98

Constituency: Chhatarpur – 46

Candidate Name	Turnout (%): 56.00	Party	Actual Vote	Vote (%)
Balram Tanwar		INC	32,406	37.22
Brahm Singh Tanwar		BJP	27,376	31.44
Kanwar Singh Tanwar		BSP	25,492	29.28
Hira Lal Singh		Independent	481	0.55
Prem Raj		RLD	440	0.51
Rest (All Other Candidates)		Others	882	1.00

Constituency: Deoli (SC) – 47

Candidate Name	Turnout (%): 56.51	Party	Actual Vote	Vote (%)
Arvinder Singh		INC	41,497	43.41
Shri Lal		BSP	24,869	26.02
Bhim Singh		BJP	22,661	23.71
Dal Chand Kapil		LJP	4,758	4.98
Rakesh Kumar		Independent	1,244	1.30
Rest (All Other Candidates)		Others	558	0.58

Constituency: Ambedkar Nagar (SC) – 48

Candidate Name	Turnout (%): 57.44	Party	Actual Vote	Vote (%)
Ch. Prem Singh		INC	30,467	43.19
Suresh Chand		BJP	25,630	36.34
Prahlad Kumar Malviya		BSP	12,362	17.53
Dalip Valmiki		LJP	1,264	1.79
Trilok		Independent	515	0.73
Rest (All Other Candidates)		Others	300	0.42

Constituency: Sangam Vihar – 49

Candidate Name	Turnout (%): 51.44	Party	Actual Vote	Vote (%)
Dr S. C. L. Gupta		BJP	20,332	27.37
Amod Kumar Kanth		INC	16,743	22.54
Ranjit Singh		BSP	11.687	15.73
Vir Singh		NCP	10,577	14.24
A. K. Gupta		SP	9,665	13.01
Rest (All Other Candidates)		Others	5,277	7.11

Constituency: Greater Kailash – 50

Candidate Name	Turnout (%): 54.48	Party	Actual Vote	Vote (%)
Vijay Kumar Malhotra		BJP	42,206	52.94
Jitender Kumar Kocher		INC	30,987	38.87
Rajendra Kumar Gupta		BSP	4,486	5.63
Raju		SHS	676	0.85
Jitendar Kumar Gupta		BPC	322	0.40
Rest (All Other Candidates)		Others	1,045	1.31

Constituency: Kalkaji – 51

Candidate Name	Turnout (%): 51.38	Party	Actual Vote	Vote (%)
Subhash Chopra		INC	38,360	51.91
Jai Gopal Abrol		BJP	24,971	33.79
Avinash Kaur		BSP	9,455	12.79
Sushil Kumar Agarwal		Independent	432	0.58
Om Prakash Abrol		Independent	353	0.48
Rest (All Other Candidates)		Others	333	0.45

Constituency: Tughlakabad – 52

Candidate Name	Turnout (%): 55.66	Party	Actual Vote	Vote (%)
Ramesh Bidhuri		BJP	32,633	40.99
Sahi Ram		BSP	24,399	30.65
Shish Pal Singh		INC	20,692	25.99
Hans Raj Nagar		Independent	519	0.65
Munna		RBCP	265	0.33
Rest (All Other Candidates)		Others	1,097	1.39

Constituency: Badarpur – 53

Candidate Name	Turnout (%): 56.67	Party	Actual Vote	Vote (%)
Ram Singh Netaji		BSP	53,416	47.30
Rambir Singh Bidhuri		INC	40,111	35.52
Khem Chand		BJP	15,621	13.83
Binod Raj Jha		LJP	1,262	1.12
Om Prakash Gupta		Independent	1,050	0.93
Rest (All Other Candidates)		Others	1,469	1.30

Constituency: Okhla – 54

Candidate Name	Turnout (%): 49.21	Party	Actual Vote	Vote (%)
Parvez Hashmi		INC	29,303	28.53
Asif Mohd Khan		RJD	28,762	28.00
Braham Singh		BSP	22,064	21.48
Surender Kumar		BJP	14,049	13.68
Wasim Ahmed Ghazi		SP	4,499	4.38
Rest (All Other Candidates)		Others	4,049	3.93

Constituency: Trilok Puri (SC) – 55

Candidate Name	Turnout (%): 59.99	Party	Actual Vote	Vote (%)
Sunil Kumar		BJP	30,781	37.28
Anjana		INC	30,147	36.51
Ganga Ram		BSP	19,417	23.52
Lovekush Sagar		RPI(A)	665	0.81
Ajay		Independent	435	0.53
Rest (All Other Candidates)		Others	1,117	1.35

Constituency: Kondli (SC) – 56

Candidate Name	Turnout (%): 59.60	Party	Actual Vote	Vote (%)
Amrish Singh Gautam		INC	36,580	45.26
Dushyant Gautam		BJP	21,594	26.72
Chander Pal Singh		BSP	19,903	24.63
Shiv Dutt		Independent	916	1.13
Madan Pal Singh		LJP	475	0.59
Rest (All Other Candidates)		Others	1,348	1.67

Constituency: Patparganj – 57

Candidate Name	Turnout (%): 54.57	Party	Actual Vote	Vote (%)
Anil Kumar		INC	36,999	42.40
Nakul Bhardwaj		BJP	36,336	41.64
Madan Singh		BSP	12,032	13.79
Shashi Kumar		CPI	613	0.70
Parmod		Independent	462	0.53
Rest (All Other Candidates)		Others	825	0.94

Constituency: Laxmi Nagar – 58

Candidate Name	Turnout (%): 56.50	Party	Actual Vote	Vote (%)
Dr Ashok Kumar Walia		INC	54,252	59.58
Murari Singh Panwar		BJP	31,855	34.99
Avinash Sharma		BSP	3,527	3.87
Yashoda Rani		Independent	374	0.41
Omvir Singh Yadav		SP	305	0.33
Rest (All Other Candidates)		Others	738	0.82

Constituency: Vishwas Nagar – 59

Candidate Name	Turnout (%): 58.73	Party	Actual Vote	Vote (%)
Naseeb Singh		INC	48,805	51.09
Om Prakash Sharma		BJP	39,176	41.01
Narendra Kumar Pandey		BSP	5,823	6.10
Deepak Gupta		DBP	528	0.55
Sudesh Kumar Jain		Independent	350	0.37
Rest (All Other Candidates)		Others	845	0.88

Constituency: Krishna Nagar – 60

Candidate Name	Turnout (%): 61.65	Party	Actual Vote	Vote (%)
Harsh Vardhan		BJP	47,852	45.50
Deepika Khullar		INC	44,648	42.45
Kamruddin		BSP	10,018	9.53
Chandan Lal Premi		CPI	703	0.67
Radha Yadav, Advocate		BJSH	359	0.34
Rest (All Other Candidates)		Others	1,595	1.51

Constituency: Gandhi Nagar – 61

Candidate Name	Turnout (%): 63.49	Party	Actual Vote	Vote (%)
Arvinder Singh Lovely		INC	59,795	64.25
Kamal Kumar Jain		BJP	27,870	29.94
Sanjay Gaur		BSP	4,024	4.32
Sunil Kumar		Independent	555	0.60
Lekh Raj		BJSH	205	0.22
Rest (All Other Candidates)		Others	624	0.67

Constituency: Shahdara – 62

Candidate Name	Turnout (%): 57.14	Party	Actual Vote	Vote (%)
Dr Narender Nath		INC	39,194	44.89
Jitender Singh Shunty		BJP	37,658	43.13
Vijay Pal		BSP	8,104	9.28
Neelam Kumari		RJD	669	0.77
Suresh Kumar		Independent	427	0.49
Rest (All Other Candidates)		Others	1,265	1.44

Constituency: Seemapuri (SC) – 63

Candidate Name	Turnout (%): 62.35	Party	Actual Vote	Vote (%)
Veer Singh Dhingan		INC	43,864	49.13
Chandra Pal Singh		BJP	24,604	27.56
Lallan Prasad		BSP	14,823	16.60
Raj Dulari		NLHP	1,714	1.92
Mange Ram		Independent	979	1.10
Rest (All Other Candidates)		Others	3,297	3.69

Constituency: Rohtas Nagar – 64

Candidate Name	Turnout (%): 61.16	Party	Actual Vote	Vote (%)
Ram Babu Sharma		INC	45,802	46.42
Alok Kumar		BJP	32,559	32.99
Lokesh Dixit		BSP	16,823	17.05
Laxman Dass		Independent	1,651	1.67
Jitendra Panchal		SP	482	0.49
Rest (All Other Candidates)		Others	1,362	1.38

Constituency: Seelampur – 65

Candidate Name	Turnout (%): 59.33	Party	Actual Vote	Vote (%)
Chaudhary Mateen Ahmad		INC	47,820	54.65
Sita Ram Gupta		BJP	21,546	24.62
Hazi Afzzal		BSP	13,445	15.37
Masood Ali Khan		SP	1,062	1.21
Mohd Badrul Haq		RJD	904	1.03
Rest (All Other Candidates)		Others	2,722	3.12

Constituency: Ghonda – 66

Candidate Name	Turnout (%): 59.03	Party	Actual Vote	Vote (%)
Sahab Singh Chauhan		BJP	35,226	38.46
Bheeshma Sharma		INC	34,646	37.82
Rohtash Kumar		BSP	21,724	23.72
Rest (All Other Candidates)		Others	–	–

Constituency: Babarpur – 67

Candidate Name	Turnout (%): 59.79	Party	Actual Vote	Vote (%)
Naresh Gaur		BJP	31,954	35.10
Hazi Dilshad Ali		BSP	28,128	30.90
Anil Kuamr Vashishth		INC	21,632	23.76
Kailash Chand Jain		Independent	7,247	7.96
Mohd. Sher Nabi Chaman		Independent	534	0.59
Rest (All Other Candidates)		Others	1,537	1.69

Constituency: Gokalpur (SC) – 68

Candidate Name	Turnout (%): 61.62	Party	Actual Vote	Vote (%)
Surendra Kumar		BSP	27,499	28.89
Balzor Singh		INC	24,442	25.68
Ranjeet Singh		BJP	23,364	24.55
Ch. Fateh Singh		Independent	10,262	10.78
Choudhary Balraj		Independent	4,920	5.17
Rest (All Other Candidates)		Others	4,686	4.93

Constituency: Mustafabad – 69

Candidate Name	Turnout (%): 58.09	Party	Actual Vote	Vote (%)
Hasan Ahmed		INC	39,838	40.70
Yogender Kumar Sharma		BJP	38,859	39.69
Sher Khan Malik		BSP	14,108	14.41
Mohd Rahis		Independent	989	1.01
Sunil Dhyani		Independent	778	0.79
Rest (All Other Candidates)		Others	3,322	3.40

Constituency: Karawal Nagar – 70

Candidate Name	Turnout (%): 52.86	Party	Actual Vote	Vote (%)
Mohan Singh Bisht		BJP	43,980	42.80
Satan Pal Dayma		Independent	22,852	22.24
Diwan Singh Nayal		INC	15,182	14.78
Harender Kumar Sharma		BSP	9,233	8.99
Anmol Choudhari		CPM	2,198	2.14
Rest (All Other Candidates)		Others	9,303	9.05

Abbreviations: Ch–Choudhary; Kr–Kumar; Mohd–Mohammed.

Appendix 2:
Detailed Results of
Delhi Assembly Elections, 1993–2003

Constituency: SAROJINI NAGAR – 1

Election: 1993	Turnout (%): 49.64	Party	Actual Vote	Vote (%)
Ram Bhaj		BJP	26,307	63.82
Prem Das Ahuja – W		INC	12,111	29.38
F. C. Pawar		JD	2,144	5.20
Deepak Mudgil		DBP	153	0.37
Dharam Pal Singh Shukla		Independent	152	0.37
Rest (All Other Candidates)		Others	353	0.86

Election: 1998	Turnout (%): 43.86	Party	Actual Vote	Vote (%)
Ram Bhaj		BJP	21,318	49.80
Mukesh Bhatt		INC	19,790	46.23
Shela Gaur – W		Independent	741	1.73
Dharam Bir Singh		Independent	521	1.22
Adersh Kumar		Independent	123	0.29
Rest (All Other Candidates)		Others	315	0.73

Election: 2003	Turnout (%): 43.61	Party	Actual Vote	Vote (%)
Ashok Ahuja		INC	21,125	52.18
Ram Bhaj		BJP	18,370	45.38
Mahesh Chabnd		Independent	648	1.60
Subhash Ahluwalia		NCP	236	0.58
Parmanand		JD(U)	105	0.26
Rest (All Other Candidates)		Others	–	0.00

Constituency: GOLE MARKET – 2

Election: 1993	Turnout (%): 48.39	Party	Actual Vote	Vote (%)
Kirti Azad		BJP	18,935	46.79
Brij Mohan Bhama		INC	15,132	37.39
Himanshu Pande		JD	3,896	9.63
Moti Lal		BSP	1,203	2.97
S. Dhanpal		Independent	295	0.73
Rest (All Other Candidates)		Others	1,008	2.49

Election: 1998	Turnout (%): 41.46	Party	Actual Vote	Vote (%)
Sheila Dikshit – W		INC	24,881	53.95
Kirti Azad		BJP	19,214	41.66
M. M. Gope		CPI	831	1.80
Romesh Sabharwal		Independent	342	0.74
Ram Kumar		SP	321	0.70
Rest (All Other Candidates)		Others	532	1.15

Election: 2003	Turnout (%): 45.62	Party	Actual Vote	Vote (%)
Sheila Dikshit – W		INC	25,156	64.44
Poonam Azad – W		BJP	12,221	31.31
Kalpana – W		JD(S)	265	0.68
Sunil Chaturvedi		Independent	236	0.60
Romesh Sabharwal		Independent	163	0.42
Rest (All Other Candidates)		Others	996	2.55

Constituency: MINTO ROAD – 3

Election: 1993	Turnout (%): 57.39	Party	Actual Vote	Vote (%)
Tajdar Babar – W		INC	18,411	43.83
Arun Jain		BJP	16,540	39.38
Manju Mohan – W		JD	5,645	13.44
P. N. Jha		CPI	229	0.55
Ranjit Singh		Independent	221	0.53
Rest (All Other Candidates)		Others	960	2.27

Election: 1998	Turnout (%): 43.49	Party	Actual Vote	Vote (%)
Tajdar Babar – W		INC	28,815	53.73
Arun Jain Engineer		BJP	14,050	26.20
Ramesh Dutta		Independent	7,656	14.28
Minoo Kaim – W		BSP	960	1.79
Anfal Nizam		JD	475	0.89
Rest (All Other Candidates)		Others	1,676	3.11
Election: 2003	Turnout (%): 44.93	Party	Actual Vote	Vote (%)
Tajdar Babar – W		INC	29,038	65.06
Manoj Jain		BJP	10,377	23.25
Riyazuddin		BSP	2,210	4.95
Baldev Singh		SP	599	1.34
Prabhu Dayal		IJP	464	1.04
Rest (All Other Candidates)		Others	1,942	4.36

Constituency: KASTURBA NAGAR – 4

Election: 1993	Turnout (%): 55.44	Party	Actual Vote	Vote (%)
Jagdish Lal Batra		BJP	25,215	55.72
Des Raj Chhabra		INC	15,159	33.50
Laxmi Chand Chechi		JD	3,671	8.11
Mithlesh Jha		Independent	608	1.34
Subhash Chander		SP	178	0.39
Rest (All Other Candidates)		Others	418	0.94
Election: 1998	Turnout (%): 48.91	Party	Actual Vote	Vote (%)
Sushil Choudhary		BJP	20,146	42.04
Ram Rattan Gupta		INC	19,247	40.16
Jagdish Lal Batra		Independent	6,825	14.24
Ramkaran Gupta		JD	922	1.92
Sunil Rawat		Independent	486	1.01
Rest (All Other Candidates)		Others	297	0.63

Election: 2003	Turnout (%): 45.15	Party	Actual Vote	Vote (%)
Sushil Choudery		BJP	17,949	45.52
Ashok Chopra		INC	17,266	43.79
Om Prakash		BSP	2,737	6.94
Rajendra Baisoya		NCP	438	1.11
Beer Singh Negi		SSGP	256	0.65
Rest (All Other Candidates)		Others	782	1.99

Constituency: JANGPURA – 5

Election: 1993	Turnout (%): 58.52	Party	Actual Vote	Vote (%)
Jag Pravesh Chandra		INC	24,200	47.40
Ram Lal Verma		BJP	21,709	42.52
P. Chakraborty		JD	3,382	6.62
Jai Kishan		Independent	464	0.91
Om Parkash		BSP	378	0.74
Rest (All Other Candidates)		Others	919	1.81

Election: 1998	Turnout (%): 49.77	Party	Actual Vote	Vote (%)
Tarvinder Singh Marwah		INC	28,384	51.47
Bir Bahadur		BJP	16,465	29.86
Tilak Raj Malhotra		Independent	8,605	15.60
Hari Lal Mandora		BSP	464	0.84
Inder Jit Singh Sethi		JD	419	0.76
Rest (All Other Candidates)		Others	807	1.47

Election: 2003	Turnout (%): 51.16	Party	Actual Vote	Vote (%)
Tarvinder Singh Marwah		INC	32,937	68.88
Kuldeep Singh Bhogal		BJP	12,710	26.58
Rajan Taneja		Independent	1,009	2.11
Naresh Kumar		JD(U)	538	1.13
Pavnesh Kumar		LJP	378	0.79
Rest (All Other Candidates)		Others	248	0.51

Constituency: OKHLA – 6

Election: 1993	Turnout (%): 52.90	Party	Actual Vote	Vote (%)
Parvej		JD	13,282	30.91
Hasan Ahmed		INC	11,975	27.87
Suraj Pracha		BJP	10,079	23.46
Ramesh Chand Pongar		SP	3,112	7.24
Amiruddin		CPI	1,083	2.52
Rest (All Other Candidates)		Others	3,432	8.00
Election: 1998	Turnout (%): 37.00	Party	Actual Vote	Vote (%)
Parvez Hashmi		INC	32,774	57.83
Krishan Kumar Mehta		BJP	14,613	25.78
Asif Mohamad Khan		SP	5,693	10.04
Asghar Khan		BSP	1,438	2.54
Amiruddin		NLP	633	1.12
Rest (All Other Candidates)		Others	1,525	2.69
Election: 2003	Turnout (%): 44.09	Party	Actual Vote	Vote (%)
Parvez Hashmi		INC	29,876	54.83
Rajpal Singh		BJP	15,227	27.94
Wasim Ahmad Ghazi		SP	6,723	12.34
Kabir Khan		NLP	704	1.29
Amiruddin		BSP	682	1.25
Rest (All Other Candidates)		Others	1,279	2.35

Constituency: KALKAJI – 7

Election: 1993	Turnout (%): 61.28	Party	Actual Vote	Vote (%)
Purnima Sethi – W		BJP	22,468	47.51
Subhash Chopra		INC	18,456	39.03
Nasib Singh		Independent	3,374	7.13
Vasantha Nanda Kumar – W		JD	1,352	2.86
Animesh Dass		Independent	356	0.75
Rest (All Other Candidates)		Others	1,285	2.72

Election: 1998	Turnout (%): 44.93	Party	Actual Vote	Vote (%)
Subhash Chopra		INC	29,948	53.62
Purnima Sethi – W		BJP	24,704	44.23
Sewa Singh		BSP	665	1.19
Jasvinder Singh		JD	203	0.36
Vijender Kumar		SJP(R)	99	0.18
Rest (All Other Candidates)		Others	229	0.42
Election: 2003	Turnout (%): 52.80	Party	Actual Vote	Vote (%)
Subhash Chopra		INC	35,721	64.13
Purnima Sethi – W		BJP	18,077	32.45
Kalpana – W		SP	654	1.17
Anil Bawa		NCP	329	0.59
Sarla Singh – W		IJP	278	0.50
Rest (All Other Candidates)		Others	644	1.16

Constituency: MALVIYA NAGAR – 8

Election: 1993	Turnout (%): 54.99	Party	Actual Vote	Vote (%)
Rajendra Gupta		BJP	19,319	42.99
Yoga Nand Shastri		INC	19,061	42.41
Ranjit Shastri		JD	4,531	10.08
Kailash Chand Panwar		Independent	1,114	2.48
Daler Singh		BJVP	341	0.76
Rest (All Other Candidates)		Others	574	1.28
Election: 1998	Turnout (%): 44.61	Party	Actual Vote	Vote (%)
Yoganand Shastri		INC	30,910	55.19
Rajendra Gupta		BJP	22,946	40.97
Pitamber Singh		BSP	1,406	2.51
Mohd Feroz Khan		JD	308	0.55
Mohd Umar		SP	247	0.44
Rest (All Other Candidates)		Others	187	0.34

Election: 2003	Turnout (%): 47.65	Party	Actual Vote	Vote (%)
Dr Yoganand Shahstri		INC	25,448	48.10
Monika Arora – W		BJP	20,928	39.56
Sukhbir Singh Panwar		NCP	3,256	6.15
Iqbal Khan		BSP	2,601	4.92
Chetan Kumar		SP	221	0.42
Rest (All Other Candidates)		Others	449	0.85

Constituency: HAUZ KHAS – 9

Election: 1993	Turnout (%): 57.44	Party	Actual Vote	Vote (%)
Rajesh Sharma		BJP	18,231	44.39
Ashok Kumar Jain		INC	16,542	40.28
Kulwant Kumar Gupta		JD	4,844	11.80
Khem Chand		BSP	354	0.86
Raghuvendra Singh		Independent	248	0.60
Rest (All Other Candidates)		Others	848	2.07

Election: 1998	Turnout (%): 45.58	Party	Actual Vote	Vote (%)
Sushma Swaraj – W		BJP	25,267	49.29
Kiran Walia – W		INC	22,652	44.19
Virender Singh		Independent	1,301	2.54
Khem Chand Jatav		BSP	835	1.63
Ram Pal Singh		JNP(JP)	407	0.79
Rest (All Other Candidates)		Others	795	1.56

Election: 2003	Turnout (%): 48.52	Party	Actual Vote	Vote (%)
Kiran Walia – W		INC	23,561	56.56
Arti Mehra – W		BJP	16,637	39.94
Kamal Kishor		BJS	420	1.01
Kishan Gaur		NCP	369	0.89
Sanjay		LJP	221	0.53
Rest (All Other Candidates)		Others	452	1.07

Constituency: R. K. PURAM – 10

Election: 1993	Turnout (%): 50.43	Party	Actual Vote	Vote (%)
Bodh Raj		BJP	17,838	40.66
Usha Krishana Kumar – W		INC	16,178	36.88
Shanti Swaroop		JD	7,009	15.98
D. B. Thapliyal		Independent	1,044	2.38
Rama Kant		Independent	884	2.02
Rest (All Other Candidates)		Others	914	2.08

Election: 1998	Turnout (%): 35.96	Party	Actual Vote	Vote (%)
Ashok Singh		INC	20,509	45.97
Bodh Raj		BJP	17,152	38.44
Ajit Singh		Independent	4,779	10.71
Rajendra Singh		Independent	1,141	2.56
Nishan Singh Cheema		Independent	746	1.67
Rest (All Other Candidates)		Others	291	0.65

Election: 2003	Turnout (%): 40.27	Party	Actual Vote	Vote (%)
Barkha Singh – W		INC	22,591	53.98
Ajit Singh		BJP	17,006	40.64
Hiren Tokas		Independent	1,477	3.53
Inderjeet Singh Mehta		Independent	278	0.66
Kapoor Singh		BJS	242	0.58
Rest (All Other Candidates)		Others	255	0.61

Constituency: DELHI CANTONMENT – 11

Election: 1993	Turnout (%): 52.41	Party	Actual Vote	Vote (%)
Karan Singh Tanwar		BJP	23,260	59.85
Kiran Chaudhary – W		INC	14,391	37.03
Emanuel Massey		BSP	428	1.10
Jawahar Singh		JD	373	0.96
Mukh Ram		Independent	154	0.40
Rest (All Other Candidates)		Others	256	0.66

Election: 1998	Turnout (%): 44.39	Party	Actual Vote	Vote (%)
Kiran Choudhary – W		INC	23,445	51.94
Karan Singh Tanwar		BJP	20,819	46.12
Rajendra		Independent	356	0.79
Ashok Choudhary		Independent	202	0.45
Baljeet Singh		Independent	173	0.38
Rest (All Other Candidates)		Others	142	0.32
Election: 2003	Turnout (%): 53.68	Party	Actual Vote	Vote (%)
Karan Singh Tanwar		BJP	21,638	52.52
Kiran Choudhry – W		INC	17,872	43.38
Anil Mittar		NCP	695	1.69
Hemant Setia		Independent	241	0.58
Yogesh Kumar		Independent	190	0.46
Rest (All Other Candidates)		Others	564	1.37

Constituency: JANAK PURI – 12

Election: 1993	Turnout (%): 56.23	Party	Actual Vote	Vote (%)
Jagdish Mukhi		BJP	33,905	62.54
Shailender		INC	17,852	32.93
Kunwar Chatter Singh		JD	755	1.39
Hans Raj		BSP	420	0.77
Moji Ram		DND	197	0.36
Rest (All Other Candidates)		Others	1,087	2.01
Election: 1998	Turnout (%): 53.01	Party	Actual Vote	Vote (%)
Jagdish Mukhi		BJP	31,115	55.86
Shiv Kumar Sondhi		INC	23,415	42.04
Rajbir Singh		LKS	750	1.35
Rajender Kapoor		Independent	224	0.40
Naresh Malik		SHS	148	0.27
Rest (All Other Candidates)		Others	49	0.08

Election: 2003	Turnout (%): 57.95	Party	Actual Vote	Vote (%)
Jagdish Mukhi		BJP	35,281	59.69
Shiv Kumar Sondhi		INC	22,390	37.88
Anil Jain		SHS	433	0.73
Dinesh Jain		NCP	411	0.70
Satbir		Independent	148	0.25
Rest (All Other Candidates)		Others	442	0.75

Constituency: HARI NAGAR – 13

Election: 1993	Turnout (%): 62.75	Party	Actual Vote	Vote (%)
Harsharan Singh Balli		BJP	31,150	59.35
Onkar Singh Thapar		INC	14,251	27.15
Gurcharan Singh Bannar		JD	2,697	5.14
Gurudayal		BSP	997	1.90
Jai Dev Vashist		ICS	778	1.48
Rest (All Other Candidates)		Others	2,609	4.98

Election: 1998	Turnout (%): 51.63	Party	Actual Vote	Vote (%)
Harsharan Singh Balli		BJP	29,136	49.79
O. P. Wadhwa		INC	28,519	48.74
Rajinder Singh		SP	333	0.57
Afroz Khan		JD	242	0.41
Navrung Paul		Independent	129	0.22
Rest (All Other Candidates)		Others	159	0.27

Election: 2003	Turnout (%): 58.61	Party	Actual Vote	Vote (%)
Harsharan Singh Balli		BJP	32,971	54.86
O. P. Wadhwa		INC	26,180	43.56
Ambika – W		Independent	342	0.57
Prakash Chauhan – W		NCP	281	0.47
Brij Raj Bhola		Independent	138	0.23
Rest (All Other Candidates)		Others	190	0.31

Constituency: TILAK NAGAR – 14

Election: 1993	Turnout (%): 63.87	Party	Actual Vote	Vote (%)
O. P. Babbar		BJP	33,911	62.04
Tervinder Singh Marwah		INC	17,341	31.73
Mukhtar Singh		JD	864	1.58
Dinesh Jain		JNP(JP)	857	1.57
Manjeet Singh		BSP	399	0.73
Rest (All Other Candidates)		Others	1,284	2.35

Election: 1998	Turnout (%): 51.01	Party	Actual Vote	Vote (%)
Jaspal Singh		INC	27,240	49.22
O. P. Babbar		BJP	25,724	46.48
Mannu Devi – W		BSP	414	0.75
Sudhir Bathla		Independent	385	0.70
Ranjit Singh		SP	330	0.60
Rest (All Other Candidates)		Others	1,250	2.25

Election: 2003	Turnout (%): 60.45	Party	Actual Vote	Vote (%)
O. P. Babbar		BJP	32,298	51.97
Jaspal Singh		INC	26,670	42.91
S. Gurcharan Singh		BSP	1,397	2.25
Ramesh Yadav		NCP	854	1.37
Bharat Bhusan		Independent	289	0.46
Rest (All Other Candidates)		Others	645	1.04

Constituency: RAJOURI GARDEN – 15

Election: 1993	Turnout (%): 66.25	Party	Actual Vote	Vote (%)
Ajay Makan		INC	28,075	50.95
Manohar Lal Kumar		BJP	24,524	44.51
Jai Prakash Tyagi		JD	1,454	2.64
Gurcharan Singh		Independent	203	0.37
Narinder		Independent	144	0.26
Rest (All Other Candidates)		Others	700	1.27

Election: 1998	Turnout (%): 50.62	Party	Actual Vote	Vote (%)
Ajay Makan		INC	36,060	65.73
Sashi Prabha Arya – W		BJP	16,763	30.55
Shakuntala – W		BSP	1,094	1.99
Subhash Bairwa		Independent	367	0.67
Jagdish Parshad Nainawat		Independent	233	0.42
Rest (All Other Candidates)		Others	345	0.64
Election: 2003	Turnout (%): 57.91	Party	Actual Vote	Vote (%)
Ajay Makan		INC	39,515	69.03
Sarabjit Singh		BJP	15,028	26.25
Sarup Singh Tur		RSP(U)	656	1.15
Moti Lal Bairwa		Independent	605	1.06
Subhash Chander		SHS	428	0.75
Rest (All Other Candidates)		Others	1,010	1.76

Constituency: MADIPUR (SC) – 16

Election: 1993	Turnout (%): 63.42	Party	Actual Vote	Vote (%)
Swarup Chand Rajan		BJP	28,861	51.10
Mala Ram Gangwal		INC	23,986	42.47
B. L. Gautam		JD	1,797	3.18
Kanta Devi – W		CPI	886	1.57
Roop Singh Ahirwar		BSP	512	0.91
Rest (All Other Candidates)		Others	441	0.77
Election: 1998	Turnout (%): 51.94	Party	Actual Vote	Vote (%)
Mala Ram Gangwal		INC	33,639	55.38
Laxman Singh Atal		BJP	25,543	42.06
Roop Singh Ahirwar		BSP	1,184	1.95
Naval Kishore		Independent	183	0.30
Om Parkash Phulwaria		RPI	146	0.24
Rest (All Other Candidates)		Others	42	0.07

Election: 2003	Turnout (%): 55.20	Party	Actual Vote	Vote (%)
Mala Ram Gangwal		INC	33,329	50.96
Kailash		BJP	26,990	41.27
Radhey Shyam		SP	2,328	3.56
Naval Kishore Bilunia		Independent	1,891	2.89
Kalu Ram		INLP	382	0.58
Rest (All Other Candidates)		Others	486	0.74

Constituency: TRI NAGAR – 17

Election: 1993	Turnout (%): 70.44	Party	Actual Vote	Vote (%)
Nand Kishore Garg		BJP	28,872	55.55
Deep Chandd Sharma		INC	20,199	38.86
Nathu Singh Garg		JD	1,202	2.31
Raj Kumar Goel		SHS	497	0.96
Suresh Kumar		Independent	339	0.65
Rest (All Other Candidates)		Others	870	1.67

Election: 1998	Turnout (%): 53.26	Party	Actual Vote	Vote (%)
Nand Kishore Garg		BJP	25,776	51.09
Chattar Singh		INC	23,493	46.56
Shiv Kumar		SP	543	1.08
Vikram Singh Khari		Independent	244	0.48
Nathu Singh Garg		SAP	200	0.40
Rest (All Other Candidates)		Others	197	0.39

Election: 2003	Turnout (%): 60.11	Party	Actual Vote	Vote (%)
Anil Bhardwaj		INC	32,449	56.47
Nand Kishore Garg		BJP	23,958	41.70
Humayun Khan		Independent	393	0.68
Raj Kumar		NCP	289	0.50
Satish Bhati		Independent	197	0.34
Rest (All Other Candidates)		Others	172	0.31

Constituency: SHAKURBASTI – 18

Election: 1993	Turnout (%): 69.55	Party	Actual Vote	Vote (%)
Gauri Shankar Bhardwaj		BJP	28,933	51.45
Kamal Kant Sharma		INC	21,437	38.12
Suresh Yadav		JD	2,289	4.07
Sukh Charan Kapil		BSP	1,701	3.02
Vijay Bhatia		CPM	499	0.89
Rest (All Other Candidates)		Others	1,378	2.45
Election: 1998	Turnout (%): 54.50	Party	Actual Vote	Vote (%)
S. C. Vats		INC	36,010	56.14
Gauri Shankar Bhardwaj		BJP	27,371	42.67
Pradeep		Independent	417	0.65
Deepak Kumar Gupta		JNP(JP)	184	0.29
Ajay Shrivastava		SHS	166	0.25
Rest (All Other Candidates)		Others	–	–
Election: 2003	Turnout (%): 58.26	Party	Actual Vote	Vote (%)
S. C. Vats		INC	39,200	56.21
Shyam Lal Garg		BJP	25,200	36.14
Banwari Lal Nagpal		Independent	3,473	4.98
Pappu		SP	317	0.45
Sanjay		Independent	305	0.44
Rest (All Other Candidates)		Others	1,241	1.78

Constituency: SHALIMAR BAGH – 19

Election: 1993	Turnout (%): 67.91	Party	Actual Vote	Vote (%)
Sahib Singh Verma		BJP	40,077	65.21
S. C. Vats		INC	18,307	29.79
Joginder Singh		JD	1,328	2.16
Amar Singh		BSP	892	1.45
Ravi Chambail		Independent	175	0.28
Rest (All Other Candidates)		Others	684	1.11

Election: 1998	Turnout (%): 52.55	Party	Actual Vote	Vote (%)
Ravinder Nath Bansal		BJP	32,623	57.37
Sarla Kaushik – W		INC	22,618	39.77
Krishan Kumar Aggarwal		Independent	656	1.15
O. P. Mittal		Independent	551	0.97
Jagdish Chandra		BSP	305	0.54
Rest (All Other Candidates)		Others	113	0.20
Election: 2003	Turnout (%): 56.74	Party	Actual Vote	Vote (%)
Ravinder Nath Bansal		BJP	34,288	54.68
B. S. Walia		INC	27,404	43.70
Ramji Lal		Independent	207	0.33
Ramesh Dhawan		JPJD	201	0.32
Sushil Jain		SHS	160	0.26
Rest (All Other Candidates)		Others	443	0.71

Constituency: BADLI – 20

Election: 1993	Turnout (%): 60.52	Party	Actual Vote	Vote (%)
Jai Bhagwan Aggarwal		BJP	30,420	48.75
Rajesh Yadav		INC	20,588	32.99
Satish Yadav		JD	5,507	8.82
Phool Chand		BSP	3,015	4.83
Ramesh Chandra Sharma		DPP	1,320	2.12
Rest (All Other Candidates)		Others	1,553	2.49
Election: 1998	Turnout (%): 45.86	Party	Actual Vote	Vote (%)
Jai Bhagwan Aggarwal		BJP	42,259	47.95
Narain Singh Yadav		INC	37,822	42.91
Phool Chand		BSP	3,808	4.32
Ramesh Chander Sharma		SAP	2,509	2.85
Manmeet Singh		Independent	997	1.13
Rest (All Other Candidates)		Others	741	0.84

Election: 2003	Turnout (%): 47.88	Party	Actual Vote	Vote (%)
Jai Bhagwan Aggarwal		BJP	69,189	53.33
Dharam Vir Yadav		INC	52,625	40.56
Ramesh Chander		BSP	4,340	3.34
Lakhan Singh		LP(S)	750	0.58
Basuki Nath Chaudhary		RJD	566	0.44
Rest (All Other Candidates)		Others	2,278	1.75

Constituency: SAHIBABAD DAULATPUR – 21

Election: 1993	Turnout (%): 55.87	Party	Actual Vote	Vote (%)
Jet Ram Solanki		BJP	25,372	48.02
Ishwar Singh		INC	16,676	31.56
Chander Prakash		BSP	3,392	6.42
Deep Chand		JD	2,860	5.41
Anand Jain Chandiwala		DPP	1,882	3.56
Rest (All Other Candidates)		Others	2,653	5.03

Election: 1998	Turnout (%): 49.00	Party	Actual Vote	Vote (%)
Ramesh Kumr		INC	35,328	44.54
Kulwant Rana		BJP	25,529	32.18
Ravinder Kumr Gupta		Independent	7,620	9.61
Hari Singh		BSP	4,040	5.09
Kanwar Singh		SHS	1,430	1.80
Rest (All Other Candidates)		Others	5,374	6.78

Election: 2003	Turnout (%): 53.84	Party	Actual Vote	Vote (%)
Kulwant Rana		BJP	48,528	47.83
Ramesh Kumar		INC	42,672	42.06
Asgar Imam		BSP	7,054	6.95
Jit Ram		INLDR	727	0.72
Satpal		Independent	509	0.50
Rest (All Other Candidates)		Others	1,976	1.94

Constituency: BAWANA (SC) – 22

Election: 1993	Turnout (%): 58.04	Party	Actual Vote	Vote (%)
Chand Ram		BJP	18,383	35.48
Rajender Singh		JD	16,188	31.24
Om Prakash Ranga		INC	14,876	28.71
Udai Singh Kataria		Independent	1,059	2.04
R. P. Gautam		BSP	754	1.46
Rest (All Other Candidates)		Others	555	1.07
Election: 1998	Turnout (%): 43.81	Party	Actual Vote	Vote (%)
Surender Kumar		INC	40,241	59.18
Om Parkash Rang		Independent	14,543	21.39
Hem Chander		INLDR	8,588	12.63
Ram Palat Gautam		BSP	2,282	3.36
Talewar		Independent	980	1.44
Rest (All Other Candidates)		Others	1,368	2.00
Election: 2003	Turnout (%): 52.97	Party	Actual Vote	Vote (%)
Surender Kumar		INC	50,327	50.81
Rajkumar		BJP	35,805	36.15
Sanjay Kumar		BSP	5,423	5.47
Neelam Kinner – W		Independent	1,851	1.87
Ved Parkash		Independent	1,703	1.72
Rest (All Other Candidates)		Others	3,942	3.98

Constituency: SULTANPUR MAJRA (SC) – 23

Election: 1993	Turnout (%): 61.25	Party	Actual Vote	Vote (%)
Jai Kishan		INC	20,890	37.75
Nand Ram Bagri		JD	13,478	24.36
Bhagwan Dass		BJP	12,562	22.70
Jagdhari Lal		BSP	2,893	5.23
Mangat Ram		Independent	2,252	4.07
Rest (All Other Candidates)		Others	3,261	5.89

Election: 1998	Turnout (%): 55.47	Party	Actual Vote	Vote (%)
Sushila Devi – W		INC	34,194	56.79
Kailash		BJP	17,261	28.67
Kiran Devi – W		BSP	3,085	5.12
Nand Ram Bagri		Independent	2,646	4.39
Ranbir Singh		JD	1,695	2.82
Rest (All Other Candidates)		Others	1,327	2.21
Election: 2003	Turnout (%): 58.77	Party	Actual Vote	Vote (%)
Jai Kishan		INC	36,164	52.27
Satish Kumar		BJP	17,243	24.92
Bhagwan Das		BSP	10,812	15.63
Nand Ram Bagri		LJP	1,550	2.24
Mangat Ram		SP	1,139	1.65
Rest (All Other Candidates)		Others	2,281	3.29

Constituency: MANGOLPURI (SC) – 24

Election: 1993	Turnout (%): 65.77	Party	Actual Vote	Vote (%)
Raj Kumar Chauhan		INC	21,344	41.50
Soran Singh Nirala		BJP	13,681	26.60
Tej Singh		JD	7,207	14.01
Daya Ram		BSP	5,569	10.83
Kameshwar Prasad		CPM	814	1.58
Rest (All Other Candidates)		Others	2,813	5.48
Election: 1998	Turnout (%): 56.25	Party	Actual Vote	Vote (%)
Raj Kumar Chauhan		INC	32,372	60.80
Lakshmi Narayan		BJP	11,358	21.33
Mahender Singh		BSP	6,707	12.60
Suraj Pal		RJD	1,500	2.82
Tej Singh		JD	844	1.59
Rest (All Other Candidates)		Others	459	0.86

Election: 2003	Turnout (%): 57.14	Party	Actual Vote	Vote (%)
Rajkumar Chauhan		INC	39,147	68.34
Megh Singh		BSP	8,832	15.42
Raju Balmiki		BJP	8,670	15.14
Shyam Kaur – W		BRPP	633	1.10
Rest (All Other Candidates)		Others	–	–

Constituency: NANGLOI JAT – 25

Election: 1993	Turnout (%): 62.38	Party	Actual Vote	Vote (%)
Davinder Singh		BJP	28,427	54.13
Bharat Singh		INC	16,287	31.02
Anil Yadav		JD	5,457	10.39
K. D. Sharma		Independent	691	1.32
Vijay Kr Rana		JNP(JP)	443	0.84
Rest (All Other Candidates)		Others	1,208	2.30

Election: 1998	Turnout (%): 43.38	Party	Actual Vote	Vote (%)
Prem Chand		INC	30,533	49.00
Devender Singh		BJP	27,706	44.46
Panmeshwari – W		SAP	1,149	1.84
Arvind Kataria		BSP	682	1.09
Jai Parkash		JD	560	0.90
Rest (All Other Candidates)		Others	1,683	2.71

Election: 2003	Turnout (%): 54.43	Party	Actual Vote	Vote (%)
Bijender Singh		INC	42,158	52.75
Devinder Singh		BJP	34,116	42.69
Mohinder Yadav		SP	1,937	2.42
Ramesh Kumar		Independent	478	0.60
Om Bir Prasad Sharma		RPD	290	0.36
Rest (All Other Candidates)		Others	942	1.18

Constituency: VISHNU GARDEN – 26

Election: 1993	Turnout (%): 58.58	Party	Actual Vote	Vote (%)
Mahinder Singh Saathi		INC	17,962	35.46
Daya Nand Chandila		Independent	12,252	24.18
R. P. Singh		BJP	11,086	21.88
Balwinder Singh Talwandi		JD	7,090	13.99
Satnam Singh		JNP(JP)	807	1.59
Rest (All Other Candidates)		Others	1,464	2.90

Election: 1998	Turnout (%): 46.83	Party	Actual Vote	Vote (%)
Mahinder Singh Sathi		INC	21,612	40.42
Dayanand Chandila		JMM	17,375	32.50
Dhanwant Singh		BJP	9,763	18.26
Gurcharan Singh Babbar		Independent	1,889	3.53
Pritpal Singh Pali		SAD(M)	1,393	2.61
Rest (All Other Candidates)		Others	1,436	2.68

Election: 2003	Turnout (%): 56.18	Party	Actual Vote	Vote (%)
A. Dayanand Chandila A.		BJP	31,211	50.78
Mahender Singh Sathi		INC	27,951	45.48
Harisharan Jeet Singh		NCP	1,157	1.88
Ravinder Yadav		SP	337	0.55
Ravinder Singh		Independent	325	0.53
Rest (All Other Candidates)		Others	483	0.78

Constituency: HASTSAL – 27

Election: 1993	Turnout (%): 60.72	Party	Actual Vote	Vote (%)
Mukesh Sharma		INC	25,193	36.97
Kamla Choudhary – W		BJP	17,723	26.01
Rajesh Gahlot		JD	12,251	17.98
Karan Yadav		Independent	11,178	16.40
Ramesh Kumar		JNP(JP)	755	1.11
Rest (All Other Candidates)		Others	1,048	1.53

Election: 1998	Turnout (%): 49.49	Party	Actual Vote	Vote (%)
Mukesh Sharma		INC	48,146	52.79
Naresh Tyagi		BJP	24,858	27.26
Karan Yadav		SAP	14,006	15.36
Raj Bharti – W		BSP	2,858	3.13
Ravi Kumar		Independent	346	0.38
Rest (All Other Candidates)		Others	986	1.08
Election: 2003	Turnout (%): 55.00	Party	Actual Vote	Vote (%)
Mukesh Sharma		INC	70,495	48.57
Rajesh – W		BJP	51,207	35.28
Rajender		NCP	14,135	9.74
Kishan Singh		BSP	5,794	3.99
Mehar Singh		Independent	738	0.51
Rest (All Other Candidates)		Others	2,768	1.91

Constituency: NAJAFGARH – 28

Election: 1993	Turnout (%): 66.42	Party	Actual Vote	Vote (%)
Suraj Parshad		Independent	19,582	35.23
Ran Singh		BJP	14,203	25.55
Jai Om Dagar		JD	8,785	15.81
Ram Kala		INC	8,629	15.53
Rameshwar		BSP	2,487	4.47
Rest (All Other Candidates)		Others	1,894	3.41
Election: 1998	Turnout (%): 61.48	Party	Actual Vote	Vote (%)
Kanwal Singh		INC	21,111	28.02
Jai Kishan Sharma		Independent	19,284	25.60
Pritam Singh		INLDR	15,382	20.42
Jagbir		RJD	6,244	8.29
Jai Om Dagar		Independent	5,980	7.94
Rest (All Other Candidates)		Others	7,338	9.73

Election: 2003	Turnout (%): 58.63	Party	Actual Vote	Vote (%)
Ranbir Singh		Independent	43,342	46.90
Kanwal Singh		INC	26,252	28.41
Jai Om Dagar		BJP	7,970	8.62
Bharat Singh		INLDR	7,460	8.07
Subhash		BSP	5,638	6.10
Rest (All Other Candidates)		Others	1,744	1.90

Constituency: NASIRPUR – 29

Election: 1993	Turnout (%): 58.82	Party	Actual Vote	Vote (%)
Vinod Kumar Sharma		BJP	23,070	38.76
Inder Singh Solanki		INC	21,012	35.31
Gian Singh		Independent	4,687	7.88
Ramzan Khan		JD	3,952	6.64
Mahender Singh		BSP	3,413	5.73
Rest (All Other Candidates)		Others	3,379	5.68

Election: 1998	Turnout (%): 43.43	Party	Actual Vote	Vote (%)
Mahabal Mishra		INC	37,774	48.28
Vinod Kumar Sharma		BJP	36,344	46.45
Ahibaran Kumar		BSP	1,860	2.38
Brij Kishor Singh		SAP	707	0.90
Raghunandan Paswan		RJD	240	0.31
Rest (All Other Candidates)		Others	1,321	1.68

Election: 2003	Turnout (%): 55.75	Party	Actual Vote	Vote (%)
Mahabal Mishra		INC	45,948	46.45
Vinod Kumar Sharma		Independent	40,430	40.87
Chandrika Thakur		BJP	4,660	4.71
Satya Prakash Swami		BSP	2,845	2.88
Kapil Kumar		SP	806	0.81
Rest (All Other Candidates)		Others	4,233	4.28

Constituency: PALAM – 30

Election: 1993	Turnout (%): 58.51	Party	Actual Vote	Vote (%)
Dharam Dev Solanki		BJP	20,671	41.23
Mukhtyar Singh		INC	16,613	33.13
Sukhbir Singh Solanki		JD	10,655	21.25
Tikam Singh		BSP	1,233	2.46
Ram Rattan Doohan		Independent	336	0.67
Rest (All Other Candidates)		Others	630	1.26
Election: 1998	Turnout (%): 46.31	Party	Actual Vote	Vote (%)
Mahender Yadav		INC	32,699	48.62
Dharam Dev Solanki		BJP	27,152	40.37
Jasbir Singh Solanki		Independent	2,196	3.27
Sarnam Singh Pal		BSP	1,889	2.81
Mahender Yadav		RJD	1,869	2.78
Rest (All Other Candidates)		Others	1,453	2.15
Election: 2003	Turnout (%): 48.77	Party	Actual Vote	Vote (%)
Dharam Dev Solanki		BJP	43,521	47.95
Sumesh		INC	41,204	45.40
L. C. Sharma		BSP	3,496	3.85
Harish Chander Jha		Independent	488	0.54
Anil Kumar Chand		RSP(U)	463	0.51
Rest (All Other Candidates)		Others	1,582	1.75

Constituency: MAHIPALPUR – 31

Election: 1993	Turnout (%): 57.64	Party	Actual Vote	Vote (%)
Satparkash Rana		BJP	17,848	36.27
Vijay Singh Lochav		INC	14,706	29.89
Yudhvir Singh		JD	11,604	23.58
Dhanvir Singh		Independent	3,087	6.27
V. Shekhar		Independent	1,066	2.17
Rest (All Other Candidates)		Others	891	1.82

Election: 1998	Turnout (%): 44.74	Party	Actual Vote	Vote (%)
Mahender Singh		INC	31,818	51.92
Surat Singh		INLDR	14,984	24.45
Yudhvir Singh		LD	8,276	13.51
Inder Malik		BSP	4,748	7.75
Ram Mehar		SJP(R)	623	1.02
Rest (All Other Candidates)		Others	831	1.35
Election: 2003	Turnout (%): 53.33	Party	Actual Vote	Vote (%)
Vijay Singh Lochav		INC	30,230	45.74
Sat Parkash Rana		BJP	25,272	38.23
Dinesh Kumar		BSP	5,975	9.04
Hariom		SP	1,706	2.58
Virender		INLDR	1,093	1.65
Rest (All Other Candidates)		Others	1,821	2.76

Constituency: MEHRAULI – 32

Election: 1993	Turnout (%): 61.58	Party	Actual Vote	Vote (%)
Brahm Singh Tanwar		BJP	24,396	46.27
Balram Singh Tanwar		INC	17,375	32.95
Nathu Singh		JD	8,889	16.86
Srichand		CPI	1,355	2.57
Balraj		Independent	350	0.66
Rest (All Other Candidates)		Others	360	0.69
Election: 1998	Turnout (%): 51.88	Party	Actual Vote	Vote (%)
Bhram Singh Tanwar		BJP	24,996	37.44
Balram Tanwar		Independent	22,389	33.53
Vijay Deep		INC	17,427	26.10
Kiran Singh		Independent	480	0.72
Ranjeet		JD	385	0.58
Rest (All Other Candidates)		Others	1,088	1.63

Election: 2003	Turnout (%): 56.37	Party	Actual Vote	Vote (%)
Balram Tanwar		INC	40,595	56.48
Brahm Singh Tanwar		BJP	28,939	40.26
Baljeet Singh Deswal		BSP	781	1.09
Raghvinder Bakshi		Independent	641	0.89
Kiran Singh		SHS	442	0.61
Rest (All Other Candidates)		Others	482	0.67

Constituency: SAKET – 33

Election: 1993	Turnout (%): 56.02	Party	Actual Vote	Vote (%)
Tek Chand		INC	13,687	32.38
Raj Rawat – W		BJP	12,938	30.61
Narjeet Singh		JD	9,041	21.39
Braham Prakash		Independent	5,454	12.90
Guru Charan		BSP	490	1.16
Rest (All Other Candidates)		Others	658	1.56

Election: 1998	Turnout (%): 44.26	Party	Actual Vote	Vote (%)
Tek Chand Sharma		INC	24,903	40.68
Vijay Jolly		BJP	17,729	28.96
Manoj Choudhary		JD	9,426	15.40
Chhotey Lal Chandra		BSP	3,073	5.02
Narjit Singh Yadav		RJD	2,983	4.87
Rest (All Other Candidates)		Others	3,102	5.07

Election: 2003	Turnout (%): 48.18	Party	Actual Vote	Vote (%)
Vijay Jolly		BJP	17,323	29.12
Rohit Manchanda		INC	17,202	28.92
Satish Gupta		Independent	13,229	22.24
Suresh		LJP	5,536	9.31
Tejpal		BSP	2,962	4.98
Rest (All Other Candidates)		Others	3,235	5.43

Constituency: AMBEDKAR NAGAR (SC) – 34

Election: 1993	Turnout (%): 61.13	Party	Actual Vote	Vote (%)
Premsingh		INC	19,621	43.85
Rajender Kumar Sonker		BJP	11,056	24.71
Sat Pal		JD	5,801	12.96
Rajbir		CPM	3,841	8.58
Ram Narayan		Independent	1,684	3.76
Rest (All Other Candidates)		Others	2,742	6.14
Election: 1998	**Turnout (%): 52.51**	**Party**	**Actual Vote**	**Vote (%)**
Ch Prem Singh		INC	27,670	52.93
Jagdish Bharti		BJP	9,662	18.48
Rajbir		CPM	3,614	6.91
Seva Das		BSP	3,330	6.37
Rajesh Chouhan		Independent	2,185	4.18
Rest (All Other Candidates)		Others	5,812	11.13
Election: 2003	**Turnout (%): 54.07**	**Party**	**Actual Vote**	**Vote (%)**
Ch Prem Singh		INC	25,880	53.15
Suresh Chand		BJP	17,519	35.98
Kailash		BSP	3,679	7.56
Siya Ram		SHS	587	1.21
Narender Malawaliya		IJP	463	0.95
Rest (All Other Candidates)		Others	567	1.15

Constituency: TUGHLAKABAD – 35

Election: 1993	Turnout (%): 61.13	Party	Actual Vote	Vote (%)
Shish Pal		Independent	14,683	30.52
Shyama Sinha – W		INC	12,151	25.25
Ramesh Bidhuri		BJP	10,434	21.68
Manoj Choudhary		JD	8,290	17.23
Dharamvir Singh		BSP	1,812	3.77
Rest (All Other Candidates)		Others	747	1.55

Election: 1998	Turnout (%): 49.64	Party	Actual Vote	Vote (%)
Shish Pal Singh		INC	39,551	49.59
Ramesh Bidhuri		BJP	30,672	38.45
Dharam Vir Singh		BSP	3,342	4.19
Babu Lal		Independent	2,834	3.55
Sunil Mehta		Independent	683	0.86
Rest (All Other Candidates)		Others	2,681	3.36
Election: 2003	Turnout (%): 55.56	Party	Actual Vote	Vote (%)
Ramesh Bidhuri		BJP	41,523	50.10
Shish Pal Singh		Independent	17,540	21.16
Vir Singh		INC	13,001	15.69
Anand Kumar Gupta		BSP	7,379	8.90
Durga Devi – W		Independent	675	0.81
Rest (All Other Candidates)		Others	2,767	3.34

Constituency: BADARPUR – 36

Election: 1993	Turnout (%): 57.25	Party	Actual Vote	Vote (%)
Ram Vir Singh Bidhuri		JD	22,102	41.61
Ram Singh Netaji		INC	15,036	28.31
Lajja Ram		BJP	10,697	20.14
Chander Pal		BSP	2,823	5.31
Jagdish		CPM	747	1.41
Rest (All Other Candidates)		Others	1,714	3.22
Election: 1998	Turnout (%): 44.65	Party	Actual Vote	Vote (%)
Ram Singh Netaji		Independent	40,548	45.50
Ramvir Singh Bidhuri		INC	26,259	29.46
Suraj Bhan		BJP	8,858	9.94
Chander Pal		BSP	5,075	5.69
Inder Raj Singh		Independent	2,361	2.65
Rest (All Other Candidates)		Others	6,025	6.76

Election: 2003	Turnout (%): 47.17	Party	Actual Vote	Vote (%)
Rabmir Singh Bidhuri		NCP	40,224	38.31
Ram Singh Netaji		INC	39,788	37.89
Brahm Singh		BSP	14,976	14.26
Virender Bahadur Singh		BJP	4,923	4.69
Gyasi Lal Sharma		RJD	1,891	1.80
Rest (All Other Candidates)		Others	3,203	3.05

Constituency: TRILOK PURI (SC) – 37

Election: 1993	Turnout (%): 57.48	Party	Actual Vote	Vote (%)
Brahm Pal		INC	17,844	37.26
Ram Charan Gujrati		BJP	14,989	31.30
Mange Ram		JD	10,088	21.07
Hari Das		BSP	4,203	8.78
Kanwar Pal		BKD	163	0.34
Rest (All Other Candidates)		Others	600	1.25

Election: 1998	Turnout (%): 48.61	Party	Actual Vote	Vote (%)
Brahm Pal		INC	22,887	43.79
Ram Charan		BJP	18,116	34.66
Ganga Ram Bairwa		BSP	9,419	18.02
Ramji Lal		Independent	448	0.86
Kamal Kishore		JD	335	0.64
Rest (All Other Candidates)		Others	1,062	2.03

Election: 2003	Turnout (%): 52.53	Party	Actual Vote	Vote (%)
Brahm Pal		INC	26,469	39.82
Sunil Kumar		BJP	20,254	30.47
Ganga Ram		BSP	13,938	20.97
A. Vijay Pal		LJP	2,307	3.47
Pritam		JD(U)	951	1.43
Rest (All Other Candidates)		Others	2,551	3.84

Constituency: PATPARGANJ (SC) – 38

Election: 1993	Turnout (%): 55.88	Party	Actual Vote	Vote (%)
Gyan Chand		BJP	17,020	35.69
Amrish Singh Goutam		JD	14,873	31.18
Rame		INC	14,065	29.49
Sakuntala – W		BSP	703	1.47
Kehar Singh		CPI	394	0.83
Rest (All Other Candidates)		Others	639	1.34

Election: 1998	Turnout (%): 44.98	Party	Actual Vote	Vote (%)
Amrish Singh Gautam		INC	33,351	58.06
Ganga Ram Pipal		BJP	17,030	29.65
Rajveer Singh		BSP	4,363	7.60
Bachan Singh		Independent	722	1.26
Ranjana – W		UKD	650	1.13
Rest (All Other Candidates)		Others	1,325	2.30

Election: 2003	Turnout (%): 47.29	Party	Actual Vote	Vote (%)
Amrish Singh Gautam		INC	36,930	53.37
Gian Chand		BJP	18,932	27.36
Dhani Ram Shankhwar		BSP	11,322	16.36
Sunil		SHS	637	0.92
Madanlal		SP	569	0.82
Rest (All Other Candidates)		Others	805	1.17

Constituency: MANDAWALI – 39

Election: 1993	Turnout (%): 56.18	Party	Actual Vote	Vote (%)
M. S. Panwar		BJP	20,872	46.51
Ashutosh Upreti		INC	12,273	27.35
C. P. Singh		JD	7,927	17.66
Dal Chand		BSP	930	2.07
D. P. Singh		CPI	921	2.05
Rest (All Other Candidates)		Others	1,953	4.36

Election: 1998	Turnout (%): 45.63	Party	Actual Vote	Vote (%)
Meera Bhardwaj – W		INC	24,150	43.62
Murari Singh Panwar		BJP	22,307	40.29
Shripal Singh		BSP	2,945	5.32
Vijay Sharma		Independent	1,408	2.54
Prahlad Singh Gusain		JD	901	1.63
Rest (All Other Candidates)		Others	3,651	6.60
Election: 2003	Turnout (%): 44.67	Party	Actual Vote	Vote (%)
Meera Bhardwaj – W		INC	27,409	42.64
Virender Juyal		BJP	21,175	32.94
Madan Singh		BSP	9,754	15.17
Ashutosh Upreti		NCP	1,872	2.91
Rishikesh Nishkar		JD(U)	1,415	2.20
Rest (All Other Candidates)		Others	2,653	4.14

Constituency: GEETA COLONY – 40

Election: 1993	Turnout (%): 68.98	Party	Actual Vote	Vote (%)
K. Walia		INC	27,265	49.90
Radhey Sham		BJP	24,394	44.65
Surat Singh Bhadoria		JD	2,007	3.67
Rajinder		Independent	197	0.36
Ishwar Dutt Sharma		SHS	185	0.34
Rest (All Other Candidates)		Others	589	1.08
Election: 1998	Turnout (%): 48.38	Party	Actual Vote	Vote (%)
Ashok Kumar Walia		INC	40,094	67.16
Darshan Kumar Bahal		BJP	17,124	28.68
Mool Chand		BSP	908	1.52
Rajiv Nagar		JD	693	1.16
Anil Kumar		Independent	220	0.37
Rest (All Other Candidates)		Others	662	1.11

Election: 2003	Turnout (%): 56.03	Party	Actual Vote	Vote (%)
Ashok Kumar Walia		INC	45,163	66.32
Naveen Kumar		BJP	20,311	29.83
Subhash		BSP	1,378	2.02
Sanjay Kumar		Independent	388	0.57
Surinder		Independent	373	0.55
Rest (All Other Candidates)		Others	484	0.71

Constituency: GANDHI NAGAR – 41

Election: 1993	Turnout (%): 68.24	Party	Actual Vote	Vote (%)
Darshan Kumar Bahl		BJP	23,093	46.76
Pyare Lal Ghee Waley		INC	20,176	40.86
Chowdhary Dharam Singh		JD	3,703	7.50
Narinder Kaur – W		Independent	431	0.87
Ashok Pathak		Independent	276	0.56
Rest (All Other Candidates)		Others	1,704	3.45

Election: 1998	Turnout (%): 57.58	Party	Actual Vote	Vote (%)
Arvinder Singh		INC	21,905	41.67
Swinderjit Singh Bajwa		BJP	15,143	28.81
Raghuvir Singh Jain		Independent	8,144	15.49
Naveen Chaudhary		Independent	5,159	9.81
Sanjay Kumar Gahlot		BSP	1,468	2.79
Rest (All Other Candidates)		Others	751	1.43

Election: 2003	Turnout (%): 56.19	Party	Actual Vote	Vote (%)
Arvinder Singh Lovely		INC	35,791	73.53
Tarjeet Singh		BJP	11,806	24.25
Ram Pratap Yadav		Independent	257	0.53
Arvind Kumar Kashyap		IJP	179	0.37
Rakesh Kumar		SHS	161	0.33
Rest (All Other Candidates)		Others	483	0.99

Constituency: KRISHNA NAGAR – 42

Election: 1993	Turnout (%): 70.87	Party	Actual Vote	Vote (%)
Harsh Vardhan		BJP	30,537	53.94
Balvinder Singh		INC	18,118	32.00
Virender Gaur		JD	4,239	7.49
Jai Prakash Sharma		ICS	2,133	3.77
Mahinder Bahal		Independent	383	0.68
Rest (All Other Candidates)		Others	1,201	2.12
Election: 1998	Turnout (%): 52.19	Party	Actual Vote	Vote (%)
Harsh Vardhan		BJP	30,358	54.82
S. N. Misra		INC	23,748	42.89
Virendra Kushwaha		BSP	567	1.02
Pramod Kumar		SHS	458	0.83
Krishna – W		JD	140	0.25
Rest (All Other Candidates)		Others	103	0.19
Election: 2003	Turnout (%): 61.76	Party	Actual Vote	Vote (%)
Harsh Vardhan		BJP	35,477	59.51
Narinder Kumar		INC	21,404	35.90
Praveen		Independent	868	1.46
Hukam Chand		Independent	712	1.19
Raj Bala – W		ABDUP	292	0.49
Rest (All Other Candidates)		Others	861	1.45

Constituency: VISHWASH NAGAR – 43

Election: 1993	Turnout (%): 65.53	Party	Actual Vote	Vote (%)
Madan Lal Gawa		BJP	27,711	50.47
Abjit Singh Gulati		INC	21,151	38.53
Ram Singh Thekedar		JD	4,519	8.23
Kamal Jeet		BSP	471	0.86
Surinder Kumar Ralli		DBP	451	0.82
Rest (All Other Candidates)		Others	598	1.09

Election: 1998	Turnout (%): 45.39	Party	Actual Vote	Vote (%)
Naseeb Singh		INC	30,380	48.18
Ved Vyas Mahajan		BJP	29,924	47.45
Narender Kumar		BSP	1,500	2.38
Surinder Kumar		Independent	621	0.98
Jai Chand		Independent	159	0.25
Rest (All Other Candidates)		Others	476	0.76
Election: 2003	Turnout (%): 53.02	Party	Actual Vote	Vote (%)
Naseeb Singh		INC	48,897	61.55
Madan Lal Gaba		BJP	26,948	33.92
Rakesh Tyagi		BSP	2,852	3.59
Vijay Sharma		Independent	265	0.33
Ramesh Kumar		Independent	101	0.13
Rest (All Other Candidates)		Others	380	0.48

Constituency: SHAHDARA – 44

Election: 1993	Turnout (%): 65.32	Party	Actual Vote	Vote (%)
Ram Niwas Goyal		BJP	28,253	53.32
Chaman Lal Yadav		INC	16,086	30.36
Ram Kishor Gupta		JD	4,549	8.58
Dal Chand		BSP	1,777	3.35
Rajesh Chand		Independent	567	1.07
Rest (All Other Candidates)		Others	1,756	3.32
Election: 1998	Turnout (%): 49.91	Party	Actual Vote	Vote (%)
Narender Nath		INC	29,929	55.86
Jyotsna Aggarwal – W		BJP	20,689	38.61
Dharmendra Kumar		BSP	1,130	2.11
Prayagraj Gupta		SHS	818	1.53
Mahinder Singh		JD	348	0.65
Rest (All Other Candidates)		Others	669	1.24

Election: 2003	Turnout (%): 56.87	Party	Actual Vote	Vote (%)
Narender Nath		INC	26,423	42.86
Jitender Singh Shunty		Independent	13,238	21.47
Ved Vyas Mahajan		BJP	13,155	21.34
Chaman Lal Yadav		BSP	8,032	13.03
Laxman Singh Sisodia		Independent	237	0.38
Rest (All Other Candidates)		Others	561	0.92

Constituency: SEEMAPURI (SC) – 45

Election: 1993	Turnout (%): 58.19	Party	Actual Vote	Vote (%)
Balbir Singh		BJP	14,579	38.80
Giri Lal		INC	12,817	34.11
Mam Chand Rewaria		JD	6,736	17.93
Bhoop Singh		Independent	1,266	3.37
Shri Nath		BSP	752	2.00
Rest (All Other Candidates)		Others	1,421	3.79

Election: 1998	Turnout (%): 51.70	Party	Actual Vote	Vote (%)
Veer Singh		INC	30,330	63.26
Chander Pal Singh		BJP	13,647	28.46
Brij Pal Singh		BSP	1,813	3.78
Madan Lal		SHS	571	1.19
K. K. Gothwal		ICS	430	0.90
Rest (All Other Candidates)		Others	1,157	2.41

Election: 2003	Turnout (%): 52.02	Party	Actual Vote	Vote (%)
Veer Singh Dhingan		INC	31,051	50.49
Kamala – W		BJP	13,961	22.70
Jai Bhagwan		BSP	6,749	10.97
Nand Kishor		NLP	5,673	9.23
Narayan Singh		SP	1,611	2.62
Rest (All Other Candidates)		Others	2,450	3.99

Constituency: NAND NAGARI (SC) – 46

Election: 1993	Turnout (%): 61.96	Party	Actual Vote	Vote (%)
Fateh Singh		BJP	13,429	30.18
Rup Chand		INC	12,648	28.42
Amar Pal Singh		JD	11,440	25.71
Bhim Sen		Independent	2,747	6.17
Pran Singh		BSP	2,091	4.70
Rest (All Other Candidates)		Others	2,147	4.82

Election: 1998	Turnout (%): 47.64	Party	Actual Vote	Vote (%)
Roop Chand		INC	25,742	46.78
Fateh Singh		BJP	15,006	27.27
Satish Kumar		BSP	6,997	12.72
Shishu Pal Singh		Independent	2,922	5.31
Rajesh Kumar		Independent	1,580	2.87
Rest (All Other Candidates)		Others	2,775	5.05

Election: 2003	Turnout (%): 54.28	Party	Actual Vote	Vote (%)
Baljor Singh		INC	30,408	44.65
Satish Kumar		BSP	19,063	27.99
Ranjit Singh		BJP	14,950	21.95
Ram Prakash		SP	734	1.08
Jeet Singh		RLD	648	0.95
Rest (All Other Candidates)		Others	2,306	3.38

Constituency: ROHTAS NAGAR – 47

Election: 1993	Turnout (%): 64.23	Party	Actual Vote	Vote (%)
Alok Kumar		BJP	24,324	47.12
Babu Krishan Lal		INC	16,508	31.98
Ratan		JD	8,148	15.78
Mahesh Chand		BSP	1,095	2.12
Dhanajay Kumar		SHS	256	0.50
Rest (All Other Candidates)		Others	1,290	2.50

Election: 1998	Turnout (%): 47.26	Party	Actual Vote	Vote (%)
Radhey Shyam Khanna		INC	22,746	43.19
Alok Kumar		BJP	22,579	42.87
Prem Prakash		BSP	3,497	6.64
Janardhan		Independent	1,465	2.78
Damodar Joshi		UKD	741	1.41
Rest (All Other Candidates)		Others	1,641	3.11

Election: 2003	Turnout (%): 60.44	Party	Actual Vote	Vote (%)
Ram Babub Sharma		INC	29,886	48.70
Alok Kumar		BJP	23,523	38.33
Surender		BSP	6,457	10.52
Dhannjoy		SHS	360	0.59
Puneet Dhawan		IPP	276	0.45
Rest (All Other Candidates)		Others	864	1.41

Constituency: BABARPUR – 48

Election: 1993	Turnout (%): 65.42	Party	Actual Vote	Vote (%)
Naresh Gaur		BJP	21,023	53.32
Bhopal Singh		INC	5,722	14.51
Rifaqt Ali		Independent	4,251	10.78
Sunil Vashist		Independent	3,241	8.22
Ishwar Pal		JD	2,985	7.57
Rest (All Other Candidates)		Others	2,203	5.60

Election: 1998	Turnout (%): 50.39	Party	Actual Vote	Vote (%)
Naresh Gaur		BJP	22,606	42.96
Abdul Hameed		INC	21,643	41.13
Sunil Vashisht		ICS	4,618	8.78
M. A. Chand		RAS	1,007	1.91
Usha Yadav – W		SP	899	1.71
Rest (All Other Candidates)		Others	1,842	3.51

Election: 2003	Turnout (%): 52.84	Party	Actual Vote	Vote (%)
Vinay Sharma		INC	25,630	47.52
Naresh Gaud		BJP	21,371	39.62
Mohd Said		NLP	2,617	4.85
Satya Narain Kaushik		Independent	1,479	2.74
Mohd Jafar		SP	703	1.30
Rest (All Other Candidates)		Others	2,134	3.97

Constituency: SEELAMPUR – 49

Election: 1993	Turnout (%): 71.21	Party	Actual Vote	Vote (%)
Chaudhry Mateen Ahmed		JD	16,518	42.54
Jai Kishan Dassgupta		BJP	15,080	38.84
Sultan Ahmed		INC	6,309	16.25
Nand Kishore Kashyap		JNP(JP)	244	0.63
Ayub Ali Khan		CPI	194	0.50
Rest (All Other Candidates)		Others	481	1.24

Election: 1998	Turnout (%): 54.88	Party	Actual Vote	Vote (%)
Chaudhry Mateen Ahmed		Independent	27,376	49.68
Data Ram		BJP	11,001	19.96
Salauddin		INC	7,497	13.60
Mohd Nahid		BSP	2,317	4.20
Sultan Ahmad		JD	2,148	3.90
Rest (All Other Candidates)		Others	4,771	8.66

Election: 2003	Turnout (%): 55.81	Party	Actual Vote	Vote (%)
Chaudhry Mateen Ahmed		INC	34,085	62.64
Sanjay Kumar Jain		BJP	12,373	22.74
Haji Ikram Hasan		JD(S)	5,323	9.78
Mohd Yusuf		NLP	1,060	1.95
Haider Ali		Independent	512	0.94
Rest (All Other Candidates)		Others	1,060	1.95

Constituency: GHONDA – 50

Election: 1993	Turnout (%): 65.60	Party	Actual Vote	Vote (%)
Lal Behari Tiwari		BJP	21,614	48.80
Dhiraj Singh		INC	13,841	31.25
Balraj Singh		JD	3,915	8.84
Kumarji Lal Rajoria		BSP	1,583	3.57
Jai Prakash Sharma		Independent	1,301	2.94
Rest (All Other Candidates)		Others	2,035	4.60

Election: 1998	Turnout (%): 47.45	Party	Actual Vote	Vote (%)
Bheeshm Sharma		INC	25,014	50.89
Sarvesh Sharma – W		BJP	14,594	29.69
Jai Pal Singh		BSP	2,551	5.19
Ashok Kumar		Independent	1,539	3.13
Nathu Singh		Independent	1,479	3.01
Rest (All Other Candidates)		Others	3,980	8.09

Election: 2003	Turnout (%): 58.47	Party	Actual Vote	Vote (%)
Bheeshma Sharma		INC	26,785	48.23
Rohtash Kumar		BSP	13,177	23.73
B. D. Sharma		BJP	12,439	22.40
Sunder Lal		NCP	829	1.49
Hari Ram		JPJD	528	0.95
Rest (All Other Candidates)		Others	1,777	3.20

Constituency: YAMUNA VIHAR – 51

Election: 1993	Turnout (%): 63.97	Party	Actual Vote	Vote (%)
Sahab Singh Chauhan		BJP	23,665	48.63
Bhisham Sharma		INC	13,211	27.15
Nasir Ali Alvi		JD	8,670	17.82
Sobha Ram		Independent	1,459	3.00
Harish Tyagi		SUCI	322	0.66
Rest (All Other Candidates)		Others	1,336	2.74

Election: 1998	Turnout (%): 44.85	Party	Actual Vote	Vote (%)
Sahab Singh Chauhan		BJP	24,258	44.63
Pushkar Singh Rawat		INC	22,974	42.27
Pramod Nagar		JD	2,206	4.06
B. D. Phuloriya		Independent	1,785	3.28
Abdul Sattar		NLP	984	1.81
Rest (All Other Candidates)		Others	2,148	3.95
Election: 2003	Turnout (%): 53.79	Party	Actual Vote	Vote (%)
Sahab Singh Chauhan		BJP	31,001	46.09
Diwan Singh		INC	29,442	43.78
Manohar Lal		BSP	3,431	5.10
Munnu Singh		CPM	831	1.24
Mohd Fakhruddin		NLP	497	0.74
Rest (All Other Candidates)		Others	2,053	3.05

Constituency: QARAWAL NAGAR – 52

Election: 1993	Turnout (%): 60.42	Party	Actual Vote	Vote (%)
Ram Pal		BJP	18,322	29.97
Kalyan Singh		INC	12,816	20.96
Chand M. A. A.		SP	9,292	15.20
Kadam Singh		JD	8,514	13.92
Jagdish		Independent	6,320	10.34
Rest (All Other Candidates)		Others	5,878	9.61
Election: 1998	Turnout (%): 56.11	Party	Actual Vote	Vote (%)
Mohan Singh Bisht		BJP	23,191	29.17
Zile Singh		INC	20,133	25.33
Hazi Mangta		Independent	9,410	11.84
Jagdish Pradhan		Independent	8,530	10.73
Keshu Prasad		SP	5,657	7.12
Rest (All Other Candidates)		Others	12,573	15.81

Election: 2003	Turnout (%): 55.92	Party	Actual Vote	Vote (%)
Mohan Singh Bisht		BJP	44,884	42.35
Hasan Ahmed		INC	29,657	27.98
Sher Khan		BSP	20,291	19.15
Sher Khan Malik		SP	3,076	2.90
Anand Trivedi		SHS	1,743	1.64
Rest (All Other Candidates)		Others	6,331	5.98

Constituency: WAZIRPUR – 53

Election: 1993	Turnout (%): 68.79	Party	Actual Vote	Vote (%)
Deep Chand Bandhu		INC	26,150	43.13
Mange Ram Garg		BJP	25,671	42.34
Umesh Khari		JD	7,176	11.84
Phool Chand Yada		BSP	780	1.29
Rajendra Prasad		Independent	254	0.42
Rest (All Other Candidates)		Others	599	0.98

Election: 1998	Turnout (%): 55.19	Party	Actual Vote	Vote (%)
Bandhu Deep Chand		INC	36,010	59.69
Shyam Lal Garg		BJP	21,132	35.03
Rajender Rpasad		BSP	1,450	2.40
Umesh Khari		JD	1,413	2.34
Chhimma Prasad		Independent	140	0.23
Rest (All Other Candidates)		Others	186	0.31

Election: 2003	Turnout (%): 59.11	Party	Actual Vote	Vote (%)
Mange Ram Garg		BJP	27,052	45.29
Rattan Chand Jain		INC	24,545	41.09
Janesh Kumar Bhadana		BSP	5,965	9.99
Kalpu Ram		BKRP	325	0.54
Adarsh Bhalla		NCP	242	0.41
Rest (All Other Candidates)		Others	1,601	2.68

Constituency: NARELA (SC) – 54

Election: 1993	Turnout (%): 60.43	Party	Actual Vote	Vote (%)
Inder Raj Singh		BJP	18,386	42.01
Charan Singh Kendera		INC	10,733	24.53
Dharam Pal		JD	7,526	17.20
Om Parkash		Independent	6,207	14.18
Surender Kumar		BSP	498	1.14
Rest (All Other Candidates)		Others	413	0.94

Election: 1998	Turnout (%): 55.51	Party	Actual Vote	Vote (%)
Charan Singh Kandera		INC	19,143	37.63
Laxman Singh		BJP	16,549	32.53
Om Parkash Ranga		Independent	7,881	15.49
Indraj Singh		Independent	4,796	9.43
Kishori Lal		BSP	1,981	3.89
Rest (All Other Candidates)		Others	520	1.03

Election: 2003	Turnout (%): 57.63	Party	Actual Vote	Vote (%)
Charan Singh Kandera		INC	36,501	48.40
Laxman Singh		BJP	28,698	38.06
Ram Phool Jatav		BSP	8,018	10.63
Rajender Lahari		Independent	594	0.79
Kailashwati – W		RLD	428	0.57
Rest (All Other Candidates)		Others	1,169	1.55

Constituency: BHALSWA JHANGIRPURI – 55

Election: 1993	Turnout (%): 62.85	Party	Actual Vote	Vote (%)
Jitendra Kumar		Independent	21,946	36.75
Ramphal Tyagi		BJP	14,124	23.65
Shyam Sunder Tyagi		INC	11,775	19.72
Chhatar Pal Khari		JD	9,765	16.35
Brahm Pal		BSP	961	1.61
Rest (All Other Candidates)		Others	1,139	1.92

Election: 1998	Turnout (%): 55.04	Party	Actual Vote	Vote (%)
J. S. Chauhan		INC	31,991	41.73
Jitender Kumar		DVP	16,749	21.85
Roshan Kanshal		BJP	13,094	17.08
Ram Phal Tyagi		Independent	6,790	8.86
Samay Singh		BSP	2,829	3.69
Rest (All Other Candidates)		Others	5,200	6.79

Election: 2003	Turnout (%): 54.75	Party	Actual Vote	Vote (%)
J. S. Chauhan		INC	39,356	40.20
Jitender Kumar		NCP	27,084	27.66
Mahesh Chand		BSP	12,925	13.20
Niranjan Parshad Sharma		BJP	12,097	12.36
Shishu Pal Singh Rawat		Independent	2,089	2.13
Rest (All Other Candidates)		Others	4,354	4.45

Constituency: ADARSH NAGAR – 56

Election: 1993	Turnout (%): 64.84	Party	Actual Vote	Vote (%)
Jai Parkash Yadav		BJP	17,020	34.18
Mangat Ram		INC	16,980	34.10
Guru Surender Vig		Independent	5,930	11.91
Lakshmi Chand Singhal		JD	4,335	8.71
Shiv Charan		BSP	3,958	7.95
Rest (All Other Candidates)		Others	1,571	3.15

Election: 1998	Turnout (%): 50.08	Party	Actual Vote	Vote (%)
Mangat Ram		INC	37,818	61.75
Jai Parkash Yadav		BJP	18,300	29.88
Shiv Charan Bhaskar		BSP	3,620	5.91
Pardip Skhokin		JD	839	1.37
Krishan Kumar Goyal		Independent	223	0.36
Rest (All Other Candidates)		Others	448	0.73

Election: 2003	Turnout (%): 48.81	Party	Actual Vote	Vote (%)
Mangat Ram		INC	29,290	47.12
Ravinder Singh		BJP	19,958	32.11
Rajesh Chauhan		BSP	8,296	13.35
Ajay Tyagi		NCP	2,677	4.31
Inderjeet		RJD	749	1.20
Rest (All Other Candidates)		Others	1,189	1.91

Constituency: PAHARGANJ – 57

Election: 1993	Turnout (%): 67.13	Party	Actual Vote	Vote (%)
Satish Chandra Khandelwal		BJP	22,889	41.76
Hari Chand Verma		INC	18,875	34.44
Shakeel Ur Rehman		JD	11,148	20.34
Mohanlal		CPI	685	1.25
Naresh Kumar		JNP(JP)	180	0.33
Rest (All Other Candidates)		Others	1,032	1.88

Election: 1998	Turnout (%): 53.52	Party	Actual Vote	Vote (%)
Anjali Rai – W		INC	31,065	63.89
Nirmal Khandelwal		BJP	14,217	29.24
Iqbal Ahmed		JD	2,275	4.68
Ram Gopal		BSP	512	1.05
Jagdish Manocha		CPM	173	0.36
Rest (All Other Candidates)		Others	377	0.78

Election: 2003	Turnout (%): 56.09	Party	Actual Vote	Vote (%)
Anjail Rai – W		INC	28,225	59.48
Virender Babbar		BJP	16,885	35.58
Manoj Narain		JD(S)	1,176	2.48
Mirza Mehtab Beg		JKNPP	421	0.89
Mahender Kumar		TRMC	236	0.50
Rest (All Other Candidates)		Others	513	1.07

Constituency: MATIA MAHAL – 58

Election: 1993	Turnout (%): 69.64	Party	Actual Vote	Vote (%)
Shoaib Iqbal		JD	27,617	62.77
Begum Khurshid – W		BJP	7,672	17.44
Memood Pracha		INC	4,221	9.59
Saeed Khan		SP	2,068	4.70
Khalil		Independent	677	1.54
Rest (All Other Candidates)		Others	1,743	3.96
Election: 1998	Turnout (%): 56.54	Party	Actual Vote	Vote (%)
Shoaib Iqbal		JD	28,872	65.18
Aziz Ahmad Siddiqui		INC	8,956	20.22
Aslam Sadar		BJP	5,230	11.81
Mohd Asif		RJD	406	0.92
Mohd Irfan Qqureshi		AP	335	0.76
Rest (All Other Candidates)		Others	496	1.11
Election: 2003	Turnout (%): 55.46	Party	Actual Vote	Vote (%)
Shoaib Iqbal		JD(S)	25,222	52.21
Azhar Shagufa – W		INC	17,524	36.28
Qasim Malik		BJP	3,114	6.45
Abdul Jabbar		RJD	1,185	2.45
Nazar Mohd		JKNPP	362	0.75
Rest (All Other Candidates)		Others	901	1.86

Constituency: BALIMARAN – 59

Election: 1993	Turnout (%): 64.53	Party	Actual Vote	Vote (%)
Haroon Yusuf		INC	20,217	39.03
Vihsambhar Dutt Sharma		BJP	18,726	36.15
Raj Kumar Jain		JD	10,146	19.59
Abdul Matin		IUML	1,725	3.33
Sheikh Alimuddin		BSP	320	0.62
Rest (All Other Candidates)		Others	667	1.28

Election: 1998	Turnout (%): 57.08	Party	Actual Vote	Vote (%)
Haroon Yusuf		INC	38,105	70.05
Vishwamber Datt Sharma		BJP	14,262	26.22
Syed Hamid Hussain Khizar		BSP	811	1.49
Naved Yar Khan		JD	399	0.73
Javed Ashraf Khan		SP	395	0.73
Rest (All Other Candidates)		Others	425	0.78
Election: 2003	Turnout (%): 55.53	Party	Actual Vote	Vote (%)
Haroon Yusuf		INC	31,357	64.60
Satish Chand Jain		Independent	8,766	18.06
Raj Kishore Gupta		BJP	5,584	11.50
Jamiluddin		NCP	1,010	2.08
Mohd Akram Ansari		BSP	709	1.46
Rest (All Other Candidates)		Others	1,111	2.30

Constituency: CHANDNI CHOWK – 60

Election: 1993	Turnout (%): 64.87	Party	Actual Vote	Vote (%)
Vasdev Kaptain		BJP	25,910	50.56
M. M. Agarwal		INC	21,456	41.87
Ram Kishan		JD	1,142	2.23
Ratttan Lal Bairwa		Independent	515	1.00
Vinod		LD	459	0.90
Rest (All Other Candidates)		Others	1,765	3.44
Election: 1998	Turnout (%): 52.42	Party	Actual Vote	Vote (%)
Prahlad Singh Sawhney		INC	24,348	47.90
Viresh Pratap Chaudhary		BJP	16,186	31.84
Amod Kumar Sharma		Independent	6,574	12.93
Chakresh Kumar Jain		Independent	3,214	6.32
Manoj Kumar		Independent	293	0.58
Rest (All Other Candidates)		Others	220	0.43

Election: 2003	Turnout (%): 53.64	Party	Actual Vote	Vote (%)
Prahlad Singh Sawhney		INC	26,744	59.91
Dharamvir Sharma		BJP	15,878	35.57
Iswar Pai Singh		SHS	600	1.34
Seema – W		Independent	509	1.14
Vipin Kumar Gupta		Independent	174	0.39
Rest (All Other Candidates)		Others	737	1.65

Constituency: TIMARPUR – 61

Election: 1993	Turnout (%): 66.70	Party	Actual Vote	Vote (%)
Rajender Gupta		BJP	27,232	50.57
Hari Shanker Gupta		INC	22,176	41.18
Nathi Singh Baghel		JD	2,569	4.77
Bhola Nath Babbar		Independent	501	0.93
Arun Kaushik		Independent	302	0.56
Rest (All Other Candidates)		Others	1,071	1.99

Election: 1998	Turnout (%): 50.03	Party	Actual Vote	Vote (%)
Jagdish Anand		INC	27,411	52.27
Raghuvansh Singhal		BJP	19,559	37.30
Surinder Pal Singh		Independent	2,809	5.36
Bhagwan Singh		SP	555	1.06
Tilak Raj Jatav		JD	529	1.01
Rest (All Other Candidates)		Others	1,576	3.00

Election: 2003	Turnout (%): 52.81	Party	Actual Vote	Vote (%)
Surinder Pal Singh		INC	29,952	53.86
Rajendra Gupta		BJP	23,978	43.12
Anand Singh		ABHM	298	0.54
Suraj Parkash		Independent	281	0.51
Rajni Sodhi – W		NCP	255	0.46
Rest (All Other Candidates)		Others	845	1.51

Constituency: MODEL TOWN – 62

Election: 1993	Turnout (%): 64.82	Party	Actual Vote	Vote (%)
Chatri Lal Goel		BJP	23,870	44.29
Kanwar Karan Singh		INC	21,532	39.95
Suresh Kumar Sonkar		JD	5,789	10.74
Pati Ram		BSP	1,319	2.45
Ashish Bhasin		SHS	445	0.83
Rest (All Other Candidates)		Others	938	1.74
Election: 1998	Turnout (%): 52.31	Party	Actual Vote	Vote (%)
Kanwar Karan Singh		INC	32,315	55.75
Bhola Nath Vij		BJP	21,276	36.70
M. L. Ram		BSP	1,791	3.09
Suresh Kumar Sonkar		JD	1,023	1.76
Tara Shankar		Independent	399	0.69
Rest (All Other Candidates)		Others	1,163	2.01
Election: 2003	Turnout (%): 51.33	Party	Actual Vote	Vote (%)
Kanwar Karan Singh		INC	24,660	45.17
Ashok Aggarwal		BJP	19,944	36.53
Vinod Nagar		LJP	6,277	11.50
Makhan Lal		BSP	2,727	4.99
Shambhu Nath Mishra		Independent	308	0.56
Rest (All Other Candidates)		Others	680	1.25

Constituency: KAMLA NAGAR – 63

Election: 1993	Turnout (%): 66.72	Party	Actual Vote	Vote (%)
P. K. Chandla		BJP	28,450	51.07
Rajinder Sharma		INC	22,429	40.26
Inder Mohan		JD	2,281	4.09
Dev Raj		Independent	839	1.51
Ram Dhari Goel		Independent	651	1.17
Rest (All Other Candidates)		Others	1,055	1.90

Election: 1998	Turnout (%): 50.95	Party	Actual Vote	Vote (%)
Shadi Ram		INC	26,326	49.50
P. K. Chandla		BJP	19,940	37.50
Suresh Gupta		Independent	6,696	12.59
Suresh Chand		Independent	96	0.18
Sudhir Yadav		Independent	68	0.13
Rest (All Other Candidates)		Others	54	0.10
Election: 2003	Turnout (%): 59.73	Party	Actual Vote	Vote (%)
Shadi Ram		INC	27,789	53.59
Surya Parkash		BJP	22,627	43.64
Taiyab Hussain		SP	459	0.89
Anil Sharma		NCP	276	0.53
Ramesbh		AIFB	176	0.34
Rest (All Other Candidates)		Others	523	1.01

Constituency: SADAR BAZAR – 64

Election: 1993	Turnout (%): 65.70	Party	Actual Vote	Vote (%)
Hari Krishan		BJP	27,125	46.93
Harcharan Singh Joshi		INC	25,786	44.61
Mohammed Ilyas		JD	1,615	2.79
Jagan Nath		Independent	812	1.40
Rajender Singh Mathoo		BSP	514	0.89
Rest (All Other Candidates)		Others	1,946	3.38
Election: 1998	Turnout (%): 53.15	Party	Actual Vote	Vote (%)
Rajesh Jain		INC	32,555	63.00
Hari Krishan		BJP	16,187	31.33
Rajender Singh Matthu		BSP	1,072	2.07
Sumit Pal Singh		JD	919	1.78
Chander Shekhar Gupta		SHS	381	0.74
Rest (All Other Candidates)		Others	560	1.08

Election: 2003	Turnout (%): 56.61	Party	Actual Vote	Vote (%)
Rajesh Jain		INC	33,144	66.07
Raghuvansh Singhal		BJP	15,065	30.03
Mohd Imran Ansari		SP	665	1.33
Balbir Singh		ABHM	257	0.51
Ravi Kumar		Independent	222	0.44
Rest (All Other Candidates)		Others	815	1.62

Constituency: MOTI NAGAR – 65

Election: 1993	Turnout (%): 70.41	Party	Actual Vote	Vote (%)
Madan Lal Khurana		BJP	33,503	54.10
Anjali Ram – W		INC	24,365	39.34
Ram Avhal		BSP	2,115	3.42
Kedar Nath Jha		JD	907	1.46
Jathedar Trilochan Singh		Independent	267	0.43
Rest (All Other Candidates)		Others	771	1.25

Election: 1998	Turnout (%): 53.35	Party	Actual Vote	Vote (%)
Avinash Sahni		BJP	29,589	49.87
Kanwaljit Singh		INC	26,280	44.29
Moti Ram		BSP	2,640	4.45
Subhash Goel		SHS	616	1.04
Ashok Kumar Munna		Independent	127	0.21
Rest (All Other Candidates)		Others	86	0.14

Election: 2003	Turnout (%): 62.34	Party	Actual Vote	Vote (%)
Madan Lal Khurana		BJP	37,051	61.35
Alka Lamba – W		INC	21,861	36.20
Anil Kumar Chadha		AB	313	0.52
Kishore Gohri		NCP	255	0.42
Ram Niwas Chandervansh		JD(S)	249	0.41
Rest (All Other Candidates)		Others	664	1.10

Constituency: PATEL NAGAR – 66

Election: 1993	Turnout (%): 61.81	Party	Actual Vote	Vote (%)
M. R. Arya		BJP	24,058	44.85
Manohar Arora		INC	21,911	40.85
Braham Prakash		JD	3,717	6.93
Mahender Pratap		BSP	1,090	2.03
Mansa Ram		Independent	1,052	1.96
Rest (All Other Candidates)		Others	1,814	3.38
Election: 1998	Turnout (%): 50.32	Party	Actual Vote	Vote (%)
Rama Kant Goswami		INC	26,135	47.38
Mewa Ram Arya		BJP	20,541	37.24
Dilvinder Singh		Independent	5,861	10.63
Vinita – W		BSP	1,630	2.95
Kiran Kapoor – W		Independent	370	0.67
Rest (All Other Candidates)		Others	625	1.13
Election: 2003	Turnout (%): 51.50	Party	Actual Vote	Vote (%)
Rama Kant Goswami		INC	32,833	60.04
Mahesh Chadha		BJP	18,657	34.11
Asha		Independent	1,043	1.91
Brijesh Kumar Singh		IFDP	860	1.57
Sudesh Chug – W		Independent	535	0.98
Rest (All Other Candidates)		Others	761	1.39

Constituency: RAJINDER NAGAR – 67

Election: 1993	Turnout (%): 65.06	Party	Actual Vote	Vote (%)
Puran Chand Yogi		BJP	23,847	47.75
Brahmi Yadav		INC	22,234	44.52
Ram Asish		JD	2,519	5.04
Vijay Kumar		BSP	971	1.94
Surinder Singh		LD	101	0.20
Rest (All Other Candidates)		Others	271	0.55

Election: 1998	Turnout (%): 44.99	Party	Actual Vote	Vote (%)
Puran Chand Yogi		BJP	21,150	37.63
Brahm Yadav		Independent	19,767	35.17
Ram Ashish Singh		INC	12,189	21.69
B. K. Parsad		JD	1,037	1.84
Shyam Sunder		Independent	651	1.16
Rest (All Other Candidates)		Others	1,414	2.51

Election: 2003	Turnout (%): 50.64	Party	Actual Vote	Vote (%)
Puran Chand Yogi		BJP	22,069	41.84
Raj Kumar Kohli		INC	21,178	40.15
Trilok Chand Sharma		Independent	8,514	16.14
P. L. Premi		Independent	365	0.69
Usha Singh – W		IJP	314	0.60
Rest (All Other Candidates)		Others	303	0.58

Constituency: KAROL BAGH (SC) – 68

Election: 1993	Turnout (%): 62.06	Party	Actual Vote	Vote (%)
S. P. Ratwal		BJP	26,794	51.73
Sunderwati Naval Prabhakar – W		INC	15,405	29.74
Shyam Babu		JD	7,182	13.86
Karan Singh Tanwar		Independent	665	1.28
Trilok Chand Sanwariya		Independent	590	1.14
Rest (All Other Candidates)		Others	1,164	2.25

Election: 1998	Turnout (%): 52.44	Party	Actual Vote	Vote (%)
Moti Lal Bokolia		INC	26,466	50.91
Surender Pal Ratawal		BJP	24,154	46.46
Rohtash		BSP	588	1.13
Ajay Harit		JD	300	0.58
Krishan Kumar Rajora		Independent	262	0.50
Rest (All Other Candidates)		Others	220	0.42

Election: 2003	Turnout (%): 54.30	Party	Actual Vote	Vote (%)
Surender Pal Ratawal		BJP	21,812	46.85
Durgesh Mohanpuria – W		INC	20,953	45.00
Y. R. Dhuriya		BSP	2,544	5.46
Yogesh Narayan		SHS	293	0.63
Dev Dass		TRMC	289	0.62
Rest (All Other Candidates)		Others	671	1.44

Constituency: RAM NAGAR (SC) – 69

Election: 1993	Turnout (%): 64.49	Party	Actual Vote	Vote (%)
Moti Lal Soddi		BJP	23,181	43.01
Babu Ram Solanki		INC	19,760	36.66
Nathu Prasad		CPM	7,111	13.19
Rajender Singh		JD	1,897	3.52
Sushila Gihara – W		BSP	1,159	2.15
Rest (All Other Candidates)		Others	786	1.47

Election: 1998	Turnout (%): 54.41	Party	Actual Vote	Vote (%)
Darshna – W		INC	31,794	56.88
Moti Lal Sodhi		BJP	19,811	35.44
Nathu Prasad		CPM	2,568	4.59
Gopal Chauhan		BSP	546	0.98
Ramesh Kumar		JD	526	0.94
Rest (All Other Candidates)		Others	655	1.17

Election: 2003	Turnout (%): 54.55	Party	Actual Vote	Vote (%)
Moti Lal Sodi		BJP	22,319	44.94
Darshna – W		INC	21,221	42.73
Nathu Prashad		CPM	3,564	7.18
Raj Kumar Indoria		NCP	670	1.35
Lekh Raj		RJD	656	1.32
Rest (All Other Candidates)		Others	1,236	2.48

Constituency: BALJEET NAGAR (SC) – 70

Election: 1993	Turnout (%): 61.64	Party	Actual Vote	Vote (%)
Krishna Tirath – W		INC	21,796	47.51
K. C. Ravi		BJP	20,211	44.05
Sahatam		BSP	1,343	2.93
Budh Priya Rahul		JD	1,281	2.79
Laxmi Narain Nawara		Independent	347	0.76
Rest (All Other Candidates)		Others	900	1.96
Election: 1998	Turnout (%): 43.28	Party	Actual Vote	Vote (%)
Krishna – W		INC	28,832	55.83
Yogendra Chandoliya		BJP	17,047	33.01
Jai Singh Bharti		BSP	3,611	6.99
Man Mohan Singh		Independent	1,723	3.34
Bimla Devi – W		LKS	375	0.73
Rest (All Other Candidates)		Others	54	0.10
Election: 2003	Turnout (%): 52.23	Party	Actual Vote	Vote (%)
Krishna Tirath – W		INC	30,132	55.35
K. C. Ravi		BJP	19,202	35.27
Darshan Kumar		BSP	2,664	4.89
Nanda		NCP	794	1.46
Manmohan Singh		Independent	506	0.93
Rest (All Other Candidates)		Others	1,145	2.10

Abbreviations: Ch–Choudhary; Kr–Kumar; Mohd–Mohammed; W–Woman.

References

Government Publications

Census of India (various years). Government of India.
Economic Survey of Delhi (various years). Government of Delhi.

Books and Articles

Abrams, Charles. 1964. *Man's Struggle for Shelter in an Urbanizing World.* Cambridge, MA: MIT Press.

Ahmed, Bashiruddin. 1970. 'Caste and Electoral Politics', *Asian Survey,* 10 (11): 979–92.

Antony, Margaret and G. Maheswaran. 2001. *Social Segregation and Slums: The Plight of Dalits in the Slums of Delhi.* New Delhi: Indian Social Institute.

Bass, B. M. 1990. 'From Transactional to Transformational Leadership: Learning to Share the Visio', *Organizational Dynamics,* (Winter): 19–31.

Birdsall, Nancy and John Nellis. 2002. 'Winners and Losers: Assessing the Distribution Impact of Privatization'. Working Paper No. 6, Centre for Global Development.

Bourdieu, P. 1986. 'The Forms of Capital', in J. Richardson, *Handbook of Theory and Research for the Sociology of Education*, pp. 241–58. New York: Greewnood.

Bukharin, N. 1921. *Historical Materialism.* Ann Arbor: Ann Arbor Paperbacks.

Cadene, Phillipe. 2000. 'Delhi's Place in India's Urban Structure', in Véronique Dupont, Emma Tarlo and Denis Vidal (eds), *Delhi: Urban Space and Human Destinies*, pp. 241–250. Delhi: Manohar.

Clarke, S. 2002. 'Hindutva, Religious and Ethnocultural Minorities, and Indian-Christian Theology', *The Harvard Theological Review*, 95 (2): 197–226.

Consultation Report. 2003. Presented by Action Aid. Commissioned by MCD.

Dahrendorf, R. 1959. *Class and Class Conflict in Industrial Society.* California: Stanford University Press.

Daly, Gerald. 1996. *Homeless: Policies, Strategies, and Lives on the Street.* London and New York: Routledge.

Dirks, N. 2001. 'Discriminating Differences: The Postcolonial Politics of Caste in India', in André Burguière and Raymond Grew (eds), *The Construction of Minorities: Cases for Comparison Across Time and Around the World*, pp. 213–43. Ann Arbor, MI: University of Michigan Press.

Deshpande, Anirudh. 2000. 'Caste and Electoral Politics', *Economic and Political Weekly,* 35 (5): 267–70.

Dupont, Véronique, Emma Tarlo and Denis Vidal (eds). 2000. *Delhi: Urban Space and Human Destinies.* Delhi: Manohar.

Engels, Friedrich. 1936. *The Condition of the Working Class in England in 1844.* London: Allen and Unwin.

Gardner, Howard. 1996. *Leading Minds: An Anatomy of Leadership.* New York: Basic Books.

Giddens, A. 1973. *The Class Structure of the Advanced Societies.* New York: Harper and Row.

Gimpel, James G. and Jason E. Schuknecht. 2001. 'Interstate Migration and Electoral Politics', *The Journal of Politics,* 63 (1): 207–31.

Government of Delhi. 2012. *Delhi Statistical Handbook 2012.* Retrieved from http://www.delhi.gov.in.

Harris-White, Barbara. 2003. 'Destitution in India', paper presented at the *Conference on Inequality, Poverty and Human Well-being*, Helsinki, Finland, 30–31 May.

Hindustan Times. 1998 and 2003. CSDS Delhi Surveys, New Delhi Edition.

Jaffrelot, C. 2003. *India's Silent Revolution: The Rise of the Lower Castes in North India.* London: C. Hurst & Co. Publishers.

Kanth, Amod K. n.d. 'Housing for the Urban Poor: A Case for the Homeless in Delhi'. Retrieved from http://www.prayaschildren.com.

Kaur, Guneet. 2004. 'Revival of Satellite and Ring Cities', *40th Annual Congress of The International Society of City and Regional Planners (ISOCARP)*, Geneva.

Kaur, Ravinder. 2007. *Since 1947: Partition Narratives among Punjabi Immigrants of Delhi.* New Delhi: Oxford University Press.

Kothari, Rajni. 1970. *Politics in India.* New Delhi: Orient Longman.

Kothari, J. 2002. *India Together.* Bangalore: VOICES.

Lenin, V. I. 1914. 'A Great Beginning', in *The Essentials of Lenin.* London: Lawrence and Wishart.

Lukács, Georg. 1922. *History and Class Consciousness.* Cambridge, MA: MIT Press.

Lynch, Philip and Jacqueline Cole. 2003. 'Homelessness and Human Rights: Regarding and Responding to Homelessness as a Human Rights Violation', *Melbourne Journal of International Law,* 4 (1): 139–76.

Michelutti, L. 2004. 'We (Yadavs) Are a Caste of Politicians: Caste and Modern Politics in a North-Indian Town', *Contributions to Indian Sociology* 38(3): 43–72. (Reprinted in Gupta, D. 2004. *Caste in Question: Identity or Hierarchy*. New Delhi: SAGE Publications.)

Mills, C. Wright. 1956. *The Power Elite*. London: Oxford University Press.

Mitra, Subrata. 2010. 'Citizenship in India: Some Preliminary Results of a National Survey', *Economic and Political Weekly*, 45 (9): 46–53.

Mumford, Lewis. 1961. *The City in History*. London: Secker and Warburg.

National Capital Region Planning Board. n.d. *Urban and Regional Planning: Study on Counter Magnet Areas to Delhi & NCR*. Retrieved from http:// ncrpb.nic.in/pdf_files/06_Chapter3_cma.pdf.

Nayyar, D. 2011. 'Discrimination and Justice: Beyond Affirmative Action', *Economic and Political Weekly*, 15 October.

Parsons, T. 1970. 'Equality and Inequality in Modern Society, or Social Stratification Revisited', in E. O. Lauman (ed.), *Social Stratification: Research and Theory for the 1970s*. Indianapolis: Bob–Merill.

Parry, K. and D. Melling (eds). 1999. *The Blackwell Dictionary of Eastern Christianity*. Malden, MA: Blackwell Publishing.

Premi, Mahendra K. 1986. 'Migration to Cities in India', in M. S. A. Rao (ed.), *Studies in Migration: Internal and International Migration in India*. Delhi: Manohar.

Raj, Pushkar. 2004. 'Benefiting from Two-Layered Incumbency', *Economic and Political Weekly*, 39 (51): 5502–4.

Rao, M. S. A. 1986. *Studies in Migration: Internal and International Migration in India*. Delhi: Manohar.

Ravestein, E. G. 1889. 'The Laws of Migration', *Journal of the Royal Statistical Society*, 52: 241–305.

Reddy, D. S. 2005. 'The Ethnicity of Caste', *Anthropological Quarterly,* 78 (3): 543–84.

Rudolph, Lloyd I. and Susanne Hoeber Rudolph. 1967. *The Modernity of Tradition: Political Development in India*. Chicago: University of Chicago Press.

Savarkar, V. D. 1969. *Hindutva: Who is a Hindu?* Bombay: Veer Savarkar Prakashan.

Shahri Adhikar Manch [Urban Rights Forum]. 2009. *Begharon Ke Liye* [For the Homeless]. Press Release. Retrieved from http://www.hic-sarp.org.

Shamir, Boas, Robert J. House and Michael B. Arthur. 1993. 'The Motivational Effects of Charismatic Leadership: A Self-Concept Based Theory', *Organization Science*, 4 (4): 577–94.

Singh, Indu Prakash. 2001. 'Census of the Homeless: A Painful Farce and Assault'. New Delhi: First City.

———. 2004. 'Urban Poverty Approach Paper', (unpublished). New Delhi: Action Aid International.

Singh, V. B. 2000. 'Political Profile of Delhi and Support Bases of Parties: An Analysis', in Veronique Dupont, Emma Tarlo and Denis Vidal (eds), *Delhi: Urban Space and Human Destinies*. Delhi: Manohar.

Srinivas, M. N. 1957. 'Caste in Modern India', *The Journal of Asian Studies*, 16 (4): 529–48.

———. 1962. *Caste in Modern India: And Other Essays*. Bombay: Asia Publishing House.

sub Terrain. 2007. 'Housing Is a Human Right: An Interview with Miloon Kothari, UN Special Rapporteur', *sub Terrain*, #2, July.

Thakur, Sudarshan. 2005. 'Alive in the Pyramids', *Tehelka*, 15 October.

Times of India. 2011. 'Flow of Migrants Highest to Delhi, not Maharashtra', *Times of India*, 6 December, New Delhi.

United Nations Human Rights Commission (UNHRC). 2001. *CCPR General Comment 25: The Right to Participate in Public Affairs, Voting Rights and the Right of Equal Access to Public Service*, [1], UN Doc HRI/GEN/1/ Rev. 5.

United Nations Office of the High Commissioner for Human Rights (UNOHCHR). 2002. *Draft Guidelines: A Human Rights Approach to Poverty Reduction Strategies*. Retrieved from http://www.fao.org/.

Warner, W. L. 1949. *Social Class in America: A Manual of Procedure for the Measurement of Social Status*. New York: Harper and Row.

Weber, M. 1922. *Economy and Society*. New York: Bedminster Press.

World Bank. 2006. *India: Strengthening Institutions for Sustainable Growth*. Retrieved from http://siteresources.worldbank.org/INDIAEXTN/ Resources/295583-1176163782791/ch1.pdf.

Wright, E. O. 1985. *Classes*. London: Verso.

———. 1979. *Class Structure and Income Determination*. New York: Academic Press.

Yadav, Y. 1999. 'Electoral Politics in the Time of Change: India's Third Electoral System, 1989–99', *Economic and Political Weekly*, 21–28 August, 2393–9.

Zaidi, Annie. 2005. 'Homeless in Delhi', *Frontline*, 22 (1), 14 January.

Index

anti-corruption movement (2012), 3
anti-Emergency movement (1975–77), 3
anti-Mandal movement (1990), 3

'Babri Masjid' campaign, 35
Backward Classes Commission (Mandal Commission), 34, 57
Bahujan Samaj Party (BSP), 3, 28, 37
   between 2003 and 2008 poll, 79–84
   rise in Delhi politics, 73–74, 76–79
Baker, Sir Herbert, 1
Bharatiya Janata Party (BJP), 3, 28, 35–37, 86
   failure of, 89–93
bipolar contest between BJP and Congress, 74–77
Bose, N. K., 32
Bourdieu, Pierre, 120

caste, role in electoral politics, 6–7, 36–55
   Brahmin vote, 37–39
   Dalits voters, 50–51
   Gujjars Vote, 43–45
   Jat Vote, 45–47
   Muslim voters, 52–53
   OBC voters, 47–49
   Punjabi Khatri vote, 39–40
   Rajput vote, 41
   Sikh voters, 53–55
   Vaishya/Bania Vote, 41–43

Centre for the Study of Developing Societies (CSDS), 4
'centre–periphery' relationship, 22
class
   Dalit voters, 71–72
   definitions and interpretations of, 58–60
   Jat voters, 70
   lower-class voters, 67–68
   middle-class voters, 65–66
   politicization of, 60–61
   Punjabi Khatri voters, 69–70
   Sikh voters, 70–71
   struggles, 57–58
   upper-class Brahmin voters, 69
   upper-class voters, 64–65
   voting behaviour, 61–72
class consciousness, 120
Congress, 3, 28, 86
Constitution (69th Amendment) Act, 1991, 89

Dalit–Bahujan social critique, 33
Delhi, 1
   changed class profile of, 2
   changes, 2
   cultural conditioning of population, 120
   density of, 13
   development since Independence, 15
   electoral politics, 3

geographical distance with other metropolitan cities, 15
language diversity, 2
old and new, 1, 117–18
overcrowding of, 17
physical growth and underdevelopment of, 22
refugee camps, 1
settlement pattern, 18–19, 119–20
Trans Yamuna localities, 19, 119
unauthorized colonies, 26–27
voters of, 4
Delhi Urban Environment and Infrastructure Improvement Project, 128
Dikshit, Sheila, 3, 86
popularity of, 88, 93–96
diversity of people in Delhi
conceptual framework, 98–99
homelessness without identity, 99–101
houseless population, 101–16

electoral politics of Delhi, 3–4
caste, role of, 6–7, 36–55
factor for voters' mobilization, 8
impact of migration, 5–6
personality factor, 9
trajectories of main political parties, 8–9
voting patterns, 10–11, 56–72
voting rights, 9

four-fold hierarchy of caste system, 31

Goel, Vijay, 92

Harappan Civilization, 1
houseless population, 101–16
assessment of, 101–4
causes for, 104–7
life on street, 113–16
National Housing and Habitat Policy, 1998, 110–11
night shelter for urban shelterless, 111–13
state's sensitivity to, 108–13

Indian Institute of Human Settlement, 5

Janata Dal, 75

Kalekar, Kaka, 32
Kalekar commission, 33
Khurana, Madan Lal, 89–91

Lutyens, Sir Edwin, 1

Maken, Ajay, 89
Malhotra, Vijay Kumar, 90, 92
'Mandalization' of India, 34–35
'Metropolis–Satellite' syndrome, 22
migration, 5–6
after partition, 16
analysis of, 20–24
from Bihar, 12–13, 18, 27
census of 2011, 12
changes in last three decades, 12–13
economic prosperity of migrants, 24
educational attainment as a reason, 21, 23
employment as a reason for, 20
historical view, 15–17
occupational pattern of migrants, 22–23
pattern of, 17–18
proportions of Jats and Punjabis, 25, 27–28
sizeable proportion of voters, 25–26
social composition, changes in, 25–28
state-wise pattern of, 18
in terms of push and pull factors, 14–15, 20–21
theorizing, 13–15

from 1911 to 2011, 16
voting behaviour of migrants, 17–20

National Housing and Habitat Policy, 1998, 110–11
national politics *vs* Delhi's politics, 87–89

party performance in Delhi, 75
people perception about Delhi
  basic facilities, 133–37
  Bus Rapid Transit (BRT) system, 126–28
  'cleaning' and 'beautification' of city, 128
  Delhi Transport Corporation (DTC), 122–23
  Delhi Urban Environment and Infrastructure Improvement Project, 128
  issue of beggars and homeless, 131–33
  JJ clusters, 129
  Metro rail, 122, 126
  public and private transport, 122–28

removal of jhuggis, 130–31
Revised Resettlement Policy, 129
slum resettlement, 129
support for privatization, 121–22
political leadership, 87
politicization of caste, 57

Rashtriya Janata Dal (RJD), 36
Rashtriya Swayamsevak Sangh (RSS), 90

Savarkar, V. D., 31
settlement patterns in Delhi, 18–20
slums and unauthorized colonies, 10
social and economic conditions of houseless, 9
Srinivas, M. N., 33
Swaraj, Sushma, 90–91

Trans Yamuna localities, 19, 119

urban population in mega cities, 13

Verma, Sahib Singh, 90
voters of Delhi, 4
voting patterns, 10–11, 56–72

About the Author

Sanjay Kumar is Fellow at the Centre for the Study of Developing Societies (CSDS), Delhi. His areas of research for past several years have been studying electoral systems, analyzing electoral politics and mapping changing patterns of democracy. Being a specialist in survey research, he has directed various national- and state-level election surveys at the CSDS.

Sanjay's writings draw heavily from survey research, which he pursues as his research tool. He has co-edited (with Christopher Jaffrelot) *Rise of the Plebians? The Changing Face of Indian Legislative Assemblies* (Routledge, 2009) and co-authored (with Peter R. deSouza and Sandeep Shastri) *Indian Youth in a Transforming World: Attitudes and Perceptions* (SAGE, 2009) and (with Praveen Rai) *Measuring Voting Behaviour in India* (SAGE, 2013). He has also authored various research reports, contributed articles for several edited volumes and published in many international and national research journals.